The Strategic Producer

Today's technologies and economic models won't settle for a conventional approach to filmmaking. *The Strategic Producer: On the Art and Craft of Making Your First Feature* combines history, technology, aesthetics, hard data, decision-making, and time-tested methods into powerful new producing strategies. Ideal for all aspiring filmmakers, *The Strategic Producer* orients the reader's mindset towards self-empowerment by sharing essential and timeless techniques producers need to get the job done while also embracing the constantly evolving production landscape and its new parameters.

- Written in clear, succinct, and non-technical prose.
- Includes six sidebar in-depth interviews with industry professionals providing additional perspectives.
- Clearly presented line drawings help readers quickly understand complex ideas like production timelines, story structure, and business models.
- Includes samples from key documents such as script pages, budgets, shooting schedules, and business plans for potential investors.

Federico Muchnik has been making films for 30 years. He studied film at NYU's Tisch School of the Arts and worked as a producer for PBS. He has also produced content for Disneyland, ABC Television, and HBO. He played the lead role in *The Golden Boat*, directed by Raul Ruiz, shown at Sundance, New York, and Toronto, and distributed by Strand Releasing. He co-wrote and co-edited *Secret Courage*, a documentary about the Jewish resistance movement during World War 2. He has made many fiction-based long form series for the educational markets and filmed numerous projects throughout North America, Europe, and Latin America. He has taught filmmaking at Boston University, Emerson College, and in New York and Los Angeles. Most recently, he produced and directed the feature length *This Killing Business* distributed by Filmbox Arthouse in Europe and shown at numerous festivals in the U.S. More at his production company site www.mightyvisual.com and his film blog http://filmadvisor.blogspot.com.

The Strategic Producer

On the Art and Craft of Making Your First Feature

Federico Arditti Muchnik

Routledge
Taylor & Francis Group
NEW YORK AND LONDON

First published 2017
by Routledge
711 Third Avenue, New York, NY 10017

and by Routledge
2 Park Square, Milton Park, Abingdon, Oxon OX14 4RN

Routledge is an imprint of the Taylor & Francis Group, an informa business

© 2017 Federico Muchnik

The right of Federico Muchnik to be identified as author of this work has been asserted by him in accordance with sections 77 and 78 of the Copyright, Designs and Patents Act 1988.

All rights reserved. No part of this book may be reprinted or reproduced or utilised in any form or by any electronic, mechanical, or other means, now known or hereafter invented, including photocopying and recording, or in any information storage or retrieval system, without permission in writing from the publishers.

Trademark notice: Product or corporate names may be trademarks or registered trademarks, and are used only for identification and explanation without intent to infringe.

Library of Congress Cataloging in Publication Data
Names: Muchnik, Federico author.
Title: The strategic producer : on the art and craft of making your first feature / Federico Muchnik.
Description: New York : Routledge, 2016.
Identifiers: LCCN 2015049211 (print) | LCCN 2015050108 (ebook) | ISBN 9781138123670 (hardback : alk. paper) | ISBN 9781138123625 (pbk. : alk. paper) | ISBN 9781138123625 (ebk.) | ISBN 9781315648729 (eBook)
Subjects: LCSH: Digital cinematography. | Digital video. | Motion pictures—Production and direction.
Classification: LCC TR860 .M83 2016 (print) | LCC TR860 (ebook) | DDC 778.5/3—dc23
LC record available at https://lccn.loc.gov/2015049211

ISBN: 978-1-138-12367-0 (hbk)
ISBN: 978-1-138-12362-5 (pbk)
ISBN: 978-1-315-64872-9 (ebk)

Typeset in Sabon and Gill Sans
by Florence Production Ltd, Stoodleigh, Devon, UK

Printed and bound in Great Britain by
TJ International Ltd, Padstow, Cornwall

Contents

Acknowledgments   vii

Introduction   1

PART 1
BACK STORY   5

1 History   7

2 Story   21

The Artistic Impulse 21
Why Stories 22
Oral to Visual Storytelling 23

3 Working the Material   25

Suspension of Disbelief 25
Character 26
Suspense, Surprise, and Mystery 28
Originality 29

4 Writing the Script   31

Elements and Structure of the Script 32
Style 35

PART 2
GETTING TO WORK   39

5 Development   41

The Producer/Director Relationship 42
Proof of Concept 43
SIDEBAR: Interview with Piotr Reisch, Producer 44

6 Money — 49

The Producer–Investor Relationship 49
What Do Investors Want? 50
The Business Entity 51
Investor Sources 52
Your Money 52
No Budget Filmmaking and the Compilation Film 53

7 Preproduction — 55

SIDEBAR: Interview with Brian Falk, Producer 58
The Casting Session 60
Location Scouting 62
Shooting on a Soundstage 66
Hiring People 66
SIDEBAR: Interview with Michael Bowes, Producer 68
Budget 71
Scheduling 76

8 Production — 85

Camera Setups and Block/Light/Shoot 86
Directing Actors 88
Working with the Crew 95
Meals and Breaks 98
Common Problems 99
End of Production 103

9 Post-production — 105

Workflow and Story Structure 106
SIDEBAR: Interview with Anne McCabe, A.C.E., Editor 108
Test Screenings and Finishing the Film 112
Deliverables 115

10 The Marketplaces: History, Deal Structures, Distribution, Exhibition, and Film Festivals — 117

What Distributors Want 118
Deal Structures 120
SIDEBAR: Interview with Francois Yon, distributor 121
Film Festivals 124
SIDEBAR: Interview with Larry Jackson, producer's rep. 126
The Larger Distribution Landscape 129
In Closing 132

Appendix: The Business Plan — 135
Index — 159

Acknowledgments

I am indebted to the following collaborators whose admirable work has informed mine over the years: James Schamus, Michael Donaldson, Ted Hope, Christine Vachon, Marin Karmitz, Raul Ruiz, Valeria Sarmiento, Fred Barzyk, Olivia Tappen, Antonio Mayans, Francisco Torregrossa, Matt Campbell, Bob Nesson, Franco Sacchi, Tom Robotham, Vincent Liota, Howard Phillips, Greg McLeary, Geof Thurber, Richard LaBrie, Stewart Clifford, Juan Mandelbaum, Gary Henoch, Tom Robotham, and Alex Cook.

My thanks to Anne McCabe, Michael Bowes, Brian Falk, Francois Yon, Piotr Reisch, and Larry Jackson for the interviews included in this book.

Thanks to Michael Shrum for help with the illustrations and Natalia Ruiz for help transcribing interviews.

Friends and family who directly or indirectly contributed to this book project: Rita, Mario, Nicole, Estelle, Layla, Katherine, Naima, Peter, Bob and Martha, Elijah, Nicolas, Dan, Anatole, Michel, Irene, Natalia, and Alejandro.

The hundreds of filmmaking students I've had the good fortune to meet over the course of my teaching career at Boston University, Emerson College, and The Center for Digital Imaging Arts at BU.

The cast and crew members I've had the opportunity to work alongside throughout the U.S., Europe, and in Central and South America.

Finally, my thanks to Emily McCloskey and David Williams at Routledge/Focal Press for their interest and support.

Introduction

If you are holding this book there's a strong chance you are a first time feature film producer or director and, by extension, not making a multi-million dollar production with an established star, director, or guaranteed distribution strategy. In other words, you are an independent David to Hollywood's studio-system Goliath. Multi-million dollar movies come with A-list stars and massive marketing campaigns you cannot compete with. You are the underdog and, no matter how hard you try to come across as a Goliath by making a Hollywood-style film, keep in mind there will always be a *bigger boat* downstream that will make your production look like a dinghy.

If, on the other hand, you eschew the urge to look and sound like the big boys and take a moment to unpack the advantages of being the underdog, you've immediately accomplished two things: a) you've accepted to play in the playground that best suits you and b) you've differentiated yourself from the studio-driven films or the films that pretend to be as much. Let's take a moment to see how using your opponent's weight (and girth) against them can further lead you to building a *better* (if not bigger) boat. Or, as director Mike Nichols said: *"The only safe thing is to take a chance."*

Studios are operating in highly institutionalized and conventional ways. They exist as complex, multi-layered organizations with hundreds of employees hoping to deliver the next *blockbuster du jour*. Because their production pipeline has become so dependent on frequent releases of big movies into theatres, studios are essentially stuck playing Goliath. The system they've built demands it. The system wants a predictable product and strategy: a big budget star driven special effects laden movie with a predictable story told in a conventional manner and released onto thousands of screens nationwide followed by a long post-theatrical distribution strategy on small screens accompanied by a large foreign sales campaign. If a movie does not promise the roadmap I've just mentioned, the studios and the distributors will reject it just as an organism rejects a virus.

You, on the other hand, are free to move about the cabin, keeping in mind that:

- Independent producers succeed by applying *unconventional methods* to their production and distribution strategies.
- *Effort* plus *strategy* is the best alternative to not having unlimited financial resources or being part of the studio system.
- With effort and strategy, *the size of a project does not matter*.
- By working outside the system independent producers become immune to problems incurred by the studios.

- The experience gained from making a film outside the system turns the novice or underdog producer into a seasoned and more hardened filmmaker able to take on bigger and more ambitious projects.
- Working outside the system comes with the necessary and inevitable *fear quotient*. It really is the wild, wild west. Novice producers need to keep in mind the all too human tendency to over-predict failure. Over-estimating the possibility of failure comes with being a small fish in a pig pond. Acknowledging our tendency to imagine worst-case scenarios is the first step towards diminishing the fear quotient.
- Independent producers understand that *disadvantage* does not mean *failure*. They examine the potential consequences of a given disadvantage, convert a deficit into an asset, and make an informed decision moving forward.
- Just as there are benefits to a crisis-free production process, there are benefits that come with adversity, innovation being one of the most important ones. Having an easy time of it can be constricting. One example: if you're a prestigious filmmaker you're essentially forced by the studios to make what audiences know you for. You can forget about innovation, originality, creativity, and self-expression. Those traits almost always emerge from outliers, independents, or filmmakers far from the top of the studio system food chain. In other words: newcomers are more inclined to come up with fresh ideas.

The Strategic Producer is divided into two parts. Part 1, *Back Story*, addresses film history, its technological evolution, and its basic aesthetic principles. I have written this section because I believe it provides the context necessary to producing *and completing* films. Good producers need to recognize good scripts, so I devote a considerable part of this section to story and storytelling. Part 2, titled *Getting To Work*, addresses the nuts and bolts of film producing from the development to the marketing and distribution stages and includes many valuable production-related strategies. Additionally, throughout the book I've provided six *Sidebar* segments consisting of interviews with three producers, a producer's rep, a film editor, and a distributor. And there's an *Appendix* dedicated to business plans.

A word about gear and technology. By the time you read this the current filmmaking technologies that are presently available will more than likely be en route to becoming obsolete or nearly so. Moreover, the internet provides information on the latest/greatest technologies; more than I could possibly hope to cover in this book. So I will refrain from going into detailed explanations of how to use a given camera or editing app. I will, however, make the *general* case here for two undeniable technologies that—as far as anyone can tell—are here to stay: digital cameras and computer-based editing. Films today are made on everything from tiny hand held *prosumer* camcorders to high-end cameras like the Arri Alexa. As of this writing at least one feature film presented at Sundance and picked up by a distributor was filmed on a *modified* iPhone. As for post-production, we are seeing films edited on state of the art AVID editing platforms, on PCs with Premiere Pro, or on Apple laptops with iMovie. So, if once there was a single technology used in making movies (using negative film stock and flatbed editing tables), today there are literally dozens of digital technology workflows, each one outdoing the next, and with new technologies on the way every month. Good producers understand the evolving nature of technology and work with the gear and workflow that best suits their project *at the time* they are making it.

Producing a feature length film, large or small, is a daunting task. Unlike a short, a feature contains innumerable variables. From the intricate story and script, to the complex production logistics, and from the numerous shooting days to the countless editing choices during post-production, making a feature length film can feel like battling that mythical Greek monster, the Hydra. Chop its head off and three new ones grow back. With producing, solving one problem means that at least three more are on the way. Eventually, however, the Hydra dies. The good producers, the *tenacious* ones, the ones that actually *complete* their films, are the ones that calmly accept the chaos that comes with making a feature. They are the ones that jump in, eager to solve the challenges inherent in filmmaking. And if they stumble or suffer a setback, no matter. They get up, regroup, and jump right back in. Moreover, I would argue that good producers *seek out* these challenges. Overcoming obstacles requires strategic thinking, discipline, persistence, and street smarts. You cannot give up. It is a test of one's character, one's *will*, and in the process one learns a great deal about oneself. *The Strategic Producer* aims to offer producers a viable roadmap to getting a feature film *across the finish line* and in front of a distributor. Combine the strategies contained in this book with the resolve to get the job done, and there's no part of the filmmaking monster that can't be slayed.

Part 1

Back Story

Chapter 1

History

All I need to make a comedy is a park, a policeman, and a pretty girl.—Charlie Chaplin

I steal from every single movie ever made. If people don't like that, then tough tills, don't go and see it, all right? I steal from everything. Great artists steal, they don't do homage.—Quentin Tarantino

For millennia humanity has been playing with images and telling stories. Prehistoric cave paintings suggest stories about humanity and hunting. Before language and the spoken word we assembled around the campfire and acted out stories about how our day went, what to watch out for during the hunt, who was sleeping with whom, and what gods we feared or loved. Happy, sad, thoughtful, informative, scary, reassuring, comic, tragic ... there's a story and an audience for every aspect of the human condition. And we've always needed to do this collectively. We've always wanted to share. Some of us developed into better storytellers than others who chose to listen instead, delighted by the increasing sophistication of the storytellers' techniques and the stories they spun.

In China, shadow plays dating back 2,000 years to the Han dynasty can be viewed as precursors to today's motion pictures. Sophisticated characters in complex narratives entertained and enlightened audiences for centuries before the invention of cinema.

And when it comes to live action storytelling we can look to early Greek civilization and plays by Euripides, Sophocles, and others.

But alongside the artists on the frontlines and in the spotlight were the individuals and groups of people who facilitated things. Someone had to help prehistoric artists select the cave and wall on which to paint. Someone had to build the shadow puppets and provide a venue for the performances. Someone had to assemble the wood frame onto which a canvas was stretched. And someone had to invent the first cameras that took the first pictures. In other words: artists have never worked alone. Everything from materials, to venue, to personnel, to salaries, to getting the work seen had to have been done by people other than the artists creating the work. Is it a stretch to call these people *producers* of one sort or another?

Let's go to the moment the movies were born. In the late 1800s technology was being developed and shared across continents. Cinema officially saw the light of day

Figure 1.1 Cave painting at Bhimbetika Rock Shelter by Nikhil Shah
[Credit: Licensed under CC BY SA 3.0]

Figure 1.2 Chinese shadow play figures by S. Meierhofer
[Credit: Licensed under CC BY SA 3.0]

Figure 1.3 Amphitheater in Epidaurus by F. Ingalo
[Credit: Licensed under CC BY SA 3.0]

in a darkened theatre in Paris in 1895 with a film by the Lumière brothers entitled, *Workers Leaving the Lumière Factory in Lyon*. The film, made using an all-in-one camera/projector called the Lumière Cinématograph, is approximately 48 seconds long. *Workers* must have been an astonishing sight for audiences. The eye and the mind had never been fooled in quite this way. The degree of photographic realism combined with motion must have felt radically different, even superior to the most realistic paintings and photographs of the time.

The birth of the American film industry is generally attributed to Thomas Edison and his invention, the Kinetoscope. At first Edison imagined his camera and projector as nothing more than a home consumer product, much like today's camcorder and now obsolete VCR.

The major distinction between Edison's Kinetoscope and the Lumière Cinematograph is that Edison's device was designed to be used by individual viewers—very much like today's smartphones, whereas the Cinématograph's design and purpose was geared toward a collective viewing experience, very much like today's multiplexes. As filmgoers, we all understand the difference between watching a film at home alone and watching one in a packed movie theater. As individual viewers we're left to our own devices (phones, laptops, etc. . . .). Will we react differently to the same film depending on the conditions we see it under? While the question is beyond the scope of this book, it's nonetheless worth posing.

So, while it's good to know when the movies were born or how the first filmmaking technology worked, it's nowhere near as important as knowing how the movies evolved. Before stories, actors, and editing, before the arrival of fiction filmmaking, movies

Figure 1.4 The poster advertising the Lumière brothers Cinématographe, showing a famous comedy (L'Arroseur Arrosé, 1895).

[Credit: Public domain]

Figure 1.5 Today's multiplex echoes the first collective viewing experiences presented by the Lumière brothers over a hundred years ago.

[Credit: Photograph by the author]

History 11

Figure 1.6 Publicity photo of the 1895 version of the Kinetoscope in use, showing the earphones that lead to the cylinder phonograph within the cabinet.

[Credit: Public domain]

Figure 1.7 Smartphones and their ability to stream audio and video are modern day examples of what Thomas A. Edison invented over a hundred years ago.

[Credit: Photograph by the author]

were more like short—very short—documentaries. They captured street scenes, people tending to their gardens, trains pulling into stations, workers leaving a factory, and so on. Daily life captured on celluloid and projected to audiences for their diversion and entertainment.

Even by today's YouTube cat videos standards, the very first films were ridiculously short because cameras like the Lumière Cinematograph could only hold one 50-second long strip of film negative. Remember, we are talking about film before the invention of editing, which involves stringing together a series of shots allowing for something longer. So at the dawn of cinema one shot equaled one movie, filmed in black and white, without sound and with a camera locked onto a tripod that neither panned from left to right nor tilted up or down. Moreover, the framing of that single shot was rarely—if ever—a close up or wide shot. It consisted of one 50-second *proscenium*-style shot. A proscenium-style shot essentially involves placing the camera at eye level 20 to 30 feet away from the subject allowing for a full body shot of people plus some degree of background environment. Imagine you are sitting in a small theater, about halfway back, in the center of the orchestra seating area, with a perfect view of the actors and the stage. That's your proscenium shot.

So how did movies evolve from a basic single shot unit to today's highly complex productions?

Up until the introduction of the Latham Loop, which became a standard feature on cameras and projectors in 1905, movies were short not only because cameras could hold just 50 seconds of film, but also because projectors could only project films of that length. In the case of the film projectors, as a film finished un-spooling the tension on the take-up reel became so powerful that it literally snapped the remaining film on the feed reel. How, the loop's inventors wondered, could they remove the tension from the feed reel and prevent the film from snapping in two? Their ingenious idea was to invent two small cylindrical barrels which sat above and below the projector's lens and the registration pins. The barrels have sprockets on them which hold the film in place, creating two loops, taking the tension off both the feed and take-up reels. The loop isolates the filmstrip from vibration and tension, allowing movies to be continuously shot and projected for extended periods. All of a sudden, with this tension gone, filmmakers could connect many 50-second shots without snapping the fragile film strip. Mr. Woodville Latham and his colleagues had just invented a way to show longer films. And when films became longer, they were no longer limited to merely showing daily life events like people leaving a factory or trains coming and going.

Now movies could tell stories.

The Latham loop is important not only because it allowed film to become a long form storytelling medium but also because it illustrates an important concept with regard to art and technology: throughout film's history, technological innovation leads to artistic development.

Let's jump to the mid-1920s with the introduction of sound. Here, a new technological advancement allowed producers to give voice to actors, to convey the sound of a door slamming, or to underscore a dramatic moment with a music cue.

Later, with the advent of color film, cinematographers, production designers, and art directors could create the illusion of three-dimensional space using color as well as focus the audience's eye on a particular part of the screen. Movies were able to work with a much wider palette, creating new feelings and atmospheres using the new color technology.

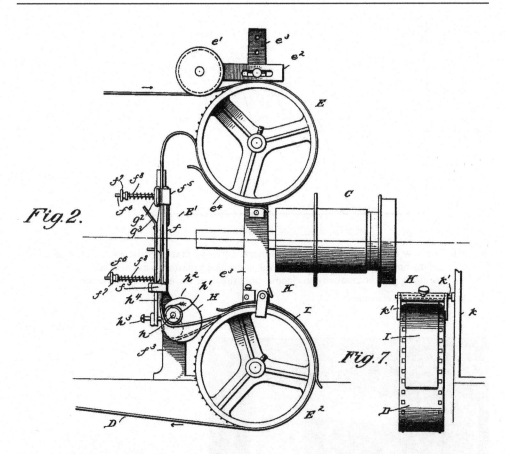

Figure 1.8 U.S. Patent Office illustration of the Latham Loop. The two barrels above and below the lens effectively removed tension and torque from the projector's feed and take up reels allowing for longer films to be made—and shown.

[Credit: Public domain]

More recently the invention of computer generated imaging in the mid-1990s has led to a new kind of cinematic artistic expression, one in which every single pixel is available to the filmmaker to imagine and manipulate.

But with every technological innovation motion pictures experienced a temporary artistic set back.

The first sound movies were visually earthbound. Cameras could no longer soar with the same fluidity they did during the last years of the silent era. With the arrival of sound the new microphones could hear the whirring noises from the camera forcing filmmakers to encase them inside large soundproof room-sized boxes that couldn't budge. An awkward transitional period had these large boxes moving on rails but it wasn't until smaller soundproof cameras were perfected that cinema began to find and improve upon the virtuosic camerawork developed during the silent era.

The arrival of sound also brought temporary artistic compromises. Scriptwriters may have had experience writing silent movies built entirely out of action scenes and

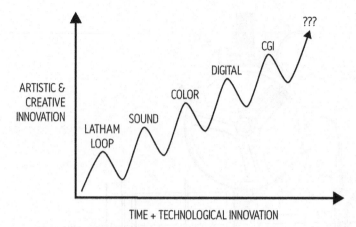

Figure 1.9 As new technology was introduced there were—at first—artistic and creative setbacks or compromises. Over time, however, filmmakers mastered the new technology, bringing greater creativity to cinema, until the next technological innovation.

[Credit: Illustration by the author]

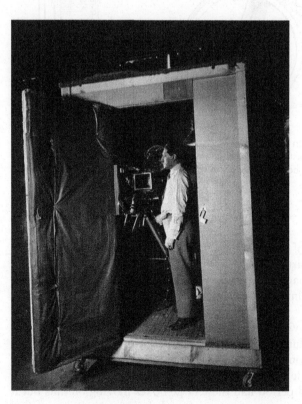

Figure 1.10 With the advent of sound, the camera lost the fluidity gained during the silent era. Here, a cameraman stands inside a soundproof camera booth with a Vitaphone camera, circa 1926.

[Credit: Courtesy of the Library of Congress]

Figure 1.11 Today's smartphones have effectively freed the camera to film everything everywhere and with great fluidity, turning us all into camera operators.

[Credit: Photograph by the author]

the occasional title card, but when it came to dialogue they had little or no idea about what they were doing. It took several years before dialogue began to sound natural. And even once dialogue began to find its feet filmmakers were faced with the problem of delivering it in a believable way. Actors used to acting in silent movies who could not make the transition to performing in dialogue scenes were out of a job, replaced by actors who could. *Singin' in the Rain* (1952) provides not only plenty of entertainment but also uses the transitional years from silent to sound film as a central plot device.

Similarly, the first color movies faced major technical challenges. Images were oversaturated and color negative film didn't hold well, leading to unintended colors. Actors' faces looked otherworldly, their skin tones either overly reddened or pasty white. There were also setbacks in the artistic areas. Cinematographers and production designers had little knowledge about color's ability to help create the illusion of depth and perspective or direct the audience's attention to a specific part of the frame. Consequently the first color films appear unfocused or flat.

More recently, technical and artistic setbacks with the first generation of computer generated imagery (CGI) included artificial looking special effects and movies that were oddly cold and sterile. As CGI matures we are beginning to see it used in not only special effects laden blockbuster movies but in more subtle and nuanced ways smaller movies with engaging characters and unique stories. So, as filmmakers learn to use CGI better, they begin to use it as a background and more support-related tool.

What new technological developments are in store for the movies? We might come up with a theatre in the round holographic 3D movie with characters projected onto surfaces in the theatre and engaging with audience members who will affect the story's outcome. What we can say with some degree of assurance is that technological innovation will bring new artistic possibilities for creative expression. Only after a period of setbacks and adjustments will the new technology integrate itself into a filmmaker's toolkit to allow movies to grow into their future—much improved—stage. As producers working today, we need to keep abreast of technological innovation and the new artistic opportunities it brings.

Allow me one more flashback to cinema's early years and a defining moment. In order for Thomas Edison's cameras and projectors to succeed as commercial products, Edison took it upon himself to produce his own short films to show on the machines he made. These films were at first nothing more than very short documentaries which he licensed to the first exhibitors of his films. These exhibitors paid Edison a fee and screened his films to growing audiences across America. To Edison it seemed like a perfect plan: manufacture the machinery and create the content to show it. But the exhibitors soon came to feel that Edison was charging too much for his films and three major changes occurred. The first was that before sending the films back to Edison, they began trading the films among themselves, sending movies that had played in their market to other exhibitors in exchange for fresh and unseen content—without paying Edison his fee. Second, eventually they simply held on to the films, forcing Edison to go after the exhibitors, a time-consuming and costly endeavor. The third change—and it was to be the most important one—was that the exhibitors learned how to make and present their own movies. Edison sent lawyers after them and persuaded his wealthy east coast bankers to refuse credit lines to these budding producers. His efforts were to be of little or no avail. The exhibitors, having been excluded from Edison's elite group, realized they could manage without him and moved west, Southern California, to be specific, farther west than Los Angeles even, and to what was at the time a one horse town called Hollywood.

The first films needed powerful, heavy, and expensive lamps to generate enough light to burn an acceptable image onto the film stock being used. But the bright and constant Southern California sun soon made it possible to work without cumbersome and expensive lighting. Even interior scenes were filmed outdoors against sets designed to look like living rooms, kitchens, and bedrooms. Add to this a newfound distance and freedom from Edison (who had no idea what Hollywood was to become) and one can imagine how self-sufficient and primed for explosive growth the nascent American film industry was.

One of the great historical ironies of the Hollywood studio system is that it began as a collection of outcasts fleeing the east coast establishment. Today Hollywood is at the apex of mainstream, studio-driven film and television production, but Hollywood's first filmmakers were independents.

Producers today need to ask two important questions of film history; the first is: what are the major film movements and trends, both artistic and commercial, that took place; and secondly: how did these movements and trends influence the present filmmaking landscape? By learning about the first aspect we'll have an easier time understanding the second.

Earlier I told you about how the first films were short documentaries about daily life; workers leaving a factory, a train pulling into a station. But it wasn't long before

Figure 1.12 Hollywood circa 1903.
[Credit: California Historical Society Collection, 1860–1960. Public Domain]

filmmakers began staging micro-scenes for the cameras: a man watering his lawn, a family out on a picnic. These were scenes which, but for the camera's presence, would not have existed. Someone had to produce the scene, find and hire the man, cue the hose, get the props for the picnic, and film the scene. As you might have already guessed, the growing distinction between short documentaries and staged scenes is—today—none other than the same distinction we make between fiction and documentary films, but there is a much higher degree of complexity in today's fiction and documentary films, with documentary-like elements in fiction films and fiction-like elements in documentaries.

Today's audiences have a far more complex understanding of movies than their antecedents from over a century ago. Consequently they have come to expect more complex films. Yet audiences *will* accept a simple story if there's a reason for it. If a story is sufficiently compelling audiences will forgive its lack of complexity and even its production values. Moreover, if a film's overall *feel* is sufficiently appealing and presents characters they empathize with, they may forgo narrative *coherence*, which is why sometimes we come out of the multiplex saying "*it was a lot of fun but the story made no sense whatsoever!*"

The historical split between documentary and fiction led to another very important distinction which impacts upon our work as producers today. Let's put documentaries aside for a moment and take a look at fictional films. Alongside that little staged scene of a man watering his lawn, a new kind of story world emerged. Its most famous proponent was Georges Meliès. His *Voyage dans la lune (A Trip to the Moon*, 1902) is considered the classic example of the fantasy film. We can take every film that has been made since our "realistic" gardener movie and the "fantasy" moon movie and draw a direct line back to one of those two films and genres. *Titanic*? Realism. *12 Monkeys*? Fantasy. *Jaws*? Realism. *Star Wars*? Fantasy. *Casablanca*? Realism. *The Day the Earth Stood Still*? Fantasy.

Naturally, I am speaking in very broad terms. You might argue that *Jaws* is a fantasy—in a sense all movies are. But *Jaws* wants you to believe its fantasy and so aims for realism, while *Star Wars* is asking you to forgo realism and accept its fantasy-driven characters and story. It's also true that fantasy and realism each have sub-genres. Within realism we get neo-realism (*Bicycle Thieves*), magical realism (*Birdman*), social realism (*The French Connection*), and more. Fantasy offers science fiction (*Star Wars*), horror (*Night of the Living Dead*), musicals (*The Sound of Music, West Side Story*), animation (*Snow White and the Seven Dwarfs, The Incredibles*), and more. As producers, knowing what tradition our film is descended from empowers us to better understand the movie we're making and, consequently, make a better film. Documentary, fiction, realism, fantasy. Pick a favorite film and see which of these

Figure 1.13 Workers Leaving the Lumière Factory in Lyon (France, 1895). Considered to be the first motion picture ever made. One can trace today's documentaries and realism-based films back to this film.

[Credit: Public domain]

Figure 1.14 A Trip to the Moon (France, 1902). Often referred to as the first fantasy film. Made by special effects pioneer Georges Meliès. Today's sci-fi and fantasy films can be traced back to Meliès.

[Credit: Public domain]

four categories it fits into. You may find that given today's complex movies and audiences, the film you pick contains elements that fit into *all four*.

The ability to mix up documentary, fiction, realism, and fantasy in differing doses and to come up with an entirely new style or storytelling method is rooted in technological innovation which, starting in the late 1950s in the U.S. and Europe, led to massive aesthetic and economic changes. Half a century ago when the godfather of American independent filmmaking, John Cassavetes, was in his backyard making movies like *Husbands* (1970), and *A Woman under the Influence* (1974) with his wife Gena Rowlands and pals Peter Falk and Ben Gazzara, the only cameras available were clunky 16 and 35 millimeter behemoths that weighed anywhere from 25 to 40 pounds or more. Hand-held work was a chore, film stock was expensive, and lenses and film stocks weren't as sensitive to light as they are today. By today's standards Mr. Cassavetes still worked with cumbersome cameras and plenty of lighting gear and, while he was able to keep to a small crew size, he nonetheless needed gaffers and grips. Yet, when compared to the films being made by the studios at the time, his crews were microscopic. Cassavetes was upending the standard economic filmmaking model and also forging a new aesthetic. It was an aesthetic born out of desire as much as it was born out of having to work with very limited resources. Today, filmmakers work with small, digital cameras requiring almost no lighting and crews as small as two or three people. Thanks to film movements like Dogme 95 audiences around the world have embraced the scruffy, hand-held, unlit look. We see it in films, television, advertising, the internet, everywhere. The hand-held look forged by Mr. Cassavetes and others has by now become deeply ingrained in American mainstream fiction and fantasy filmmaking. In *Cloverfield* (2008), a Godzilla-like monster destroys Manhattan. The film is a collection of documentary-style scenes, apparently found on a set of tapes left inside camcorders whose owners fled the scene (or were eaten!). In *Chronicle* (2012), a group of high school students develop superhuman powers, the entire tale told through hand-held camcorder-like, *verité* footage. The *Paranormal Activity* franchise is all about the documentary look at the service of a fictional story. Its predecessor, *The Blair Witch Project*, is considered by many to be the turning point when mainstream audiences embraced that cinematic style at the multiplex.

Thanks to the changes in technology and the new economic models surrounding film production it is no longer essential for a film to have a polished, classic Hollywood look. If in the past there was one predominant aesthetic audiences gravitated to, today there are myriad aesthetic choices to choose from. Today anything goes. It all means one thing: *if you have something to say that audiences want to hear, and you say it in a new, interesting, innovative, and compelling way, the technology or budget doesn't matter.* Sometimes a film can ignite the passions and imaginations of large groups of people without high production values, a movie star, or a name director. If what you've made resonates, you may have a shot at festivals and—eventually—distribution.

Chapter 2

Story

There is no suspense in the bang, only in the anticipation of it.—Alfred Hitchcock

A story should have a beginning, a middle and an end ... but not necessarily in that order.—Jean-Luc Godard

Our species has spent thousands of years telling stories. We invented our own creation myths to help explain who we are, why we're here, and where we're going. Fairy tales are allegorical, symbolic, or metaphorical stories we tell our children to help them understand the world they are growing up in. They convey the so-called wisdom that we—as adults—have learned from living life. Wisdom which we—as children—got from our parents and antecedents. Stories, in other words, help us become fully formed human beings.

Good producers need to have a nose for what is in the air, circulating among the culture at large; what ideas, themes, concerns, and interests people have, and they need to be willing to wager that their story will resonate with society. They must be able to converse persuasively with their key collaborators about the ins and outs of their story, must be able to speak about the whys and wherefores of their tale, and must be able to move forward and lead a successful film production. Moreover, good producers need to understand story archetypes and structures. They need to see, question, and affect or change the story at the beat, scene, sequence, act, and script level.

The Artistic Impulse

When novelist Stephen King was asked where he got his ideas from he answered with *"How should I know and if I did why would I tell you? They've been good to me."* Mr. King knows that his ideas come from deep inside his subconscious and that attempting to describe the journey his ideas take from there up and out to his word processor runs the risk of tampering with and maybe even destroying his creative process. King is saying that he doesn't like to think too deeply about his process. He prefers seizing the artistic impulse and running with it until it turns into another one of his page turners. King does not want to upset his Muse. If he discovers where his ideas come from they will cease being "good" to him, meaning they will disappear and along with them, his livelihood.

Mr. King's quote speaks to the essence of the creative process. The artistic impulse may be inexplicable to the artist, yet there exists a human need to express oneself that is fulfilled through art. In movies the artistic impulse is also present, either in the mind of a scriptwriter, a director, an actor, or any number of other members of the cast and crew, each of them expressing that impulse at various times and in various ways. Producers may also feel the artistic impulse, but as producers they are by definition business people, choosing the story and marshalling the cast and crew who perform the actual artistry audiences will hopefully enjoy. While the lives of a novelist and a film producer could not be more different, the successful ones share the desire to create something that connects with people. Wanting to share a movie is different from wanting to make a movie for oneself or because "*I want to.*" Bestselling novelist James Patterson adds: "*If you want to write for yourself, get a diary. If you want to write for a few friends, get a blog. But if you want to write for a lot of people, think about them a little bit. What do they like? What are their needs? A lot of people in this country go through their days numb. They need to be entertained. They need to feel something.*" His words could be applied to the mindset of a successful producer.

So let us agree that we need to make something that goes beyond something we'd make for ourselves. There are too many people involved, too much money at stake, and too large of an audience required for the film for it to be just for us.

Why Stories

When there is a story being told on the screen, people respond. If you're going to be a producer you're going to need to know how a story is built, what its components are, how it operates, what it can and cannot do, and what makes a story work or not work.

At the root of any story is an idea that conveys some aspect of the human condition. A story can be a morality play, that is: through a story we are taught a lesson about how to perhaps live our lives in a more altruistic way. Sometimes, instead of portraying an upstanding hero, the *moral of the story* is conveyed through the absence of morality or the destruction of the morally good guy. We say, "*Isn't that awful! The good guy lost! It goes to show you that sometimes bad guys win. We have to watch out.*" By modeling immoral behavior sometimes a story can show us how *not* to live.

Sometimes stories infantilize us, entertain us for no other purpose than to make us momentarily forget our cares or worries or anxieties. And sometimes a story is a way to make us feel like we're part of a larger group of human beings sharing the same trials and tribulations. Stories can be *on the nose* or they can be highly metaphorical, symbolic, or allegorical, meaning that their true purpose isn't self-evident at first glance but only after some deliberation and reflection do we understand them—perhaps in a deeper way than if that story had been told directly and without mystery.

Our minds are wired to listen to and tell stories. Throw a seemingly random set of scenes at us and we'll figure out a way to connect them into a narrative. You may see a shot of a skyscraper, followed by a shot of a man coming home, followed by a shot of a deer in the forest, followed by a shot of a woman emerging from a supermarket, and you will somehow find a way to connect these disparate images (and sounds) into something that means something to you.

Oral to Visual Storytelling

Storytelling happens every day, everywhere, and comes in all shapes and sizes. A friend begins with *"you won't believe what happened to me today."* In her mind's eye she is already formulating an engaging way to tell you what happened, and she wants you to know about it because it affected her in some way and she believes you will be entertained, learn, or benefit from hearing it. If I were to ask you to tell me about one of the most joyous experiences you've ever had you would probably frame it within the context of a short story. *"We were walking along a ridge and suddenly, there they were . . . the Northern Lights. We couldn't believe how beautiful they were. I turned to the other hikers who were looking at their smartphones and complaining about not getting a signal!"*

What you need to know as a producer—and as a writer—is that the anecdotal story, the one told casually in a bar by one person to another, contains the basic information required for a scene in a screenplay. Think about it. The Northern Lights anecdote contains: location (a mountain ridge), characters (hikers), and action (fumbling with cameras). As a storyteller you could develop each of these elements. It was a rocky and forbidding, precarious ridge. The hikers were tired or happy, and the cameras were smartphones that needed re-charging. These details come with story development and make the story more authentic, believable, or real. But the essence remains unchanged and essential to telling the story. If you were to ask "what's the moral of that Northern Lights anecdote?" the answer might be *you won't find beauty if you're not open to it*, or *in the battle between technology and nature, technology has won.*

Oral storytelling forces the storyteller's mind to come up with the least amount of words necessary to effectively tell the story. It forces the storyteller to edit out extraneous material and hew very closely to the storyline. And the storyline's main goal is to keep the listener wanting to know one thing: *what happens next.*

Chapter 3

Working the Material

A natural story is what we're after. If a story feels right, it probably is. If a story feels like it needs to be improved or enhanced with a chase scene or a big finish, it probably needs work. It's a well-known maxim that *writing is re-writing*. To get to a place where a story feels right requires improving that story. How does a producer, working with a writer, get to that point? How are you going to know which changes are good and which ones are not?

Creativity is a messy enterprise. The surest way to fail at improving a story is to believe there's a clear-cut, clean, and logical method to it. There isn't. The most common mistake storytellers make when rewriting a story is believing there are elements to their story that must be kept, no matter what. Once a story has been outlined, a stubbornness is born in the minds of the writers—and many producers—and no matter how wrongheaded or misguided a character, story point, or theme may be, no one is prepared to throw it out and start over. It just feels like it would mean too much work to go back to the drawing board. This is how bad ideas become fixtures inside a story's structure. Removing them later on becomes even more difficult. So, to get to a place where the story feels right requires the willingness to go back to the drawing board and re-conceive the very nature of the story.

Authenticity, willingness to explore alternative scenarios, getting under your character's skin and imagining their hopes, needs, wants, aspirations, and desires, coming up with scenes that help illustrate the story you're trying to tell; all of these elements and qualities will help you clarify your story's central idea. And the more you work on it the more it will evolve. You may start out wanting to tell a coming of age story but as you develop it you come to realize you've been trying to tell a story about the impossibility of going home. Good storytellers realize this shift in their thinking and immediately start reworking their story to reflect the new direction it's taking. We'll be coming back to the idea of change and adapting throughout the book. Producing means being able to think on your feet and—when necessary—make decisions that lead to immediate and important changes in your production.

Suspension of Disbelief

> Cinema should make you forget you are sitting in a theater.—Roman Polanski

Hovering above the story is *suspension of disbelief*. No matter how fantasy-driven or reality-based the theme, characters, and storyline may be, the movie does not work if audiences are unwilling to give themselves over to it. If audiences are not emotionally invested in the movie, if they have not bought into the movie's story world, they will sit passively thinking about how they've just wasted two hours of their life watching something they don't care about. The movie has failed because it has not transported them from their computer screen or their seat in the multiplex sufficiently deep into the movie's story world. So how does a movie succeed in getting audiences to start believing in the reality or fantasy it proposes?

Believability is a tricky business. When a moviegoer sits down to watch a movie they are entering into an agreement—almost like a contract—between themselves and the filmmakers. That agreement goes something like this: in exchange for your $10, for the next two hours you will be transported. Where we (the filmmakers) take you, has already been addressed when you (audience member) watched our trailer, read about our movie, and decided to see it, for whatever reason, including but not limited to: liking the poster, finding the story to be of interest, talking about the film with friends, enjoying the previous films of our movie's star, etc. Furthermore, dear moviegoer, as we un-spool our tale, we promise to set up rules and conventions which you can trust the film will abide by. Superman can fly but is vulnerable to kryptonite. The Titanic will indeed eventually sink, but not before we tell you a memorable love story. The shark is not a vegetarian. The force is the province of the Jedi. The blue pill does one thing, the red another. As you can imagine, should the movie renege on these rules and conventions, audiences will feel let down. They will stop believing in the story. They will feel betrayed, will *suspend their suspension of disbelief*, and will lose interest in the movie.

What you are doing as a storyteller is casting a spell on your audience. Every story point, every story turn, every character action, line of dialogue, every shot, scene, and sequence is about sustaining and enlarging that spell. Producers must never lose sight of the idea of casting a spell. The story's believability, no matter how outrageous the premise, depends on the audience's suspension of disbelief (which could be re-phrased as *acceptance of the film's story world*). As a budding producer, for every technical, logistic, and creative decision you make, you will need to pose the question: will this contribute or take away from the audience's suspension of disbelief? We'll delve deeper into the idea of combining creative thinking with logistics when we look at the nuts and bolts of production. For now, as producers concerned about story let's remember the importance of transporting the audience by casting a spell through suspension of disbelief.

Character

Good producers recognize the value of stories with characters audiences can *empathize* with. Think about it. Who wants to spend two hours with an unlikable dolt? But there's a paradox here: without unlikable characters audiences won't have the necessary conflict all stories need; the conflict between *our* hero and their nemesis, that unlikable dolt I just mentioned. Note how I've italicized *our*, placing the good person on our side of the fence and moving the unlikable one to the other side. Positioning the good hero as one of *us* and the antagonist as one of *them* is one of the most time honored story devices ever used in movies. Even *bad* heroes like Tony Montana in *Scarface* manage to elicit our empathy before they—inevitably—pay for their sins. And pay for their sins they must, because when they don't we feel that not all has been made right with the world. Balance has *not* been restored and we can *not* go home satisfied that justice has been served. But occasionally we do like to see bad heroes triumph. It is a peculiar talent on behalf of the adept storyteller to create empathy for a *bad* protagonist. While we, the audience, would never deign to lie, cheat, steal, betray, or kill, we nonetheless enjoy a vicarious form of temporary satisfaction in empathizing with the antagonist, perhaps even rooting for them, as long as we may resume our lives when the lights come up and justice has been served. When it hasn't, as in—for example—*No Country For Old Men* (2007)—we are left in an intentional moral limbo, unsure of what to make of the fact that *the bad guy got away*. Is it more appealing for the audience to have a *good* hero at the center of a story than it is to have a *bad* one? Is the *us* always better than the *them*? Both options are available. We can exhibit self-interest and altruism, compassion or malevolence, kindness or brutality, all within the space of a few days, hours, minutes, or seconds. The truth is that we are conflicted beings and—as such—the characters we create should also exhibit these conflicts. Creating this nuanced, fluctuating state is one of the most difficult tasks a scriptwriter faces. It is—however—very appealing to audiences precisely because it reflects the core nature of the human condition. Good producers understand these nuances and recognize them in the story they're producing.

A principal character in a story has to want something. A promotion. A lover. Money. Peace of mind. Revenge. Power. Respect. The ability to fly. To be invisible. To time travel. The story is what happens when the character does or does not get what they want. Principal characters need to have eureka moments. That instance when a light bulb goes on and they realize something they didn't realize before. And principal characters must undergo or want to undergo change. They must have a moment, or a series of moments when they believed one thing but now—given this most recent revelation—must believe another. They must have been wrong. Even if it is momentary or even of they don't—in the end—change permanently, they must at least seriously consider it. The most difficult aspect of character creation is making them human, fully formed, three dimensional. It is as hard to create a real character with feelings as it is to paint a portrait that moves us. As difficult as it is, we should not be discouraged. To the contrary. We should accept that the first of many iterations of that character and their story will be awful and that we are in it for the long haul, working to make our characters (and stories) authentic, original, and human.

But how?

One method has to with the character and their *wants*. The most common error storytellers make is to plug the character into a story, any story. The thinking goes that the character—a "stand in" for the audience—plus the story's forward movement will keep audiences watching because—as I note above—they'll want to know *what happens next*. But *what happens next* doesn't mean anything unless we add *to whom*? If, on the other hand, we know our hero wants to be the greatest women's boxing champ of all time, we can begin to deduce what scenes we'll need in order to allow—or disallow—our hero to reach her goal. But we cannot stop there. We must unpack our hero's life, from the moment she was born right up to the present dilemma she faces. We need to think about where she's coming from, what she wants, and where she's going. We need to ask questions like "would she throw a fight in order to get a shot at a title later on?" or "Why is she boxing? What is it about her past that's brought her to the sport?" We need to determine our heroine's *values*. With our values clear, whatever we throw at our heroine will be met with a clear response, even if that response is confusion. Our character has been developed to such an extent that any event or development we confront her with is met with an authentic response; just as a real person would respond to the request to throw a fight, our character will respond in the same way.

We will unpack character, dialogue, action, style, structure, and more when we talk about the actual writing and producing of screenplays. For the time being, let's stay away from the messiness of writing and look at how stories can be suspenseful, mysterious, and original.

Suspense, Surprise, and Mystery

A good story—and by extension a good screenplay—makes you want to know what happens next. There are a number of ways a talented storyteller can achieve that constant curiosity. One method is to make endearing characters audiences empathize with, characters whose fate or destiny audiences are going to want to stick around until story's end to find out what becomes of this person they've gotten to know. Empathy for a character can be created through obvious means, like having the heroine save a distressed kitten from atop a tree or in less obvious ways, like having the hero perform a selfless act that remains unknown to everyone in the story.

Another method for sustaining the audience's curiosity is by creating suspense. Suspense can be created over a number of seconds, minutes, or throughout an entire movie. What is a suspenseful sequence, then? How is it created and does it keep audiences watching your movie?

At the start of *Jaws*, a woman goes for a swim. A few feet below the water's surface is a hungry shark. The woman doesn't know about the shark, but the audience does. Suddenly the audience is asking itself if—and when—the shark is going to attack. The film is called *Jaws*, so that certainly helps with the question "will the shark attack?" Having answered that question, the audience now needs to know when the attack is going to happen. They'll keep watching until it does. Meanwhile, the story, told using every possible cinematic device available to the filmmakers, builds and builds, delaying and dancing around the moment of the attack for as long as possible, making the audience increasingly anxious, perhaps even hoping the swimmer will somehow get away. Music, long, ponderous shots of the water's calm surface, underwater shots of the swimmer's legs swaying gently, the appearance of normality—all work to counter the knowledge the audience has that there's a hungry shark about to strike. Talented filmmakers know how to milk suspenseful sequences for all they're worth until the last possible moment.

Alfred Hitchcock, whose quote begins this chapter, was known as the "master of suspense." He was asked to define suspense and his quote does an excellent job. But Hitch went on to provide an archetypal suspense scene as an example. In a restaurant two people are sitting at a table having a conversation. They talk about nothing in particular—they may even meander from topic to topic. We cut back and forth between them until we cut to a package underneath the table. We come in closer and hear a ticking sound emanating from inside the package. We go back to the two people talking nonchalantly and suddenly the conversation they're having has taken on a new sense of urgency. If we had never seen a shot of the ticking package under the table and if the restaurant suddenly explodes into a million pieces we would not have been treated to a suspenseful scene. We would have been surprised.

Suspense—and surprise—can be far more subtle and nuanced. For example: the audience may know that a longtime employee is about to be fired. She doesn't have a clue and is putting the finishing touches on buying a home. When will she learn she's been let go? How will she react? What will the impact of getting fired be on her ability to buy a home? Audiences are going to be more inclined to stick around to find out.

As a producer, you need to understand the difference between surprise and suspense and be able to spot it in a story, then in a script, and finally in your movie.

Mystery is another way stories keep us wanting to know what happens next. But not so much mystery that we become confused and lose interest. Mystery is such an effective story device that the word appears in thousands of movie titles and television series. Mystery is what keeps us watching *Close Encounters of the Third Kind* (1977) because we need to know what the extraterrestrials look like. Mystery is why we enjoy *Murder on the Orient Express* (1974) or *Seven* (1995), which offers puzzles for audiences to put together. As with all good storytelling, mystery keeps us wanting to know what happens next.

If the central reason we are attracted to mysteries is because we want to know what happens next, it follows that we will be satisfied when we finally learn—or solve—the mystery presented to us. The murders are solved. The extraterrestrials show themselves. And yet it's also true that a purposefully ambiguous, unresolved, ending (*Zodiac*, 2006) works as well as one in which the mystery is solved. Some stories are supposed to end when the movie does. Others, we imagine, are supposed to continue after the final fade to black. The lesson here is to have *developed the story sufficiently well so that the ending is unpredictable yet inevitable.*

Originality

Wise first-time producers understand that, absent A-list movie stars and studio-backed multi-million dollar production and marketing budgets, their film is going to have a hard time getting noticed. If your film is going to stand a chance at attracting distributors you will have to work with talented writers creating moving stories told with original storytelling methods. As we're about to see, there are many examples of films whose story and storytelling methods are so innovative, so unique, so different and original, that distributors and audiences could not turn away. The idea is to come up with a story and storytelling method that has broken free from the traditional narrative and storytelling techniques which the studios are tied to because of their need to keep their production and distribution pipeline flowing with cookie cutter (sequel anyone?) movies told in a conventional way.

What are some examples of moving stories told in original ways?

Take a look at *Betrayal* (1983) from Harold Pinter's stage play. A failed marriage told in reverse, set in a couple of apartments, with only four characters.

Or *Memento*, (2000). A man loses his short-term memory and must play out the same scene over and over, cobbling together his narrative (and ours) through a series of Polaroids.

Sex, Lies, and Videotape (1989). The medium of film itself plays a central character in the lives of a group of people testing sexual boundaries.

Timecode (2000). A real time narrative unfolding before us with the screen divided into four smaller screens, filmed by four cameras simultaneously, the actors synched to interact at various time and places during the telling of a story about betrayal.

Birdman (2014). One seemingly *continuous and unedited* set of scenes in the life of an actor trying for a comeback.

Brick (2005). A film noir complete with a murder and staccato street-wise crime novel 1940s dialogue spoken by today's teens and set in a modern day suburban high school.

Or *Fantastic Mr. Fox* (2009). A stop-frame animated film for adults about a talking fox and his adventures.

Or *Italian For Beginners* (2000). The paths of six characters cross at an Italian class at the local adult education center.

Or *Locke* (2013). One man. One car. One cell phone. A real time drive on a British highway at night during which time Ivan Locke's life either falls apart or is saved.

Or *The Atomic Café* (1982). One of the very first of the so-called found footage, or compilation, films.

In each of these and many other examples the filmmakers distinguished themselves sufficiently enough to elicit the attention and interest of distributors and audiences. Good producers understand the value of being innovative, authentic, and different, and pick their stories and storytelling methods accordingly.

Chapter 4

Writing the Script

> We're told every day that America's future is basically in service but our history is in building things—railroads and cars and cities—but Steve Jobs, in building something that's taking us to our future, has also taken us to one of the best parts of our past. Now all I have to do is turn that into three acts with an intention, obstacle, exposition, inciting action, reversal, climax and denouement and make it funny and emotional and I'll be in business.—Aaron Sorkin

Many producers believe anyone can write. It's just writing. How hard can it be? Not everyone can compose a soundtrack or set up a complex lighting scheme. But writing seems to be one of those activities that is available to everyone and, as such, need not be remunerated as royally as other activities. If you're a producer that can also write good scripts, great! You're all set. If you can't write, have the honesty to accept it and hire someone who can. Perhaps the question is academic, but it should be posed: why bother writing a script in the first place?

Good producers don't need to be good scriptwriters. They just need to be able to recognize good scripts. Earlier I told you about the need for audiences to empathize with the story's central characters. If that empathy is missing from the script it's going to have a hard time appearing on the screen. A popular adage from the world of theater has it that: *if it ain't on the page, it ain't on the stage*. Additionally, as I pointed out earlier, not only should audiences empathize with characters but they also need to see those characters undergo some kind of personal *transformation*. How stories become memorable is when change comes to the protagonist. If at one point she believed something, now she must—in the face of the facts before her—believe something else. If a character remains unchanged throughout the story they are basically at the helm of a forgettable story.

One way to look at a script is to tell yourself that you need to have something on paper which you and your collaborators can call a road map. Story and character aside, the script could be viewed as *a series of technical and aesthetic instructions to your cast and crew*. For example:

- Actors need a script to know what their lines and actions are.
- Art directors need a script to know what sets they need to build and dress.
- Cinematographers need a script to know when they're filming outside, inside, during the day or night.
- Sound engineers need a script to know if they'll be recording dialogue, how much of it, and whether it's happening indoors or outside.

- Hair and makeup artists need a script to know how many actors they'll be working with, what the breakdown is gender-wise.
- The wardrobe department needs a script to know how many costumes and costume changes they'll need to prepare.
- Script supervisors need a script to know if the lines actors are saying match the lines on the script. They also need to know the story's continuity; what is the timeframe over which the story takes place, where are the points of demarcation between, for example, a Tuesday and a Wednesday in the story and how does this affect everything from wardrobe to makeup to props and much more.

The need for a script is so critical to a successful production that even outlying, maverick directors known for their so called script-less approach to filmmaking understand that eventually data has to be communicated to cast and crew. For months at a time British director Mike Leigh will work out scenes with a group of actors using nothing more than character objectives, themes, or conflicts. As his story and characters take hold he begins to firm things up, and by the time production starts his cast and crew—whether they are actually holding a script in hand or not—has the data listed above and can come to work prepared. Mike Leigh is an outlier and has a solid production support team that can take the scenes he's spent months developing which his team shepherds into production. And since that production support team comes in on time and on budget there's a good chance Leigh is going to succeed and be allowed to make another film. But Leigh's technique is rare. Most of us don't have the many months Leigh uses to develop his story and characters through improvisation. So, as budding producers, *let's agree up front to make a script a requirement*, if only to make sure we don't waste time and money. And, to confirm that a script doesn't have to wreck a film (as in: suffocate it), let's remind ourselves of the script to Billy Wilder's *The Apartment* (1960) which, when compared with the finished film, is 99 percent *verbatim*. This is a very rare occurrence except that Mr. Wilder repeated that feat with a subsequent film, *The Fortune Cookie* (1966). Like Mr. Leigh, Mr. Wilder is also an outlier, but in the opposite direction, aiming and successfully replicating word for word the script he had authored.

Whether you are writing a script or commenting on someone else's writing you must never lose sight of the fact that first drafts are always clumsy, forced, and just plain bad. That's why they are called *first drafts*. Their job is to be awful or nearly so, and your job is to bring that draft from *suck* to *doesn't suck*. Time and time again producers, directors, and writers genuinely believe a script to be *camera ready* when in fact it's not. If you adopt the mindset that you will be writing and re-writing up to and including the actual shoot, you'll be relieved to know that, come what may, you and your writer(s) gave the script your all.

Elements and Structure of the Script

> A producer can be described as a dog with a script in its mouth.—Linda Obst

> People have forgotten how to tell a story. Stories don't have a middle or an end any more. They usually have a beginning that never stops beginning.—Steven Spielberg

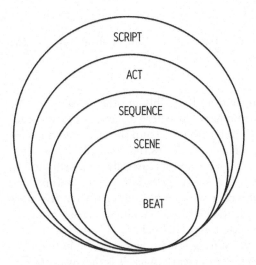

Figure 4.1 A script can be broken down into its basic components of beat, scene, sequence, and act. Actors perform the beats. Directors work the scenes, sequences, and acts while producers are more concerned with making the overall project/script into a finished film.

[Credit: Illustration by the author]

The smallest, most basic, unit of measurement in a script is often called the *beat*. Beats are simple actions like a facial expression or a gesture, individual lines of dialogue, pauses, breaks, or short transitional elements like an establishing shot of a building or a dissolve or fade to black. Beats are what the audience is consuming at the ground level. They are what the audience sees and hears. They do not announce the story's theme in a grand fashion. They do not overtly state the story's overarching theme or emotional arc. When a director is directing he is aware of or in the act of *discovering* these beats and is working with his cast and crew to capture them with the camera and microphone. When an actor is acting, her job is to perform the beat, not the theme. She looks out of her office window and sighs (beat). She does not get up and tell us that her soul sucking job is keeping her from spreading her wings and flying away, and that she is bored and lost (theme). Or, put another way, she *is* telling us about the theme but she is doing it *indirectly*, through the *beats*. As with all of the creative arts, there are no absolute rules. Sometimes she *does* spell out her character's central conflict. That, in and of itself, constitutes a series of beats she'll deliver—perhaps in a *confessional monologue*. However they are expressed, beats are building blocks to the next unit of script measurement, the scene.

Take a series of beats and artfully string them together and you have a *scene*. A scene is defined as a single unit involving a set of characters interacting in a single location. A scene that begins in a shoe store and ends in a baseball stadium isn't a scene. It's a sequence (more on sequences below). A scene in a shoe store starts and ends there. There is a reason why this is important for producers to understand. The first is that informed producers will be able to judge whether a script is well written or not based on how scenes are presented. If a scene begins with the slug line:

```
INT. SHOE STORE—DAY
```

and after a page or two we find ourselves in a baseball stadium without having read

```
EXT. BASEBALL STADIUM—DAY
```

we know the script is flawed at least in format and possibly in other areas.

Another reason why producers need to understand where a scene starts and ends has to do with the scene's content. A well-crafted scene sets up the character's wants, pits those wants against an obstacle, either delivers or denies that want, and then sends the characters and story into the next scene. This sounds awfully simplistic and of course it is. The deeper, nuanced nature of a scene's rhythm, color, texture, and ambience are the province of the talented writer who fleshes out character and story to such an extent that the audience suspends their disbelief, willingly setting aside the idea that they are watching actors performing a work of fiction.

Beats and scenes can be *overwritten*. Overwriting is a tendency among both novice and experienced script writers to want to state too clearly what it is they want to say. Overwriting manifests itself through excessive and unnecessary dialogue and action, rendering the script far less efficient than it could be. This *fat*, if you'll allow the term, is deadly to knowledgeable producers because more often than not, after time and money has been spent filming, it's edited out of the finished film. Good producers know how to assess a script to determine where it is *overwritten* and then act swiftly, in tandem with the script writer and director, to correct the situation. It's worth adding here that despite our culture's incredibly sophisticated audio-visual literacy (meaning: our ability to tell and receive complex stories through images and sounds and our unconscious understanding of symbols and language), filmmakers still make the *overwriting* error. It's as if we cannot fully believe—as scriptwriters—that once we move from the script to actually making the film, new collaborators are going to be working to enhance, improve, and even transform the story we're telling. Those collaborators include actors, directors, production designers, cinematographers, editors, and many more people and skill sets. Good producers recognize that the script is not the film; it is a *blueprint* for the film. It is scaffolding. It is, in the words of Russian film director Andrei Tarkovsky, "*The film as told to a blind man.*"

If a script can be overwritten, it can also be *underwritten*. Producers need to be equally concerned about a script whose storyline doesn't appear to make sense, or if there are placeholder lines in the script like

```
INT. BAR—DAY
```

Jim enters the bar. [We'll write a really cool scene here where he talks to seven people before finding out the person he's looking for is missing.]

Signs of an underwritten script include confusing storylines, elliptical, unclear dialogue, spotty or partial action, scenes that meander, missing beats, and insufficient information about characters and overall story. One can look at storytelling as the act of relating information, but it has to be the right amount. Too much (overwritten) and the audience guesses where things are going and loses interest. Not enough (underwritten) and the audience becomes confused and—again—loses interest.

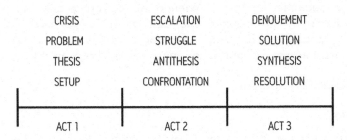

Figure 4.2 No matter how much we may try to break from a three act structure, we are hard wired to infer it in every story we read, see, or hear.
[Credit: Illustration by the author]

Take a series of scenes and artfully string them together and you have a *sequence*. A sequence is a set of scenes that are unified through either theme, character, or narrative drive—and span multiple locations. The Nazi excavation scenes in *Raiders of the Lost Ark* (1981) comprise a sequence. Luke Skywalker's scenes as he trains to become a Jedi warrior comprise a sequence. In *The Godfather* (1972), Tom Haden's (played by the actor Robert Duvall) trip to Los Angeles, culminating with the classic "horse's head" scene is a *sequence of scenes*. In *Casablanca* (1942), the flashback scenes in Paris between Humphrey Bogart and Ingrid Bergman comprise a *sequence*.

Take a series of sequences and artfully string them together and you have an *act*. String three acts together and you have a script.

The script's three acts can be named in various ways. Setup/Confrontation/Resolution. Thesis/Antithesis/Synthesis. Problem/Work/Solution. Regardless of the nomenclature, what is established in Act 1 is somehow transformed into a *struggle* in Act 2 before it becomes *resolved* in Act 3. Balance/Imbalance/Balance. Crisis/Escalation/End of Crisis. Again, many words work here. Moreover, what is fascinating about this model is how difficult it is to break. No matter how incomprehensible a film is, the human mind's ability to connect images and sounds into a coherent or semi-coherent narrative is a huge asset to filmmakers. Consciously or subconsciously, we humans can make the most nonsensical, illogical, poorly written, cliché-ridden, and non-linear story conform to the three-act model because, in order to make sense of what we're seeing, we will *impute* it. *Once upon a time . . . and then one day . . . and they lived happily (or not) ever after*. No matter how much we may want to break from it, we will do whatever it takes to apply the three-act structure to any story—in a film and in life—because as human beings we are hard-wired to do so.

Style

Celebrated screenwriter and novelist William Goldman's most famous quip is "*Nobody knows anything.*" We'll come back to this phrase when we unpack the business plan, marketing, and distribution. For now, let's look at Mr. Goldman's second most famous idea—that there are always two versions of a script: the version for the investors/producers who don't know how to read a script and the version for the director and crew who do. Before turning to the latter, we need to understand that, in the producer's or investor's version of the script one might read something like this:

And so, our hero, because he was orphaned at a young age but triumphed over adversity to become the CEO of a large multinational company, decides to open an orphanage designed to nurture future businessmen because he just feels it's right.

In the director's version one might read this:

EXT. ORPHANAGE—DAY

A ribbon runs from one side the building's front door to the other. We reveal Sam, now taking a pair of scissors from Mayor Biggs, and turning to the townspeople, media crews, and passersby. He stops smiling. He thinks.

CUT TO: Sam at age 5 in the McGuinness Orphanage, fighting the other boys for a piece of bread.

CUT TO: Sam at age 3 being given away by his mother, on the steps of the McGuiness Orphanage.

CUT TO: The present. The scissors in Sam's hands. Biggs turns his head, his eyes moving from the crowd to Sam's face.

Sam's eyes move from the scissors up to the porch of a nearby home where he sees a BOY, about five years old, holding his MOTHER'S hand, watching the ceremony.

Back to Sam, now exchanging glances with the boy as a hand comes to rest on his shoulder.

It's Biggs. He smiles. Sam looks at him, turns to the ribbon, and cuts it.

Version 1 is a reiteration of the story's *plot*, which can be defined as the story told extemporaneously, while version 2 is a set of beats from the actual story as it unfolds; an inventory of actions that are filmable by a camera and, if we add a monologue, recordable by a microphone:

> SAM
>
> This day is a dream come true
> for me, but far more important, it's
> a new beginning for the world's
> disenfranchised, the forgotten,
> who need only to be given the chance to
> realize the greatness that lies within each and
> every one of us that aspires to . . . *(etc.)*

Furthermore, while version 1 relates that Sam is capable of empathy, version 2 illustrates it and makes the moment authentic, emotional, human.

You can film the second version but you can't film the first. Investors, financiers, and many producers understand the first version but may have problems understanding the second.

Look at the investor/backer version as resembling a novel that allows for poetic flights of fancy and purple prose, while the director version resembles a sub-genre of the novel: the hard boiled detective/crime genre which, more often than not, sticks to images and sounds a camera and microphone can capture.

A good example of how the hard boiled novel resembles a script is to consider just about any passage from James M. Cain's American noir classic, *The Postman Always Rings Twice*.

> Then I saw her. She had been out back, in the kitchen, but she came into gather up my dishes. Except for the shape, she really wasn't a raving beauty, but she had a sulky look to her, and her lips stuck out in a way that made me want to mash them in for her.
>
> "Meet my wife."
>
> She didn't look at me. I nodded at the Greek, gave my cigar a kind of wave, and that was all. She went out with the dishes, and so far as he and I were concerned, she hadn't even been there. I left them, but in five minutes I was back, to leave a message for the guy in the Cadillac. It took me half an hour to get sold on the job, but at the end of it I was in the filling station, fixing flats.
>
> "What's your name, hey?"
>
> "Frank Chambers."
>
> "Nick Papadakis, mine."
>
> We shook hands, and he went. In a minute I heard him singing. He had a swell voice. From the filling station I could just get a good view of the kitchen.

Note how Mr. Cain's writing sticks to what can be seen or heard (i.e. filmed and recorded). There are few flights of poetic fancy or long-winded musings about *how* the narrator/protagonist/hero *feels* about the events unfolding. Moreover, note how his writing situates characters in locations. The reader understands perfectly well who is where, what they're doing, and what the physical proximity the characters have to one another. And, finally, note how Mr. Cain allows the reader to fill in the blanks, creating suspense and interest with the line "*From the filling station I could just get a good view of the kitchen.*"

Good producers recognize these differences and navigate the world of scripts and script versions knowing that different people are used to different ways of reading. And they know that, come production time, they want to be working with the director's version of the script, not the investor's one.

Part 2

Getting to Work

> Everyone who makes films has to be an athlete to a certain degree because cinema does not come from abstract academic thinking; it comes from your knees and thighs.—Werner Herzog

> We are in the transportation business. We transport audiences from one place to another.—Jerry Bruckheimer

Five Stages of Filmmaking

Producers make better films when they remember that filmmaking involves a *process*. Excessive concerns with your end state or madly dashing to finish for the sake of finishing it will certainly be a learning experience, but a) you won't enjoy the ride and b) you risk making an inferior film. The desire and drive to complete the film—regardless of how it turns out—is not unwarranted. It's rooted in the natural human anxiety of what will happen if the film is *not* completed. There are countless films that *languish in post*. The reasons vary; from running out of money, to a loss of momentum or interest on behalf of the filmmaker, to the realization that what's been filmed and edited to date is simply un-releasable because the material is just plain awful, to infighting among the filmmakers for control of the project. A producer may sink a lot of time and money into making a film only to decide she does not want her name associated with the project. These and other reasons are why there is such a large inventory of films living in purgatory, a junkyard of half-baked, unfinished and—eventually—orphaned films.

Filmmakers agree there are five stages to making a film: development, preproduction, production, post-production, and distribution. But these five stages are not as clearly delineated as their titles imply. They are not stand-alone stages, working independently of each other. Better to look at the five stages more as a continuum and not a set of steps with strict lines of demarcation. The five stages of production are blurred, squishy, flexible, not crisp, binary, or stiff. Of course there are milestones or flag posts along the way. For example, the first day of location scouting, or the first day of shooting, or the first day of editing. But once you start making movies you will be surprised at how much overlap takes place and how malleable filmmaking actually is. One typical example is that post-production and production often begin simultaneously. From the moment the film's first scenes are shot, editors are already at work. We will go into greater detail with regard to the overlapping of stages. For now, banish the idea of five separate steps to filmmaking and keep the image of a fuzzy, malleable continuum in mind.

40 Getting to Work

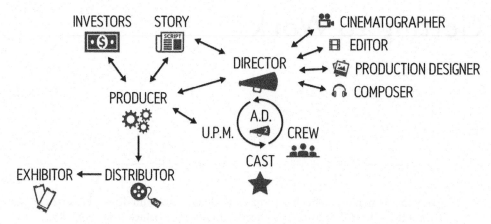

Figure II.1 A producer may be defined as someone involved in a film from concept to completion. In the above illustration the producer functions as the central figure responsible for assembling the human and material resources necessary to making a film. The arrows indicate the "must have" links between people or elements. While distributors and exhibitors are very interested in a film's cast, they don't always control or dictate casting decisions, hence no arrow linking them to the cast. The initials *U.P.M.* are for Unit Production Manager, the person responsible for managing the actual production of the film. The initials *A.D.* are for Assistant Director, the person running the set, assuring the director can do their job.]

[Credit: Illustration by the author]

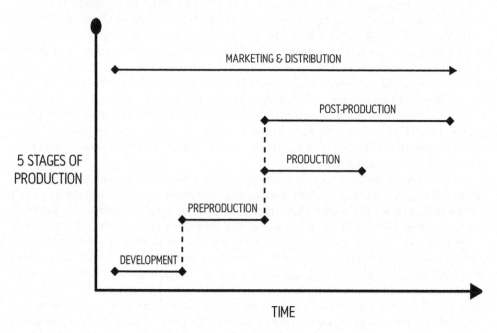

Figure II.2 The five stages of production are not always clearly delineated, compartmentalized, sequential processes. They are often overlapping, layered, and *more or less* sequential stages with diffuse borders.

[Credit: Illustration by the author]

Chapter 5

Development

Development means taking an idea from a conceptual stage to a stage where elements, both abstract (story) and concrete (money and human resources) are at a stage where preproduction begins. It's the stage where, among other questions, producers ask "*What are we going to make a film about?*" and "*Why are we going to make it?*" The beauty of the development stage is that, compared to every other stage of production, it is much less expensive. The development stage is inexpensive because there are simply not enough people involved in the production yet. Fewer people, fewer salaries. Development is when ideas are incubated, tested, *developed*, and firmed up. If there are films that, as I said earlier, *languish in post*, it is also true that there are ideas that, to borrow a term from the Hollywood studio system, end up in *development hell*. And, of course, many ideas die there. That's okay. Not all ideas turn into movies and that's as it should be. Producers knowledgeable of the high casualty rate of ideas during the development stage wisely choose to develop more than one idea, carefully monitoring the growth of each one, and eventually deciding to focus on one over another depending on how good and feasible a given idea becomes.

Where, during development, is money spent, and how much of it are we talking about?

Producers spend money during the development stage on *properties*. A property is a piece of IP (intellectual property) that the producer has decided she wants to turn into a movie. The sources for this IP are quite varied and bear mentioning. They include long form magazine articles, short stories, novels, works of non-fiction, songs, poems, and original *spec* scripts. This last source, the original script, written *speculatively* (with the expectation that it will be made into a movie), is one of the most often seen types of scripts, yet it's one of the most challenging types of IP to turn into a movie. Take a look at any film playing at the multiplex, on demand, or on Netflix, and see for yourself. From *The Lord of the Rings* (saga) to *Brokeback Mountain* (2005, short story first published in The New Yorker), to *The Bridges of Madison County* (1995) (novel) to *Orange Is The New Black* (2013, personal memoir), non-spec, or pre-existing source material accounts for a staggeringly high amount of film production.

Studio-based producers gravitate to pre-existing material over spec scripts for the brand recognition. A producer options a bestseller and suddenly has built in audience interest. Moreover, because the studios are owned by large media conglomerates who also own major publishing companies, pre-publication versions of manuscripts of forthcoming novels are routinely sent from the publishing companies to their sister companies, the studios in Los Angeles and New York. In other words: budding producers do not get easy and early access to Stephen King's latest novel. A producer who can attach a director or star Stephen is fond of may find the author and his agent more inclined to negotiate film rights. If you are a budding producer, getting that director or star is going to be, to put it mildly, a challenge. Not impossible, but no picnic either. Which brings us back to the *spec* script and its ubiquity at the independent film level. A *spec* script is *unattached*. It is free from the constraints and conditions of a publishing company connected to a film studio. It is the original *source material*, and it's become the preferred type of script for independent filmmakers operating outside the studio system.

But *what if* a budding producer chooses to adapt a pre-existing piece of IP into a script and then a movie? Earlier I told you about spending money during development. Here is where that money is spent. The term used in the film industry for the first stage in the acquisition of a piece of intellectual property is *option*. An option is an initial agreement formalized through a legally binding contract between a producer and the copyright holder of the intellectual property. It is neither an outright purchase of the property nor is it a temporary transfer of copyright. An option essentially says that—for a fee—the copyright holder will accord the producer a series of rights subject to certain terms and time limits. More specifically: when a producer options a piece of IP they are reserving the right to be the first person to buy the right to adapt that IP into a movie. Options are ways for producers and copyright holders to agree—for a predetermined period of time—to do business. For example: An 18-month $1,500 option on a novel means that from the time of signature, the producer, having paid the copyright holder $1,500, has a year and a half to raise the money to purchase audio visual rights for the IP. The option protects the producer as well as the copyright holder; the producer is confident they have exclusivity for a predetermined period of time, and the copyright holder is comfortable knowing they retain copyright. At the end of the option agreement, if the producer hasn't found the money to purchase the IP, the option expires and the copyright holder is free to option the IP to someone else or renew their agreement with the producer.

If I have not persuaded you to consider producing a *spec* script or a little-known, easy to option piece of intellectual property for your first production and you still want to option Stephen King's latest novel, by all means, be my guest. But whether you are adapting a bestseller, a little known short story, or producing an original spec script, in all cases you will need a talented, focused, and disciplined screenwriter to provide you with a script you can feel good about showing to the growing number of close collaborators you'll be approaching during the next step of the development stage. And one of the first people good producers want to bring on board during development is the director.

The Producer/Director Relationship

The producer/director relationship is perhaps the single most important relationship on a film shoot. Everything flows from this collaborative, challenging, and potentially brilliant union. Keep in mind that while a good union necessitates a shared, altruistic vision between these two opinionated and strong-willed individuals, both will also have their own priorities aimed at serving their own self-interests. This is the way it's always been.

Veteran producer Christine Vachon, when asked about choosing directors offers: *pick a director who isn't a psychopath*. Her advice should tell you a lot about what a producer needs to know about directors as well as the degree of control a director has on a film set.

Throughout cinema's history there have been many exceptional producer/director relationships. Unions so fraught with (creative) tension yet so positive that both parties determined the relationship was worth sustaining over multiple film projects. Alfred Hitchcock and David O'Selznick, Claude Chabrol and Marin Karmitz, Ang Lee and James Schamus, Woody Allen and Jack Rollins and Charles Joffe, Quentin Tarantino and Harvey Weinstein, Jim Jarmusch and Sarah Driver; the list is long. As fruitful as these collaborations were, they could not have been a walk in the park. For every line item in a budget which the director felt needed more money, there was his producer pushing back.

Good producers understand the need for a shared vision with a talented director brought on during the development stage. They also understand that directors have their own self-interest to look after. We will look at the art and craft of directing in greater detail as we unpack the prep, production, and post-production stages. For now, let us make sure as we bring on a director, that they are not a psychopath, that they share our vision for the material, and that they have enough of an independent mind to allow for the creative tension so vital to successful producer/director relationships.

Proof of Concept

The history of cinema provides us with plenty of excellent stories where a proof of concept played a central role in persuading investors to back a film. At the same time, a solid proof of concept allowed directors to visualize ideas adopted by the production team. Moreover, a writer's dialogues taken through this stage provide immediate opportunities for improvement because the lines aren't just words on a page; they're audible and one step closer to what audiences are going to hear. For his *Lord of the Rings* trilogy director Peter Jackson spent many months creating a short film using animation, puppets, and whatever other special effects he could get his hands on. His proof of concept played a key role in persuading Robert Shaye of New Line to back all three films. Legendary director Akira Kurosawa could not gain financing for his epic *Ran* and spent years creating gorgeous gouache and watercolor-based concept art of the characters and sets for the film. His commitment to seeing through his vision must no doubt have impacted on his backers' decision to finance the film. And in what is perhaps one of the most impressive examples of proof of concept, Chilean director Alejandro Jodorowsky, working with a team of comic book artists, illustrators and musicians, created a massive archive of images and sounds for his cinematic interpretation of the Frank Herbert sci-fi classic *Dune*. Moreover, Mr. Jodorowsky storyboarded virtually every shot. The film was never made but a documentary, *Jodorowsky's Dune* (2013), offers an in-depth look at his proof of concept. It was eventually assembled into a book which producer Jerome Seydoux delivered to all of the major film studios. As Jodorowsky himself says (in broken English), in the documentary: *"If somebody take this script . . . even if I am not alive . . . and do a picture in animation . . . Now is possible. I can die, they can do my picture."*

Producers seeking money, directors wishing to bring their ideas to fruition, writers sorting out ideas and turning them into words and actions . . . all of these individuals understand the need for an incremental development process where ideas are tested, re-jiggered, refined, and eventually turned into a film. Audiences are watching the end of a very long and complex creative process begun months if not years earlier with the earliest drafts of a script. Beyond the script are tools and methods producers use today, available at little or no cost, which enable them to bring to life a compelling proof of concept for their production, allowing them to raise money, visualize ideas, and test dialogue and action before the start of the costly production stage. Some of those tools and methods include:

- Assembling a group of actors for a round table, audio-only recording the script. Once recorded, the audio file can be played back and edited inside software like AVID or Final Cut Pro, yielding a *radio-friendly* version of the script. Useful in identifying redundancies, story problems, timbre, and tone of dialogue. Allows streamlining of the story or, where necessary, deepening of character and conflict.
- Editing static or film images over the radio version of the script. The internet, that bottomless repository of images and sounds, can deliver just about any character type or location setting imaginable. Need a young, preppy ingénue? Looking for a barroom? Does the script call for a plane flying across the Atlantic? All of these images are available for free. A mock up of the entire film becomes not just a dream, but a reality.
- Temp music tracks. Have a favorite piece of music you imagined in the film? You're free to use anything in any way to make your case to investors. A proof of concept mock up of the film is not a commercial product. Until financing comes along that permits hiring a composer or clearing music rights, temp tracks will do the job.
- Sound effects hit home the feeling you want the film to have—and they are free.
- Storyboards, concept art, poster art; all legitimate tools useful in communicating vision and persuading people to come on board.
- Filming scenes with non-professional actors using a camcorder can allow for a demo of the entire film, much like the music industry creates demos.

SIDEBAR INTERVIEW | Piotr Reisch, Producer. Feature films, television series, animated films. Warsaw.

FM: How would you describe your profession as producer?

PR: Being a producer is a form of *creative venture capitalism*. You need to have a solid knowledge of how show business works and a nose for good material. There are two types of producers: those who *facilitate* projects and those who *originate* and *develop* them.

A producer that *facilitates* an existing project has to be a creative businessman. He has to arrange the financing and then has to produce the film using the best team the budget allows. But let me be clear: this type of producer is always serving the director's vision.

A producer that *originates* a project involves a much more *creative* line of work. You're selecting the material, or commissioning a specific script, then working with the scriptwriter on the story. Additionally you're looking for a director and—eventually—you're producing the project be it a feature film, a pilot for a series, or an animated film.

FM: What are the skills a producer needs to have in order to best perform their job?

PR: You have to have brains, business acumen, patience, the ability to stay calm. And you're going to need strong social skills. You have to know everything there is to know about filmmaking. Additionally you have to have a *feel* for what the audience wants and which director is going to be best suited for the script you're producing.

You need to patiently wait for script revisions, money, contracts, director and actor availability, and more. Good producers wait for the perfect location, the right weather, and good distribution deals. Moreover, there are constant pressures like negotiating book rights, contracts with stars, budget issues, missed shooting days, lack of money, and missed deadlines. Your job is to manage all of these challenges with a smile on your face, giving everyone the impression that everything is under control.

Keep in mind that everybody will be coming to you to solve their problems. You are, in essence, a middle man moving between financiers and creators, between distributors, international sales and TV stations, between director, scriptwriter, actors and the crew. It's a tough but very rewarding job.

FM: Can you describe what a producer does during each of the five stages of production? (Development, pre-production, production, post-production and marketing and distribution.)

PR: That's a tough question because it depends on what role you want to play and to what extent you want to play it. If you treat producing as if it were assembly line factory-type work then you just need to keep an eye on budgets and deadlines. But limiting yourself to that makes you little more than an accomplished accountant. On the other hand, if you really care about your movie you will be always be near the director, working with the scriptwriters, talking to the casting director, checking set designs, looking at costumes, and so on. And you're *also* keeping your eye on the budget, asking: "*Can we afford additional lights? Can we do a few more takes? Are we in overtime? Do we have a union situation?*" And, then, once the film is done you've got to ask: "*Is this sellable? Will a broadcaster or distributor kill for it?*"

Production and post-production are delicate moments; either you are getting exactly what you imagined from the director or you have to find a way to gently steer things your way. Unless, of course, you come to realize you're wrong and the director is right.

The final stages of production are much more dependent on you than the filming stage was. You no longer have the director leading things, nor do you have the department heads. Now it's your responsibility to get the best possible distribution deal. So it's up to you to focus on festivals and marketing. You need to be absolutely sure about what are you doing or listen to the advice of people who've marketed and distributed hundreds of movies before and have an established track record.

FM: What are the key relationships a producer must have on a film production? With whom and why?

PR: Basically, you are dealing with four groups of people: creative talent, financiers, craftsmen (crew), and people distributing, marketing, and selling your product.

So talent comes first. First and foremost, we need good scripts, and in order to get them we need to let screenwriters know what type of scripts we are looking for. Types of scripts can either be a personal preference for a genre we want to work in or our *best guess* for what the market is looking for. So as producers we have a choice of whether to follow trends, producing something similar to the box office hits and popular TV series, or we can try to create trends, coming up with something new and surprising. This second option is, of course, riskier and more difficult.

Once we have the script, the basic story, or the book rights, we can start looking for the director. We, in effect, have started the packaging stage: basic description of our movie, what it's going to be about, which talent is going to be involved, what would be the required budget, and what is its financial potential. And once we have that in place we can start looking for investors, be they studios, production companies, or individuals.

With the budget finally in place production begins. Casting, locations, crew selection, and hiring of major key players like the director of photography, set designer, wardrobe people, sound recordist, composer, editor, and so on. At this stage one of the most important things is finding a reliable line producer responsible for spending the budget, keeping everything on schedule and making sure everybody is doing their job.

With regard to marketing, the time to talk to festival people and distributors is well before the film is finished, and sometimes even before the start of production.

FM: What do you enjoy the most about producing? What are the most challenging/frustrating aspects of the profession?

PR: As producers we are creating something that did not exist before. The first public screening and audience reactions are particularly rewarding. Knowing that stories, scenes, or sequences were created with your help is a priceless feeling. We can take our audience on a journey, make them feel, transport them to a different world, if only for an hour or two. This is when we feel like magicians.

I love being on the set but working with a script is what gives me the most pleasure. Telling stories, creating lively characters and putting problems in front of them to solve. Giving them emotions and making sure those emotions will be passed to the audience. It's fun and challenging but once that's over things can get very frustrating. In order to make your vision come to life you need to work with talent. I love talented people, but it took me some time to understand that they are not like the rest of us mere mortals. Quite often they come with huge egos that producers have to learn to deal with. So for the sake of the production, and in deference to the stars, producers must check their own egos at the door.

I have always believed that the product we are making is the most important thing and that for the sake of delivering it we have to sometimes conceal our personal likes and dislikes and our social skills to make sure everybody involved in the project will perform at his or her best. So as producers we have to accept that there will be plenty of moments when somebody else will take credit for our vision and our decisions. We will be the silent creators; the people behind the curtain.

FM: What does a producer look for in a director?

PR: Choosing a director is a key decision and has to be very carefully calculated. The first question you need to ask is what do you need the director for? It's not a trick question and the answer requires absolute honesty. Do you want to win an award on the festival circuit and walk the red carpet? Do you want to work with a particular movie star? Are you making a commercial movie on a tight budget that needs to be delivered on time? Do you want publicity? Do you need a draw for potential investors? Do you need to strengthen one of the aspects of the movie that is not working at the script level such as a comedic element, an emotional tone, or an action sequence? Do you want a peaceful set and fun working environment? Or maybe you're the adventurous type and want to go on an emotional roller-coaster ride with a director nobody wants to work with but who delivers excellent work? Keep in mind that there is not a single director who can fulfill all of your needs. Some are artists who are difficult to control, some are excellent craftsmen, some are superb manipulators, some are loved by the media, and some have the connections to the actors you need. Whom to choose?

So once you've decided what you need the director for, talk to the producers of their movies, crew members they've worked with, and marketing people. Do not believe printed interviews and publicity materials about them. We are in show business, an industry full of stories of which almost none are true. Keep cool and make informed decisions.

FM: What is the producer's role in the marketing and distribution of a film?

PR: A distributor can make or break your film. Choosing well is essential. Before you negotiate a deal with a distributor you need to know what type of movies they're handling and what were their successes and failures. Additionally, find out what their current and future lineup is and what relationships they have with broadcasters. How strong are their marketing and PR departments? How hungry are they? Will they commit to your movie or will they put it in a box with a note that reads: "*If somebody asks for it, we can sell it.*" This is when personal relationships and knowledge of the market play a huge role. The right choice will make you money, the wrong one will put your movie on a dusty shelf.

FM: Is producing the same in Europe as in the USA?

PR: Europe has always been geared more towards authors. It's a director's paradise. Moreover, directors here are often hyphenates, as in *writer-producer-director*. Today, most of the movies produced in Europe are finding a home on the arthouse and festival circuit and are seen in theaters by just a few thousand viewers. This unique state of affairs is due to state subsidies which make producing possible as a way of strengthening what's referred to as *cultural diversity*. The scripts that get financed are chosen by government officials. Producers are often treated as assistants to directors.

Their job is to file applications, collect the subsidies, and help the director produce his movie. More recently, the American model has started to gain popularity; producers are originating more and more film projects. I've witnessed conversations between American and European producers. The Europeans were concerned with filing the right papers and applying to the right agencies while the Americans were simply looking for financing and ways to make money from the movies they were producing. In short, there is a big difference.

FM: What advice can you offer to a novice producer?

PR: It's very simple: keep learning. Either through your own mistakes or the mistakes of others. Keep reading and talking to people. Watch movies and visit festivals. Keep developing your own network, schmooze, work as a producer's assistant, stay on the set as long as possible and read lots of scripts. Ask questions. Ask for help. Produce an indie. Put your stuff on YouTube. Stay busy! With some luck you will be successful and begin what may become a rewarding career. The only thing I can promise is that it will never be boring.

FM: Closing thoughts?

PR: Most people in this business don't work simply for the money. They work because they love to, and they want to do their best. Your job as a producer is to find the people that are the absolute best at what they do then to push them to do it. It sounds simple, but it's actually very difficult. This is a fun job. Keep it that way. Enjoy each day and produce movies people will love. There is nothing more rewarding than seeing people watching your movie in a movie theater, laughing and crying (at the right moments of course). I promise you will be satisfied. And always keep in mind that if you find an investor you will have to give him back his money. Because we are all in this for the long haul.

Chapter 6
Money

Show me the budget and I'll show you the film.—Jean-Luc Godard

Mr. Godard's quote provides a useful directive to producers to let their budget dictate their aesthetic. Moreover, there is a great deal of truth to the maxim that working with budgetary constraints often leads to better results. Filmmakers generally agree that imposing limits on spending forces them to think creatively, often concocting brilliant and inexpensive solutions to ambitious and pricey shots, set pieces, or sequences. Akira Kurosawa's *Kagemusha* (1980) provides one such example. The film, a historical epic set in sixteenth-century Japan, features numerous complex battle sequences requiring the use of hundreds of extras, horses, props, wardrobe, and so on. When the production could not provide Kurosawa with the budget for all the battles in the script, he trained his camera on the protagonist—in close up—and filmed him *watching* the battle while *hearing* the battle sounds. After the battle ends Kurosawa cuts to the carnage on the battlefield. Art directing a shot of fallen soldiers was much less expensive than staging an all out battle. *Let your budget be your aesthetic.*

But producers understand there is no movie without money. Sooner or later they have to have it, enough of it, in a bank account, ready to be spent. A novelist can type out a story without spending a nickel. A producer cannot make a movie without money.

Money has to be raised. It can come from a wide variety of sources. It can be a very large amount or an extremely small one. It often comes with strings attached. Over the life of a production money is spent in varying amounts and in a great variety of ways. Producers understand how to manage it, what its blessings and curses are, what the inherent risks of not having enough of it are, and what creative solutions can replace not having it. They also understand that having money in the bank during the development stage is smarter than being in preproduction and having to find it. Money in the bank early on gives producers the confidence they need in order to manage a successful production, allowing them to focus on the creative and logistical aspects of the project.

During the fundraising stage a producer's relationship to money is *really* about their relationship to their investors or backers.

The Producer–Investor Relationship

In spite of its high rate of failure, the film industry is responsible for some of the world's most lucrative return on investments with revenues in the tens or hundreds of millions from investments often totaling less than $5 or $6 million. The potential for profit as compared to, say, investing in a bank's certificate of deposit or any other low risk investment product is different by orders of magnitude. This makes film investing very attractive to investors attracted to risk. But even the highest of rollers prefers making an informed decision over an uninformed one. When compared to building and selling a widget the financials of the film industry make little sense. Why? Because widgets can be measured from every aspect: manufacturing, distribution, cost/benefit, supply/demand, etc. A film—because it is a work of intellectual property and in some instances a work of art—is only as valuable as the audience makes it. There are no guarantees, no formulas, no foolproof business steps assuring profit. You can only mitigate risk. If a film *catches* the public's interest, there is nothing you can do to keep them away. Conversely, if it doesn't, there's little you can do to make them show up. Film producing is—like everything in life—also a game of chance.

An investor is someone with money or access to it. An investor may be personally wealthy or they may control money belonging to an investment fund. An investor may own a string of car washes or have made a fortune on Wall Street or from selling beauty care products through multi-level marketing schemes. Investors can be old college alumni managing hedge funds you meet at a 25-year reunion. They can be acquaintances who happen to be real estate mavens. They can be friends and relatives you tap into through a Kickstarter campaign. An investor might have made money gradually, over decades, or quickly, over a couple of years. Their money can be *new* or *old* (inherited).

Money, in the end, is money but this doesn't mean you shouldn't do your homework. You can choose not to care who your investor is or where their money comes from but you do so at your own peril. With as much diplomacy, discretion, respect, and vigilance as possible, a producer ought to research a potential investor's background. There's no need to hire a private detective here. Just find out what you can and if you spot any red flags like bankruptcies, problems with the law, unethical business practices, complaints from others, and so forth, think hard before pursuing that person, regardless of how much and what kind of money they're proposing to invest.

What Do Investors Want?

Good investors may not care what the film's about but most absolutely *do* care about *who's attached* to it. They believe that if anyone with *box office potential* is attached to your business plan or production, that production will have a better chance of succeeding. Then, if their film is a hit, they get bragging rights. Other investors may not be overly concerned about who's attached to a project but share the vision and values inherent in the story. Be assured that *alongside* all these wants or shared interests is the desire to make money.

An investor, even one so attracted to chance as to consider putting money into a high risk venture like a feature length motion picture, is going to want a realistic scenario for a return on their investment. Investors may not know how wonderful your film is going to be, but they certainly know about making money. If they sense your production has a fighting chance of breaking even or better, they're going to want to see a preferred placement memorandum, an investor offering, and a contract. These legally binding documents are always—and I mean *always*—prepared by experienced entertainment lawyers, not producers, and—as such—are beyond the scope of this book. It is enough for a producer to know that in order for the project to become a reality and for the money to start flowing she will need to hire a good entertainment lawyer. Producers, however, need to understand what kind of business entity they'll need to have in place when approaching investors.

The Business Entity

The two most frequently used business entities in the production of independent motion pictures in the U.S. are the Limited Partnership (LP) and the Limited Liability Corporation (LLC). Other entities, like a corporation (Inc.) or a sole proprietorship (or a DBA, *doing business as*) come with terms and conditions that do not align well with the needs of a production company making a film. In the case of a company that is incorporated (Inc.), the downside for film producers is that it is—by definition—a constantly operating business. The assumption is that the company is in business year round, with a regular and constant number of employees on payroll. Incorporated entities have complex organizational structures with job titles that are of little or no use to independent film producers (Chairman of the board? Treasurer?). They are also subject to a set of tax laws that are complex, strategically inconvenient, and financially unwise for indie filmmakers.

On the other end of the spectrum, a sole proprietorship or DBA is a business entity centered on the individual. Aside from the pitfalls that come with pooling one's personal finances with those of a film production which the sole proprietorship or DBA inevitably engenders, these entities provide zero legal protection against the individual should someone choose to sue the production.

So, while the incorporated entity (Inc.) will protect the individual owner(s) from a personal lawsuit, it is best suited to a year-round business. Meanwhile, the sole proprietorship or DBA may be a simpler structure but offers no protection for the individual owner. Enter the Limited Partnership and Limited Liability Corporation. These two entities are best suited to the needs of film producers because they are easy to create and dissolve. Moreover, they are friendlier to companies that will not be staffed year round. And—most importantly—both the LP and LLC protect its owners from having to be personally liable to any lawsuits.

LPs and LLCs are excellent business entities for producers making one, two, or three films. If the number of films rises, the implication is that the entity will be open for business over many years—in which case it probably makes sense to look at incorporating. If you are reading this book chances are you are interested in making one film, perhaps two.

But which of the two entities do producers choose? LP or LLC? No two projects are exactly alike. There are simply too many variables; from the producer/investor relationship and agreement to the part of the world the production is taking place in. It is not the purpose of this book to provide detailed definitions of LPs and LLCs. Nor is the goal here to offer advice on which entity to select. Good producers understand the need for a savvy entertainment lawyer who'll assess their specific situation, unpack and explain the pros and cons of the LP and the LLC, and recommend the best choice for them. For our purposes let's accept that an LP or LLC will be the entity through which the film is made, handling payroll, administrative matters, and protecting the producer from being in any way personally liable.

Investor Sources

There are annual industry events dedicated to connecting investors with producers. One is Film Com (http://film-com.com), which takes place in Nashville every year. It's attended by industry reps, aspiring producers, venture capitalists, and more. There are panels on industry financing trends, panels on what film genres are currently being financed more than others, panels on new models of revenue sharing, and more. If you can live the hotel conference life for a weekend or more, if you have the financial resources (air, hotel, prospectus, media, display materials, etc.), and if—when you get home—you follow through with the networking begun at the conference, then it's not a bad idea to go.

Another, much more mainstream event, is the American Film Market, held in Los Angeles, every year. Before getting on a plane and spending your time and money walking the halls of the Loews Santa Monica Beach Hotel knocking on doors, keep in mind that for all of the AFM's claims that billions of dollars of business are done here every year, it's mostly hype. Business is certainly done at the AFM, but the vast majority of deals are initiated, developed, and all but signed months in advance of the market. Industry insiders come here to re-connect, shmooze, *and* do business. Outsiders are easy to spot here; they're the ones looking bewildered, standing by themselves. AFM's open door policy is certainly a welcome breath of fresh air to budding producers wishing to break into show business, but the reality is that if it's too good to be true, it probably isn't. The AFM will gladly take your conference fee and let you knock on the doors of the industry's biggest players but this does not mean doors will open. Producers who are not industry insiders but who want a seat at the AFM table need to take the long view, accepting that they will be attending the AFM over the course of many years, gradually but certainly becoming a familiar sight to industry insiders who will eventually develop enough interest and trust to consider doing business with them. Creative people have a difficult time at the AFM. Business-minded people do better. Industry insiders do best. Industry outsiders waltzing up to moguls with *ideas* or scripts will fail. If you're a creative producer or director working outside the industry your best bet is to make a movie distributors want. If you accomplish this your movie will sell itself.

Your Money

You'll hear industry sages insisting that investing your own money in a movie is the greatest blunder of all. Other people's money, they say, is the only way to fly. But the sages are missing stories like Francis Ford Coppola's or producer Christine Vachon's, or mine. We will tell you we've spent our own money and are happy to have done so because it was the only way to make the film we wanted to make. Filmmakers recognize the catch 22 they face when it comes to money and film. More money equals more opinions about how the film should be made. Less money equals more creative control for the core production team.

If you plan to self-finance your film make sure you a) spend what you say you will spend. Don't chicken out; you'll lose your money and won't have a film to show for it. And b) keep your assets and emerge from the production stage having incurred no risk to your quality of life/standard of living. Yes, people have had to file for personal bankruptcy while making their film. Don't be one of those people.

No Budget Filmmaking and the Compilation Film

No book on today's film production scene would be complete without some attention paid to the term *no budget filmmaking*. As misleading as this term is, every year films emerge touting the *no budget* banner, proud of having overcome incredible economic challenges and emerged with a finished product ready for distribution.

Producer James Schamus half jokingly states that the minimum cost for a feature film today is $7,000. Let's remind ourselves that there is no such thing as *no budget filmmaking*, certainly not for any film that ends up at a festival, in a movie theater, on cable, or through an online streaming service. Any distributor picking up a so-called *no budget* film is immediately going to incur costs to get it to market. Costs that will come out of the filmmakers revenue. (More on producer/distributor relationships in the Marketing section.) There is most definitely a *micro-budget filmmaking* movement and every year it's getting bigger. But take a no budget movie and buy a hard disc to copy media onto and suddenly you're talking about budgets. It takes very little to go from *zero money* to *money spent*. What people mean when they say *no budget* is *"we didn't keep track of our expenses, spent our own money, and racked up some credit card debt."*

No budget filmmaking includes producing strategies like: getting cast and crew to work for nothing, possibly not even lunch money, finding a way to get locations for zero cost, asking cast to handle its own wardrobe, filming with your own HD camcorder, shooting in short incremental bursts, perhaps on weekends when people aren't working for a living. To catalogue every imaginable way to avoid spending money on a film production is not only a fool's errand but also a denial of the reality. Making movies costs money. Having said that, there are recurring strategies producers use to eliminate out of pocket expenses. They may include but are no limited to:

- Deferred payment for cast, crew, and post-production staff and services.
- In kind goods and services including donated food, water, transportation, locations, and housing.

Each of these strategies and their variations needs to be successfully negotiated with no resentment on the behalf of the party offering the goods or services in kind. No economic remuneration for good or services opens the way for the provider to simply walk away at the last minute. Money's ability to solidify agreements cannot be underestimated here. Moreover, with each freebie, be it a deferred salary or a catered meal for cast and crew, there is a trade off. Some sacrifice must be made. For example: cast and crew may be eating pizza all week instead of a varied menu. An actor may work for nothing but only on days she wants to make herself available. Or her schedule may change at the last minute because she's been offered a paid position on another film shoot. There is little a producer can do here except have faith that the project is of sufficient interest to people so that they will show up and/or deliver the resource (food, water, housing) they've agreed to provide. What constitutes *sufficient interest* is answered by asking the question: *what's in it for them*? Is the role large enough to warrant acting for a deferred salary? Will the pizza provider reach new customers?

One way to avoid spending money on a movie is to skip the entire preproduction and production stages. A *compilation film* is a term used to describe movies made without anyone—*except for the people who first created said movies*—having to use a camera or microphone to acquire their content. The all but infinite inventory of content amassed over cinema's history has become available, much of it cleared of rights or—if not—affordable and easy to obtain—and filmmakers have realized that movies can be made using this material. One of the earliest, well known compilation films is *The Atomic Café* (1982), a film made entirely of pre-existing archival material related to the atomic bomb. At times whimsical, at times worrisome, *The Atomic Café* was a resounding success around the world. Audiences understood and accepted this new approach to filmmaking because the storyline was so compelling. It didn't matter that the material was archival. What mattered was the message. Moreover, *The Atomic Café* eschewed any use of voice over or narration, allowing for the archival material to do virtually all of the work. But even by eliminating the preproduction and production stages, the film's producers spent money, most of it their own, researching, acquiring, and editing material. Even compilation films need budgets.

Chapter 7

Preproduction

In order for the development process to stand a chance of moving into preproduction there need to be four essential documents in place. Without these materials the chances of success diminish greatly. The documents are:

- The business plan
- The script
- The budget
- The production schedule

I have chosen to unpack the business plan in an appendix at the end of this book. It is a complex document and presenting it here will only slow us down. I will, however, refer to it throughout this section. For details, see the appendix.

With regard to the *script*, we have already looked at storytelling and script structure in the first part of this book. I will, however, discuss the script from a technical and logistical perspective. We'll also look at how a script moves from page to screen and what a producer *must* know about this process.

With that, let's look at how script, budget, and production schedule work together to create a realistic, effective, and efficient production strategy. In other words, let's talk about *preproduction*.

Look at the script, budget, and production schedule as three inter-related, highly malleable but indispensable documents. Producers and their team are constantly moving between these three documents whose real-world impact on the production cannot be underestimated.

Add a scene to the script and you've just added to the budget's bottom line as well as an additional day of shooting. Collapse three scenes into one and add three characters and you've just reduced the location fees line item in the budget but added to the talent line item. Switch from an 8-hour day to a 12-hour day in the schedule and you've just saved money in the budget as well as given yourself the chance to film more script pages per day. Chop the budget in half (because you didn't get all the money you wanted from your investor) and you need to re-write your script as well as re-calculate and reduce the number of days you'll be filming.

As you can see, the possibilities—good or not so good—are truly limitless. Savvy producers not only understand this; they're adjusting to the new realities in *real time*. So it is absolutely *essential* that lines of communication be open and clear throughout the preproduction stage (and well into the production and post-production stage).

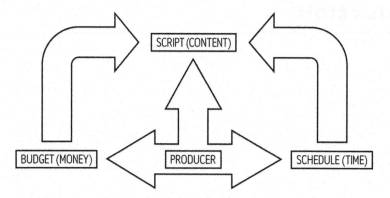

Figure 7.1 A producer knows how to manage the many different forces that will impact upon the production. The three basic forces which every decision will impact are time, money, and content.

[Credit: Illustration by the author]

It is why, for example, script revisions are printed on colored paper, indicating to the cast and crew that a white script page means a first, unrevised draft, a blue script means a first revision, pink is next, and so on. For the record, here is the Writer's Guild of America's preferred revisions color sequence.

- Unrevised draft—production white
- Blue revision
- Pink revision
- Yellow revision
- Green revision
- Goldenrod revision
- Buff revision
- Salmon revision
- Cherry revision

With the tenth draft, the sequence repeats itself, starting with blue, the assumption being that by the time the draft reaches that tenth draft, the original blue revision pages will have been long gone, replaced by pink, and so on. Sophisticated budgeting and scheduling software tools like Movie Magic Scheduling and Budgeting are programmed to adjust instantly to new information about the production. If a shooting schedule has been raised from 30 to 31 days, a unit production manager or assistant director can instantly calculate what the budget's new bottom line is. If at one time there were seven scenes scheduled to be filmed in the bar but now there are only three, the scheduling software can instantly determine how many days the production will need to spend filming in that particular location. The new information is instantly reflected in the updated budget and the script pages—colorized—are proof positive that everyone's on the same page (pun intended).

It is beyond the scope of this book to instruct producers how to use budgeting or scheduling software. Good producers *delegate* these tasks to production coordinators and assistant directors. And: much of this information is free and available on the internet. The producer's *essential* role during this *process* is to remain as *big picture* as possible, to *listen* to the advice of her trusted team members, and to make a final executive decision on what to do about a given problem. Subsequent to that, the team implements strategies based on those decisions. Let's drill a little deeper into the metrics used in calculating costs, number of shooting days, and overall scope of a production. There is a time honored unit of measurement producers use when preparing a shoot. Here it is:

One page of script equals one minute of screen time.

The one page/one minute metric is important because it helps producers determine the running time of the movie. If the average length of a feature film is two hours, it follows that a script ought to be—more or less—120 pages, or two times 60 minutes/pages.

But the one page/one minute metric also does something critically important for producers: it helps them determine production costs. The way producers estimate how much time and what human and material resources are going to be required to bring one script page to the screen is to subdivide that page into manageable sections, specifically into eighths of a page. So: half a page is equal to four eighths of a page. One quarter of a page equals two eighths of a page. Eighths are the time honored unit of measurement because experience has shown producers that using a fraction smaller than one eighth is going to provide too granular of a section to be of any practical use. A larger section (say, half pages) may be too large for a production team to accurately break down.

The one page/one minute rule is valuable to us not only during the production process. Marketers and distributors buy and sell films based in large part on their running time. So there are commercial, market-driven, and economic reasons why this rule exists.

Once we understand and accept that one page of script equals one minute of screen time we can move to the question of how many pages (or minutes of screen time), a film production cast and crew reasonably expect to film per day.

On average, the number of pages filmed per day on most independent film projects falls somewhere between three and six.

With these metrics now in hand, it becomes possible to calculate the total number of shooting days for a—for example—90-page script. At a comfortable three pages per day we are talking about a 30-day shooting schedule, not counting days off, contingency days, unforeseen snafus, or strokes of luck which, we all agree, favors the prepared.

Let's unpack those 30 days a little bit more. Some schedules opt for a five-day work week, say, Monday to Friday, giving cast and crew the weekend to rest. This is, by and large, like living in the lap of luxury. Few films observe this schedule. Other films will build a five-day, six-day alternating schedule. Work for five, rest for two, work for six, rest for one, repeat. Not a bad strategy if you want to get in, get done, and get out. Still other schedules need to take into consideration nighttime shoots.

Night shoots mean that the day leading up to that night is a non-working day. Day or night, there is an industry agreed upon *rule*, enforced by the various unions connected to film production, that stipulates a *12-hour break* from wrap to the next call.

So: if a shoot day wraps at 7 p.m., the production must accord cast and crew a minimum 12-hour break—minimum—before summoning them back to set. You can imagine the scheduling challenges that emerge when you are dealing with a film with lots of exterior night shoots.

Some films have very radical shooting schedules. Scripts may take place at various times during the four seasons. Crews assemble in the summer, shoot a week, wrap, reconvene in the fall—for the foliage shots—wrap, reconvene for the winter material, and so on. In extreme cases we get Linklater's *Boyhood* (2014), shot incrementally over a 12-year period.

What about the average *length* of an independent film production working day? Whether it's a film made over 12 years or one made in 30 days, a day is a day is a day. The stories of 18-hour days in series television are legion. Shoots in this sector of the industry are notoriously challenging for their months of stressful and demanding production days. Home and personal lives are tested, production cast and crew get little time off, children don't get the attention they need, and eventually people just get either sick or tired of the grueling routine and have to take time off or drop out.

Yet series television continues to provide highly sought-after and lucrative jobs for freelancers whose maxim is to *never refuse work*. The low budget independent film, however, is a different animal. Unlike series television, it is a *one off*. In other words: the end of production is always more or less in sight. And, unlike series television, it is not lorded over by a corporation. There are no *suits* hovering about. Independent film producers negotiate with cast and crew for 10- or 11-hour days because they cannot pay them what they make on larger jobs like series television, studio features, or advertising shoots. So it's fair not to ask people to work 14-hour days. More often than not cast and crew coming off of grueling big budget shoots are only too happy to work less for less pay. And yet it's also true that if the cast and crew are enjoying their work on your low budget film they will go the extra mile.

SIDEBAR INTERVIEW | Brian Falk, Producer. Feature films. Los Angeles.

FM: What is producing and what does a producer do?

BF: It's so varied. Producers get defined in so many ways, I think that's why producers' credits have always been something of a conundrum in Hollywood. Because what—exactly—does a producer do? The short answer, of course, is that the producer does a little bit of everything. To be called a legitimate producer, you have to have a hand in the four phases: development and preproduction, (which go together), then: the actual production of the movie followed by post-production, and finally the distribution. If you're to some degree involved in all of these then you're a producer.

FM: What are some of the life skills a good producer needs?

BF: Be quick and think on your feet. While the director is the principal decision maker on the set, the producer has to make decisions off-set. Another life skill is the ability to remain calm. A producer who loses their cool is not helpful to anyone. People take their emotional cues from the producer. With so much money on the line, exploding is not an option. A third skill would be: exude confidence, even if you're not entirely sure about everything. You have to assure people that you're going to succeed, even if privately you think things could be better.

FM: How do you pick your projects?

BF: You have to figure out what you're passionate about. What project really drives you. If you find yourself really obsessing about it, then that's your project. It's a pretty simple test.

FM: Talk about the producer's relationship to the script.

BF: It's as varied as producers themselves. I tend to be very hands-on with the script because I'm also a screenwriter. And I communicate this to my writers. But some producers are not as involved. A mistake many directors make is deciding that the script is ready when in fact it's not. Producers make this mistake as well. But as soon as you've gone into the world with your script and you want financing, it's tough to take that script back and retool it. When it comes to impressing people I believe you get one shot. Many people fall in love with the script and see nothing wrong with it; it's flawless. In reality there's no such thing as a flawless script.

FM: What are the three or four hallmark characteristics you're looking for in a good story and why is storytelling important?

BF: What you're always looking for in a story are great characters, great conflict and a meaningful resolution. I've worked on scripts that are based on true stories. I don't want to be limited to just that, but the reason those are so successful is that there is such a natural conflict in a true story that is difficult to replicate in fiction.

FM: What is a great character to you?

BF: A well-developed character, fictional or non-fictional, has a wholeness to them that is complex enough that they feel real to us. And they need to go through a transformative journey and through that we not only learn something about them, but also about ourselves. The movie takes you in for an hour and a half and during that time you're forced to confront yourself, and to me that's very intriguing.

FM: What happens when you have a script you think is ready to be made into a film?

BF: Once you have that script the next step is packaging. In a way it's the most difficult part. Scripts can be brilliantly written by one or more people sitting in a room, and concepts can be written on the back of a cocktail napkin in a restaurant. But the packaging requires so many more people: actors, agents, managers. And of course part of that packaging is financial, and trying to get financiers interested is very difficult. So that becomes the biggest grind. It can take months or years. People believe that financing is the holy grail of filmmaking but to me there are many holy grails. Financing is important but so is having the right actor, director and distribution company. You can't proceed without a dozen pieces in place and I think that's what often leaves producers tearing their hair out.

FM: In the moment of actual producing, when you zoom into the initial moments of production, what are you thinking about?

BF: There are a lot of issues to touch on. With pre-production the first thing to think about is having the right team in place; a line producer or production manager. That's a critical position and that person must execute their job fantastically. They're the drill-sergeants of the production; they make sure the trains run on time. A great script supervisor is also important because they're the ones constantly corresponding with the director. And department heads: a cinematographer, a production designer, and more. There's a core group of six or so people you need on a set and if you're missing one or two of those people the project can turn into a disaster. Producers have two main responsibilities: one is to make sure they are actually making their days while giving the director enough freedom to make the movie they want to make. The second role the producer plays is in keeping everyone calm. Actors and directors are vulnerable during a movie and they can be on edge. A movie works so much better when the atmosphere is calm and confident. So the producer plays a bit of a mother hen role, making sure they're present for everyone. In those moments when an actor and a director aren't getting along producers can come in, bring parties together, and make them see the common goal. So I'm thinking about a core team, but at the same time thinking about how to keep everyone together and marching towards our goal.

FM: If you were to compare producing to another line of work, what would it be?

BF: There's the saying that there are three great dictatorships left in the world; ship's captain, executive chef, and film director. If the director is the executive chef at a restaurant, the producer is the manager. While the chef deals with the food and the cooking, the manager deals with everything else: the house, everything. The director may have little or nothing to do with the early stages of a project. So I'd say restaurant or hotel manager or anyone who has to deal with all the pieces of their project, not just the architecture or design or presentation. That's producing.

FM: Is there an anecdote or a story that for you best illustrates what producing is?

BF: I was on a movie once where we were about two weeks into filming and I got a call from one of the two stars who was struggling with a scene that was going to be shot the next day. I received that call late into the evening and I remember already getting ready to go to bed. But I dragged myself out and went to a bar and I met the lead actor and the co-star and sat down with them with the script and ran through it. I was trying to help them understand the script and in part help the director communicate to them. I remember walking out of there having to wake up in four hours but knowing that as a result of that meeting the actors and director would be much happier.

FM: What drives you as a producer?

BF: I'm captivated by the idea of visual storytelling. I love being able to see people moved by a story. It's a lot better than a real job! I've got a million things to do every day but I'm always excited about doing them.

The Casting Session

A casting session happens when a producer has a script and posts notices online and through word of mouth that she's looking for actors. The *must have* data that goes into a casting notice includes:

- The title of the project. "Untitled Film Project" also works.
- The roles available with a brief description of the character, including gender and age and, if applicable, ethnicity or body type. Example: *Heather, Caucasian, mid-30s, worldly, cosmopolitan, but with an attitude. Exercise freak with a weakness for homemade potato chips. Says what she thinks and it sometimes gets her in trouble. Insecure, but covers it up.*
- Whether or not this is a union shoot.
- Whether or not this is a paid position. (No need to mention the amount. Save that for later.)
- An e-mail address where talent should send a head shot and resume.
- An approximate timeframe for when the project aims to be filmed.
- A brief synopsis of the film.
- The day and date of the casting session.

Create a dedicated e-mail account, in Gmail for example, to accommodate the tsunami of resumes that will be arriving. No need to list the location of the casting session until you respond to those actors you are interested in auditioning. Try to conduct your casting session near public transportation. Post your casting notice on Craigslist, reach out via Facebook, contact casting agencies and negotiate a deal for access to their files. Or just outright hire an agency to handle all the above tasks. Get the word out. Give yourself enough lead time so that actors have time to plan and schedule their audition.

Once you have sifted and sorted through the raft of resumes and headshots and come up with a short list of actors who more or less conform to the types of roles you are trying to fill, contact the actors via e-mail, text, or telephone and book them in 10 or 15 minute increments. Plan to devote the entire day to casting. If there's someone you want to see that can't make that first day consider adding a second and third casting day. Create *a schedule for the day*, entering the actor's name, contact info, and role they're auditioning for. Film the auditions by setting up a camera on a tripod next to your casting table. Hire an intern to meet and greet actors as they show up. Have water available. Make sure that there are plenty of signs at the street level indicating this is the right place. Have enough chairs in the waiting room to accommodate four or five people at a time. Make sure people know where the bathrooms are. Keep the sessions private, behind closed doors, but don't be the only person in the room with the actor(s). Have an assistant helping with headshots as well as getting actors to and from the room. As you conduct the session, be civil, put actors at ease, indicate the role you want them to read for. Hopefully you've e-mailed script pages to them or there are script pages in the waiting area for actors to peruse. Some actors bring prepared monologues, usually a comic one and a dramatic one. If they offer to perform it, accept. It never hurts to see what they can do with something they've had a chance to prepare. Once they are done you'll know if they can act or not, what you might want to tweak, and if you and they might get along on a film set. If you don't like what you see and don't want to try tweaking things, thank the actor for coming, say that you'll be in touch *either way*. If you sense the actor's got potential, see if they can *take direction* by asking them to re-do the lines faster, slower, softer, louder, more nuanced, with some hidden motive, less over the top or more to themselves. See if they follow your direction. If you really like what you see, don't offer the job on the spot—unless you really are 100 percent persuaded this is the actor for the part. Remember, the next actor you see may be even better than this one. Tell them you liked what they did and find out what their schedule is like over the next few weeks. This is code for *I'm interested in working with you* and the actor knows it. What you get is a pre-commitment of sorts that leaves the door open to continuing the conversation but also allows you to step away if someone better suited for the part comes along. If you see someone you like, consider keeping them around for a bit longer and ask if they'd be willing to read opposite another actor. Actors love being asked to stay. They didn't show up only for their 15-minute audition; they blocked off a couple of hours for you. They want the job. Consider mixing up roles. Give an actor a different part to read. Let them practice it out in the waiting room, then bring them back in. Keep an open mind.

At the end of the day you'll need to step away from everything. You will be swamped with conflicting memories about which actor did what. You'll have three stacks of headshots: *yes, no, maybe*. Start with the *yes* pile, assign roles, reach out to the actors, begin talking about dates, rates, makeup, wardrobe, script issues, and so on. Make them feel comfortable and confident. They're actors; most of them are insecure and will give you their best work if they know they can open up.

Contacting the *no* pile is an optional move. You can notify them via e-mail, phone, text, or not at all. If you said you would, you should, but no one's going to be upset if you don't. To the actor, no phone call means they didn't get the role. Should any of your *yes* actors become unavailable use the *maybe* pile as a fallback plan. There are often real finds in that *maybe* stack of headshots. In the coming days you will be referring to the casting video, so hold on to it.

Location Scouting

Once the production has a location list scouting begins. Essentially, location scouting means getting into a car and driving around. The reason you drive around is because during a scout there are often happy accidents—you literally stumble upon what you need. So the name of the game is getting out of the production office and into the field. The sooner you are out and about, the better. This is not something you put off until later. Later will be too late.

While location scouting ask yourself these questions:

Does the location align with the script and the director's vision? As a producer you have to pay attention to your director's vision. If a script calls for a warehouse scene, you, your location scout, or the director may scout out a half dozen warehouses. Each warehouse comes with a different set of characteristics and conditions which you're going to learn about as we go through this list. Your director may want the warehouse by the beach because it aligns with their vision, but you may not because the location owner wants too much money and won't negotiate. The warehouse near the turnpike is free and kind of looks like the one on the beach. After all, a warehouse is a warehouse. If your director won't budge and persuades you that the beach warehouse is *different* enough from all other warehouses, and if they tell you that using the turnpike warehouse will compromise their vision to the point of damaging the film, perhaps you need to revisit your location fee line item in your budget and see if you can either up the overall amount or redistribute part of the existing amount to accommodate the beach warehouse. Conversely, you can determine that your director's vision will be just fine in the turnpike warehouse and that there's simply no money in the budget to clear the beach warehouse. In both cases, there will be consequences that may or may not work in your favor. For example, by giving in and clearing the beach warehouse you've gained leverage for future negotiations with your director; "*Look, I got you the beach warehouse, cut me some slack on the restaurant location, okay?*" By clearing the turnpike warehouse you may have to compromise on something later on; "*Okay, I agree. We cut corners on the warehouse scene—let me see what I can do about the restaurant.*"

Can you get the location for the total amount of time you need it for? Continuing with our warehouse by the beach (let's assume we got it, persuading the owner to come down on their price in exchange for a small cameo and the name of his business prominently displayed in the scene's establishing shot), the production is going to need unfettered access to the location beyond the amount of time you plan to actually shoot there. *Advance locations* are locations being prepped by advance crew members while the production is still shooting at a previous location (which may have at one time been an advance location). Good producers know that advance location work is a *major* time saver. They dispatch grip and electric crew, art directors, and production assistants to the beach warehouse to prepare as much as possible prior to the production's arrival. They communicate with each department (lighting, grip, art) and ask them how much setup time they'll need at the advance location. Then they try to give the crew the time and resources, both human and material, so that people can do their job as well as possible. And after the scenes at the beach warehouse have been filmed producers make sure to budget enough time and money to allow for the dismantling of everything and a clean, successful rebuild of the location to the way it was before the production arrived. Good producers know that by leaving a location the way they found it they are paving the way for a future film production to have a successful engagement with a happy location owner. Trashing the place only alienates owners, turns them off to film productions and, frankly, does not send a good feeling or vibe through the ranks of your crew members. People want to take pride in their work and a good crew will always want to restore a location to its original state, but only if they're given the time to do it. In a word: you will need access to a location, before, during, and after the actual shoot.

Is the location easy or difficult to find and travel to? Our beach warehouse may align with a director's vision and also be very easy to find and get to. Conversely, that warehouse by the turnpike may be lost in a sea of other warehouses and hard to find. Getting there requires taking the exit ramp and then a sudden unmarked, hidden right turn void of any signage, then driving a quarter of a mile down a side street, etc. But, despite the complex directions, the turnpike warehouse is only fifteen minutes from town (where your cast and crew lives), while getting to the beach may be easy but requires a two hour drive. Here, again, producers must weigh the pros and cons and, in tandem with their core team, make the decision that best serves the production. One question to ask of the above scenario might be: is the location worth driving two hours for? The answer may be: *it's not worth it*, forcing the production to opt for the turnpike location. On the other hand there may be several reasons why driving to the beach is worth it; the warehouse scene may be so mercifully small in scope and so brief in length that a "*skeleton crew*" can be sent out and back, guerilla-style (smaller crews move faster and are more agile). Or perhaps the beach warehouse location fits in as a stop during a larger multi-day road trip during which time the production travels together housed and fed on the production's dime, a not uncommon occurrence.

Or perhaps the beach warehouse scene is actually a series of scenes. In fact, the majority of the film takes place inside the warehouse in which case travel times are all but eliminated because the production is housing and feeding the cast and crew over several days, by the sea. Moreover, if the budget allows it, that warehouse may function as a series of additional locations; warehouses are perfect for set construction. Apartments or offices can all be built, centralizing a production, reducing travel times, and strategically moving the film production towards completion.

Is the location free or is there a cost? We can divide locations into two broad categories: locations on public land (certain municipal or government structures, parks, sidewalks, streets, bridges, tunnels, etc.) and locations on private land (small businesses, company buildings, private homes, malls, etc.). Generally speaking, the cost of clearing rights to film on, for example, a city sidewalk is not prohibitively high. Unless they have had awful experiences with previous film shoots, municipalities will be inclined to authorize a location. They may charge a permit processing fee and request that one or more of their police officers be present and paid by the production. That officer's job is to make sure your production isn't endangering anyone passing by. Some municipalities dispense with an on-set officer but alert the police department that you're going to be filming at the appointed time and place. A public location can also be very costly. The footbridge in New York's Central Park is an iconic location and clearing it for your production will cost you many hours of work as well as more than just a permit processing fee. In addition to permitting public spaces, municipalities "sell" parking meter time in advance, allowing productions to "buy" metered parking spaces days or weeks in advance of their shoot. This is not just a great and inexpensive way to reserve space for your trucks and cars; it's also a way to free up room to set up your camera and create a playing area for the scene you're there to film. Every location is different. Each municipality has its own rules and regulations. Things get a little tricky if you're filming on a public city sidewalk in front of, for example, a privately run business. If you're pointing your camera at the business, if you're in the way of customers coming or going into the store, or if you want to film in the store's doorway, you're going to have to negotiate with the business owner. Again, as with the owner of the beach warehouse, cameos and/or including the store's signage in the film is one way to negotiate a more reasonable deal. Location fees range from free to hundreds, to thousands or tens of thousands of dollars per day. If you're reading this book chances are you are going to want to spend as little as possible on locations. How much should you be prepared to pay? Start low; perhaps $100 for an apartment. If the location owner asks for $500, they've just hit what I'd consider the maximum amount I'd consider paying for an apartment location. That number, 500, is also my limit for businesses, public spaces, company buildings, and almost all types of locations. But if a scene requires a shootout on an airport runway or a chase scene inside a supermarket I understand that I'm going to have to pay more.

A word about *stealing* locations. Most independent films steal locations. You're literally swooping in, spending minimal time with a skeleton crew, not disturbing anyone, and then you're suddenly gone. You risk getting shut down, but hopefully by the time you're caught you got the shots you needed. Here's a better way to steal a location: take advantage of today's advanced camera technology which allows for filming without having to bring in your own lights, learn what time of day the location, public or private, is the least frequented, then approach the location owner and ask them if they can spare an hour or two for you and your skeleton cast and crew. If you're filming in their restaurant tell them you'll feed your people there and assure them you'll leave the place as you found it and will be done when you say you will be.

Does the location have a holding area? Keep in mind that at every location you clear you'll need the actual space you want to film in and everything *around* that space. The space *around* the set is probably as important as the set itself. If you don't have a holding area for actors, or a place to store gear, or a place to have off set conversations with other crew, or a place to set up a table with refreshments, you're going to have a rough day.

Are the location owners easy to work with? Because filmmaking has been so glamorized, at the outset everyone wants to be a part of a film production. Location owners are no different. Early conversations will be smooth, positive, and promises will be made. You'll find people easy to deal with. After all, you're offering them money to put their home or business in your movie, because *that's how cool their home or business is*. But as you begin negotiating the days and times and the degree of access you need, the location owners will start to shut down. The more details you provide, (and you need to provide those details or at least the important ones), the less they want to hear. As the shoot date approaches people may panic and want to back out. Shooting in someone's home is a major inconvenience to that homeowner and it would be best if, during your shoot, that owner was absent. As you track your relationship with the location owner try to determine how reliable they are. If they're making noises about canceling your shoot, don't force the issue. Consider looking elsewhere. If they're being compliant, are willing to sign a location release in advance, and are not making waves prior to your shoot, chances are they are going to be easy to work with. But what if they've behaved up until the day of the shoot and now realize what they've gotten themselves into, are angry, and want you to leave immediately? In a sense, this type of situation is actually very easy to deal with. Take them off your film set, perhaps out onto the street, show them the signed location release, tell them that you have an agreement and that you've upheld your end of it by paying them the location fee. If that doesn't work and they try to sabotage your set by interrupting the shoot, let them. They will very quickly realize that stopping thirty or more people from doing their jobs is a fool's errand; your production is like a gentle but inevitable steam roller. It will simply roll over anyone trying to stop it. As your angry owner realizes this they'll either storm off the set and return when you're done or they'll embrace the chaos of production and befriend your cast and crew who'll befriend them back. Wise producers understand that difficult people need to act out on their impulses before they can become reasonable and honor their agreements. It's worth adding here that location owners that have hosted productions before yours will understand what it means to have a film crew in their home. Location managers know who these people are because they've done business with them in the past. When you meet these *veterans* you will find them to be more level headed than *first timers*.

When you find a location you think might work, take pictures. Cover it from as many angles as possible. Look at what *free, pre-existing* art direction you might benefit from (thereby reducing the work load for your production designer and art director). Upload those photos to Google docs or Dropbox. Share them with your stakeholders.

Shooting on a Soundstage

In many ways the opposite of shooting on location, in many ways similar. Parking is no longer an issue, neither are bathrooms, special insurance riders, availabilty, sound problems, lighting challenges, cast and crew holding areas, and so on. Everything is easier, safer, cleaner on a soundstage. Oddly, it doesn't necessarily make things better. You still have to build sets and populate them with props—right down to the last pencil sharpener on a desk or toothpick on a kitchen table. Add to this the need to achieve realism and you can see that a production designer that knows their stuff— as well as a lighting cameraperson that knows theirs—are essential. Unless you're going for abstract, black box, limbo lighting, fantasy-land stuff—in which case you really *do* need a soundstage.

Soundstages come with stage managers. Stage managers are a tough bunch to negotiate with because their job is to keep the stage busy at all times and yet that's kind of hard to do. They want large productions spending lots of days in their space and when you're a small indie film you don't mean that much to them. Unless they have nothing going on, in which case it's either rent you the space at an indie film production rate or don't rent it at all. Find out how much a stage manager is willing to negotiate. Have him bundle in as much lighting and grip gear as your cinematographer and lead gaffer request. Have him round out the number, then ask for a discount. Keep harping on how little money you have. Offer him a bottle of scotch but give it to him only after you wrap. Be his best friend. Remember: he normally deals with anonymous account executives from advertising firms, or *all business* production managers from large productions who just want to get this done and go home. If an auteur walks in with a vision, a stage manager can feel like they're helping an artist create something personal, unique, different. They may like that. They may enjoy the small film crew atmosphere. No teamsters, no union reps, etc. Exploit that. Build prep days into your stage rental. See if the stage manager will let you slide on the cost of that strike day.

Hiring People

Earlier I told you about the importance of hiring the right department heads and letting those hires bring their own people to the production. But what if a department head cannot get her people on board? What if everyone's booked on other projects? Usually, the department head or one of her crew members will have a backup hire to suggest. For example, a boom operator that becomes unavailable will provide the sound recordist with the name and number of an alternate boom op. The recordist—in turn— informs the unit production manager of the substitution and the new hire is entered into the production's payroll. Crew members communicate with one another constantly, both on and off a set. While it's true that the majority of crews are fixed from the start to the end of a production, illness, personal matters, other professional commitments, and unforeseen circumstances often require individual crew members to be away from a film set. When this happens, our sick or soon to be absent boom operator checks in with his network of alternate boom operators and the position is filled.

As you can see from the above example, hiring a crew member is not quite the same as hiring someone to work for a company. In the latter case there is often a formal job interview, references are requested if not required, dress code is of considerable importance, and the timeframe for the job to be done is often indefinite. Conversely, a job interview with a potential crew hire is often informal, perhaps conducted by telephone or Skype, references are important but not required, there is no agreed upon dress code, and the job's timeframe is limited to the duration of the shoot. Moreover, in a formal job interview anyone hired that chooses to pass on the job offer cannot substitute themselves with a colleague. Which brings us to two core principles about hiring people in the filmmaking world: crew members live and die on a) their reputation and character and b) word of mouth about them has a major influence on hiring decisions. If a gaffer has reputation for being reliable and good to work with, word of mouth about him travels quickly throughout the industry. If they are unreliable and hard to get along with, that information travels around just as quickly. You can imagine the consequences for someone whose reputation is not stellar.

Negotiating deals with cast and crew. Independent films rarely have the amounts of money spent on cast and crew by the studios producing big budget films and television series. It's important to understand this and—consequently—to implement a fair and equitable salary strategy. One commonly used method for paying cast and crew on a financially challenged production is to take the *favored nations* approach. This means that everyone is paid the day rate, regardless of their standing on the production totem pole. A gaffer and makeup artist will make the same day rate as a boom operator or an assistant cameraperson. With this agreement, often publicly disclosed to everyone on the production, cast and crew members no longer need to feel rivalry. Everyone is on the same page. The playing field's been leveled. If anyone is unhappy with the day rate offered, they are free to look for another job. What rates to offer crew members will vary greatly depending on what part of the world the production is taking place. I can only speak from personal experience; producing films and videos in the Northeastern part of the United States. Interestingly, the rates I have been offering to cast and crew have remained more or less the same for years—despite the increase in cost of living. Let me share some of the numbers I usually work with on a typical production.

In hiring cinematographers I've negotiated rates as low as $400 per day and as high as $1,250 per day. That's a very wide range and probably not very useful to you when it comes to negotiating your deals. But when I take a favored nations approach I can get a cinematographer for as low as $250 per day, an incredible deal. In exchange for this low day rate my cinematographer knows she will have X number of days of guaranteed work and the production will make every effort not to go beyond an 11- or 12- hour day. Our productions in this part of the world (New England) will resemble yours (unless you live and work in New York or Los Angeles, in which case, given the amount of films being produced in those cities, you'll be dealing with an extreme range of financial scenarios).

Things change, however, the moment a big budget star-driven production comes to your town. When this happens many local cast and crew members become the beneficiaries of premium wages, overtime, and union benefits. The influx of money into a regional economy thanks to the production of a big budget feature is so strong that state legislatures around the country have enacted tax credit laws providing studios with huge windfalls. For example, here in Massachusetts, if a film spends more than $50,000 inside of the state (which means just about every film made here), the producer can apply for a refund of up to 25 percent of what was spent. So if a production spends $100,000, the law allows for a refund of 25 percent of that amount, a staggeringly high percentage which becomes even more impressive when you imagine an out-of-town production coming to your area and spending $20 million. For a producer spending that much money and to have 25 percent of it come back to them, the incentive to come back is very high.

Payroll: Once cast and crew have been hired, if the hire is a freelancer and resident of the U.S., he/she should fill out a W9 form. A W9 form is a request for their taxpayer ID number. The production needs to report any monies paid to hires in excess of $600 to the Internal Revenue Service. The following January the production issues forms 1099 to each hire who in turn is responsible for reporting their income to the IRS and paying their taxes on it. Some people prefer to be paid under the table; however, the law requires a production company to inform the IRS of any amount over $600 paid to a hire over the course of filming. While the person hired may prefer that this money not be reported, the company is legally required to do so.

If the new hire is to be treated as an employee (and not as a freelancer), he/she fills out a form W4, which determines how much federal and state tax should be withheld from their paycheck. In January, the production issues a W2. In both cases, freelancer or employee, a payroll company can handle the logistics.

SIDEBAR INTERVIEW | Mike Bowes, Producer. Features, commercials, television, industrials. Boston.

FM: How did you get into producing?

MB: After college I worked for a PBS news station in Springfield, Massachusetts, and I was doing live studio lighting and more. After a year or so I realized what I was good at and I started producing with friends, and that led to more work. I was able to get some low-level producing work. Looking back I was pretty naive and I would've done things differently, but that's the way of the world.

FM: What kinds of budgets do you work with?

MB: It varies. The smaller projects I've done are just under $10,000 but I've also gone up to three million. I decided a while ago that I'd stay in Boston and make it work, and that's why I do narrative features, documentary series, commercials. I string a lot of things together. It works for me.

FM: Talk about your relationships with directors.

MB: My relationships with directors always vary. Some are very savvy and interested in the technical or mechanical side of things, and some are not. Regardless of what the director is like, I need to take their thoughts and put them into a plan in terms of schedule and resources. Living and working in a low-budget world there are always more ideas that can realistically be achieved. Some directors can make their own cuts but others have a really hard time doing that. As the producer you have to prioritize things in a way that gets you the material that is *essential* to telling the whole story. When there are scenes or shots later in the shooting schedule—or even later in the day—and you can't get to them, well, the director just has to live with that. There's only so much that can happen with the resources that you have.

FM: What do you consider to be the life skills or skill sets that you've accumulated over the course of your career that producers need to have?

MB: Fear and worrying. Every day I'm asking myself *"Do we know the right shoot date? Do we know we're really shooting on the 15th?"* I just have to make sure we are, you know? You keep going over things. Part of the job requires being resourceful. Trying to get the most out of everything and everyone working on the project. Living and working in a low-budget world I often feel like I'm asking people for what I can never give them. So you have to always be very appreciative and you have to be very kind and try to understand that you're doing the best you can for people. You want to try to make them really care about the project and not think about it as just a another job. They ought to feel like they're part of something special and different.

FM: How important is it to you as a producer to understand story?

MB: Understanding story is ridiculously important. You have to see and feel the end product as vividly as the director does because you're trying to create that end product with numbers and people, and equipment, and vehicles, and more. Everything you pull together is at the service of creating one thing. And, although it's only the nuts and bolts of it, these are things that have to be aligned in a very specific way to create feeling, and emotion, and tone, and pacing. You also need a deep understanding of film form. You have to understand shooting style. What style is more cost effective than another style. And if we can't achieve that style, can we try a different one that works? Would that new approach take more rehearsal time? There are ten thousand pieces of equipment and ten thousand different approaches you can take to accomplish something and you have to know what you can afford while still achieving what the director's looking for.

FM: Do you feel that you're a highly organized person? What tools do you use to manage a production yet also manage human beings?

MB: That's a hard one to talk about. I don't know, really. I try to be as kind as I can and also as efficient as I can. I'm asking more of people than I can give in return but, at the same time, if things aren't moving swiftly I get annoyed. In terms of tools: I use your typical movie scheduling and budgeting software. But, software aside, you must think about the flow of things and what's required to get things into place all the while understanding that the most important thing is communication. When people don't know what's happening they can get annoyed and frustrated. You have to keep a sharp eye on things both small and large at once.

FM: How do you want to be perceived by the crew and other members of the project?

MB: I want them to know that I'm there for them. I put a lot of effort in creating a congenial work environment. I want people to enjoy themselves while doing their job and I want them to feel like what they're doing means something. I hope that it comes across. Maybe it does, maybe it doesn't. And at the same time I have to be the "no" guy. *"You can't do that. You can't have that. Sorry."* I try to do that as gently and transparently as possible.

FM: What are some of your biggest frustrations?

MB: I get frustrated by people who try to impose their priorities above the project, and by that I mostly mean agents and managers. They will fight for things the actors or directors or producers don't care as much about.

FM: What are some of the joys of producing?

MB: It's when things are flowing; when the production is like a machine practically running by itself. And when a director's really happy. When you feel like you've fought for something and it's actually happening.

FM: Do you deal with investors?

MB: Sometimes.

FM: What is the producer-investor relationship like?

MB: It's always different, and it usually depends on what they're giving and what they want in return. Some people want a say over content, some people want access to Hollywood and assume giving money to a low-budget indie film will help. Again: being a creature of the low-budget world, I have to focus on the product. I try to make something I think will get into festivals and receive praise. That's how people will hear about it and want to come see it.

FM: How do you choose your projects?

MB: I just fall in love with a project and I try to push it and get a name actor or director attached. Or I seek out directors because I like their work, even if I've never met them before. I just become drawn to their work for one reason or another.

FM: What's your take on the future of film distribution?

MB: Well, no one feels good about it. That's all I know. I personally hope that content will stay king. Putting something out there means easy access for everyone, so everyone does it. But my hope is that people will always need original and creative content—and vision—because that's how projects rise to the top.

FM: Do you have any advice for a budding producer?

MB: Content is king. You want to align yourself with the right writers and directors. They're the ones that will create the content that will enable you to get actors and crew interested in working with you. There's no real building without that foundation.

FM: Ever thought about directing?

MB: I could direct a small scene, but probably not an entire movie because I'm too worried about the nuts and bolts of the project. A director shouldn't worry about those things. I've found my place as a producer.

In the U.S. many film and television actors belong to the Screen Actor's Guild. The Guild acts on behalf of actors' interests, ensuring they are paid fair rates, are not exploited or overworked with unreasonably long production days, have access to affordable health insurance, and more. Historically, the Guild was primarily concerned with advocating for actors in studio films with large budgets produced in New York and Los Angeles. But as filmmaking became increasingly affordable thanks to better and cheaper technologies (like digital cameras), producers of all stripes emerged, creating movies in just about every corner of the country. This trend, which we'll call *regionalism*, indicative of the increasing decentralization of the film industry, continues to this day and has led to changes in the Guild's *rate card*, its schedule of payments to the actors it is advocating for. Regionalism has engendered films with microscopically small budgets. It is not uncommon to see films made for $100,000 or less. Applying big budget film Guild rates to these tiny projects would prohibit the films' producers from using Guild actors, yet the Guild's mission is to put actors to work. Enter the SAG Ultra Low Budget Agreement. Also known as the Modified Low Budget Agreement, it applies to feature films with budgets of $200,000 or less and—as of this writing—stipulates a performer day rate of $268. That day rate, multiplied by a 30-day shoot and applied to a dozen union actors still adds up to a lot of money for a regional producer of independent films. It helps to know that actors are often willing to discuss having part of their day rate deferred in exchange for the chance to act. It's a hard business to work in and a good role is hard to find. When an actor is offered a *meaty* role they can really sink their teeth into, negotiating a deferred salary with that actor becomes easier.

When a producer hires an actor that belongs to the Guild, a set of protocols must be adhered to and reported. It is not the purpose of this book to detail them all. And besides, everything you need to know is on the Guild's user friendly website (www.sagaftra.org). For our purposes, suffice it to say that hiring a Guild actor brings with it a considerable amount of administrative paperwork, but nothing insurmountable. Good producers understand this and, on complex productions, bring on a *talent coordinator* to help process the actor's paperwork and make things nice with the Guild.

Budget

Earlier, I told you about investors and raising money. We looked at money as a *means to production*. In this section I'll guide you through a budget's anatomy, and how it's generated and managed.

Creating a budget without a script is an all but impossible task. What would you be assigning numbers to? It's safe to say that the guess work involved with this approach would lead to gross inaccuracies and—by extension—a boat load of headaches down the road. Best to start with a script, then move to writing up a budget. So, when a script has reached a state where a producer and his team agree it's ready to move into preproduction, an itemized budget can be generated.

One of the producer's most important responsibilities is to make a series of executive decisions about how money is going to be spent. For example, will the apartment scenes be filmed on a soundstage or on location? What about special effects? Will the explosions be real and filmed or will they be added digitally during postproduction. Naturally these decisions are made in consultation with the director, but the producer will have final say.

Budgets come in many shapes and sizes. Like movies, some are simple and basic while others are sophisticated and complex. We will look at both types, keeping in mind that while they may differ in size and sophistication they nevertheless have much in common.

It helps to look at a film's budget as if it were an itemization of costs related to running a business, albeit one without permanent offices. As with all businesses, there's a *brain trust*, usually the company's owners and directors, and there are the employees, managers, foot soldiers, the people without whom nothing gets done.

In a film's budget, the brain trust (the writers, producers, director, and principle cast) are placed in a category termed *above the line*. It follows that everyone else (production staff, casting agency, art directors, cinematographers, hair and makeup, and many more people as well as material resources) are placed *below the line*. The *above/below* distinction isn't meant to pit one group against the other. Rather, it's a time-tested method for separating two distinct camps of people who will be performing very different tasks but with a shared goal. It is also a way to quickly identify the percentage of money assigned to each camp. If the *above the line* people are taking home 50 percent of the film's overall budget, that's a problem. Good producers understand the importance of a clear, fair, and honest cost ratio between *above* and *below* the line. While there are no absolute rules, if the *above the line* cost exceeds one third of a film's overall budget, there should be cause for alarm. An ideal ratio would be to have one quarter of a film's overall budget assigned to the *above the line* people. Think about it; wouldn't you want to put as much money as possible into what ends up *on the screen* instead of in a director's or writer's pocket? Obviously this is a slippery slope; talented *above the line* writers and directors are expensive. Their work *also* ends up on the screen. But the actual *physical* work performed by the *below the line* people putting that work on that screen cannot be underestimated, nor does it come cheaply.

Budgets begin with a *top sheet* that summarizes the sheets to follow. A top sheet provides investors, producers, production managers, and others with a snapshot of the film's costs. It goes without saying that the top sheet *must accurately* reflect the information that follows throughout the rest of the budget. Experienced producers familiar with the script they are producing can glance at a top sheet and quickly assess if and where there may be cost-related issues and what line items may be too high or too low. The top sheet is also where again, at a glance, the *above the line/below the line* cost ratio is clearly visible for all to see. The top sheet is the film's opening financial *handshake* to the investors, producers, and production managers.

The top sheet is also where producers can see what the cost of post-production is going to be. Editing and delivering the finished film is a radically different process from the filming stage and producers need to know how much money's been assigned to it. And they need to make certain that the money's going to be there when the shooting stops. No one wants to take funds earmarked for post-production in order to complete the filming stage. A top sheet showing what's available for post is how producers make sure this doesn't happen.

Another line item top sheets provide is the budget's *contingency*. The contingency amount—usually around 5 percent of the total *above and below the line* amounts—is reserved for unexpected costs which, on a feature film, are going to be inevitable and numerous. And, most important of all, the top sheet provides the production's *grand total cost*, its bottom line. The film's total cost is the producer's most important number, but this is an obvious statement. Less obvious—and just as important to the producer is the following question: *is the total cost of the film less than what the film may earn?* Keeping in mind there are no guarantees, no silver bullet to success, the producer must scrutinize the film's total cost and determine if—in a word—*it's worth it*.

But if there are no guarantees, how can this question be reasonably posed? The answer is actually quite obvious and can be best relayed by posing a couple of questions: *Would you give Woody Allen $100 million to make his movies when they have a history of making a fraction of that amount?* Or: *Would you give Tom Cruise only $1 million*

FILM TITLE

Production Budget: Based on X Day Shoot Schedule

Acct #	Description	Page #	Adjustments	Notes	Total
1100	Story and Other Rights	2			-
1200	Producer	3			-
1300	Director & Staff	4			-
1400	Cast	5			-
1500	Travel and Living	6			-
1600	Miscellaneous	6			-
1900	Fringe Benefits	6			-
	TOTAL ABOVE-THE-LINE				-
2000	Production Staff	7			-
2100	Extra Talent	8			-
2200	Art Direction	9			-
2300	Set Construction	10			-
2400	Set Striking	10			-
2500	Set Operations	11			-
2600	Special Effects	12			-
2700	Set Dressing	13			-
2800	Property	14			-
2900	Wardrobe	15			-
3000	Hair & Make-Up	17			-
3100	Electrical, Rigging, and Operations	18			-
3200	Camera Operations	19			-
3300	Sound Operations	20			-
3400	Transportation	21			-
3500	Location	22			-
3600	Production Film and Lab	23			-
3700	Stage Facilities	24			-
3800	Process and Rear Projection	24			-
3900	Second Unit	25			-
	TOTAL PRODUCTION PERIOD				-
4000	Editing	27			-
4100	Music	28			-
4200	Post Production Sound	29			-
4300	Post Production Film and Lab	30			-
4400	Main and End Titles	31			-
	TOTAL EDITING PERIOD				-
5500	Publicity	32			-
5700	Insurance	33			-
5800	General Overhead	34			-
6500	Fees, Charges, and Misc.	34			-
	TOTAL OTHER CHARGES				-
	TOTAL ABOVE-THE-LINE				-
	TOTAL BELOW-THE-LINE				-
	ABOVE AND BELOW-THE-LINE				-
	Contingency				-
	GRAND TOTAL				-

Figure 7.2 The budget's top sheet summarizes the production's expenses, separating above the line (leadership, brain trust) from below the line (management, crew, employees) costs. Additionally, post-production costs are available at a glance.

[Credit: Budget excerpt provided by the author]

when his films make in the hundreds of millions? In both cases the answers are no. In other words, budgets are proportionate to track records. Good producers, even ones *without* track records, assess *where* their film stands in terms of *potential* revenue and create budgets accordingly. Later, in the section on business plans, we'll go into more detail about this most critical of producing skills when we look at *comps* (films comparable to the one you're producing) and their financial history, from production costs to revenues. For now, let's move past the top sheet and into the budget itself.

Simple or complex, big or small, all budgets are categorized and organized into *departments*. Some budgets can have a dozen or more departments, others as little as three or four. Each department has its own bottom line, the amount of money that the department head must not exceed. Standardization of budgeting formats across all departments makes it easy for us to single out one for closer inspection, knowing that, to a great extent, what we learn applies to the rest of the budget. Let's take a look at the camera department.

Scan the top of the camera department's budget and you immediately understand headings like *account number* (used for bookkeeping and payroll purposes), *description*

Acct #	Description	Amount	Units	X	Rate	Subtotal	Total
3200	**Camera Operations**						
3201	Director of Photography					$ -	
	PREP	$1,250	2		1	$ 2,500.00	
	SHOOT	$1,250	3		1	$ 3,750.00	
	WRAP					$ -	
						$ -	
3211	Camera Operator(s)					$ -	
	PREP		2		1	$ -	
	SHOOT	$200	2		1	$ 400.00	
	WRAP					$ -	
						$ -	
3221	Camera Assistant(s)					$ -	
	First Assistant					$ -	
	PREP	$250	2		2	$ 1,000.00	
	SHOOT	$1,250	5		1	$ 6,250.00	
	WRAP					$ -	
	Second Assistant					$ -	
	PREP	$250	2		2	$ 1,000.00	
	SHOOT	$1,000	5		1	$ 5,000.00	
	WRAP					$ -	
						$ -	
3231	Loader(s)					$ -	
		$950	5		1	$ 4,750.00	
3241	Still Photographer					$ -	
	misc Days					$ -	
3251	Camera Package					$ -	
		$8,000	3		1	$ 24,000.00	
3261	Expendables					$ -	
		$3,500	1		1	$ 3,500.00	
3271	Special Equipment					$ -	
						$ -	
3281	Box Rentals					$ -	
		$125	5		1	$ 625.00	
3285	Other Charges					$ -	
						$ -	
	P&W/Paryroll		30%		$ 24,650.00	$ 7,395.00	
					Total for 3200		$ 60,170.00

Figure 7.3 Film production budgets are organized by departments. Here's a summary of the costs for the camera department. Other departments include casting, art direction, set operation, set construction, wardrobe, hair and makeup, sound, transportation, location, editing, music, titles, and publicity, to name a few.

[Credit: Budget excerpt provided by the author]

(the job title), and *amount* (a fixed, agreed upon sum). Things get a little counter-intuitive after that, and require some explanation. The *units* column denotes—in this case—the total number of weeks the job title is needed for. While the actual word *weeks* is nowhere to be found, unit production managers, assistant directors, and—of course—producers, know we are talking about weeks, not hours, not days, and not months. The X header is simply a stand-in for *multiplied by* or *times* the next header, labeled *rate*. Here's where it gets counter-intuitive. The word *rate* implies an amount, not a person. There's no good explanation for this, and there are budgets that are formatted and labeled differently than the one we're looking at. For our purposes, let's let the *amount* column list the amount that job titles are being remunerated with. As for the rate column, let's agree that it will reflect *how many times* (meaning: how many people) that amount will be paid during the number of *units* (weeks) listed. So, if a film were to hire 2 Directors of Photography the *rate* wouldn't be 1, but 2. Clear?

Let's keep going.

Moving down the camera department's budget, things get a whole lot clearer: The words *Prep*, *Shoot*, and *Wrap* mean just what they're supposed to mean. Were I to ask you if the Director of Photography was going to be part of the prep and if so, for how many weeks and at what cost, what would you answer? The camera department's budget can answer that question. Or if I were to ask you if the Second Assistant Cameraman was going to be part of the wrap, what would you say? The budget will tell. Nearly every job title on a film in every department can be organized using the Prep/Shoot/Wrap model. You'll see it throughout the budget. Prep/Shoot/Wrap is an incredibly useful way to build your budget because *not everyone* is involved in every stage, and knowing who's in and who's out will save producers money and headaches down the road. Camera people are often part of preproduction, but rarely part of the wrap, but people working in the art department are almost always part of all three stages; after all, when the shooting stops *someone's* got to strike sets, return props,

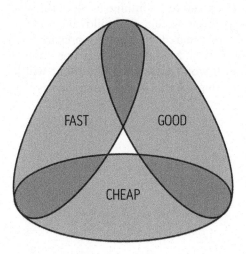

Figure 7.4 Business 101 holds that you can have two out of three. Producers are constantly weighing every decision against this simple but powerful idea.

[Credit: Illustration provided by the author]

and drive rented furniture back to the stores for a refund. The technique, incidentally, of buying furniture for a production then returning it within the store's return policy timeframe is often used on low budget productions and is incredibly effective.

Before moving on to scheduling, a word on managing the budget. Like all business endeavors, film production is subject to the three competing forces of Good/Cheap/Fast. Business 101 stipulates that you can have two but never all three. Producers can put every task, milestone, or deliverable inside the Good/Cheap/Fast paradigm and make a strategically sound decision. Don't have much money and want to work fast? You'll compromise quality. Want to work well and fast? It's going to be expensive. Want to do something well and inexpensive? It's going to take time.

Scheduling

The best production is a good preproduction. This is another way of saying that planning ahead is the only way to create the conditions under which a good production will take place. Without a solid plan, the capacity for error, waste, and even disaster is markedly increased, to say nothing of the stress cast and crew will inevitably experience. If time is money then producers want to spend as little of it as possible. Good producers know that after the filming ends they are going to need money for post-production, marketing, and distribution. But how does a film script, with its myriad scenes, actors and locations, get broken down into an effective, efficient, and strategically sound shooting schedule? Moreover, how do producers schedule (another word for *organize*) scenes taking place indoors, outdoors, during the day or night, with three actors or three hundred?

Since cinema's earliest days, producers have used the same method for breaking down a script into manageable units. These units can then be moved around, rearranged, and ordered differently from their story-driven chronology. This time tested method for creating an efficient shooting schedule is so *reliable* and error-proof that it has been incorporated into film scheduling software programs. It's a method invented by filmmakers over a century ago and producers continue using to this day.

It helps to look at the planning process as if one were a chef following a classic recipe. In order for things to work well, the right ingredients must be prepared and staged, and a certain set of steps need to be followed. Missing ingredients or skipping steps will only damage the end result; the dish won't taste good; the shoot will be flawed. Briefly, here are the ingredients and the steps. We'll list them first, then explain how to create and when to use them.

INGREDIENTS:

- Script, properly formatted, with scene numbers.
- Breakdown sheet
- Production board
- Schedule
- Call Sheets

STEPS:

- Mark up the script
- Transfer data to breakdown sheet

- Enter breakdown sheet data to production board or scheduling software
- Create schedule
- Refine schedule
- Create call sheets
- Shoot

At the very start of this process is the script. Earlier, I told you about script versions and how investors are more apt to respond to a novelistic style of script writing, while a director and their cast and crew will need a different kind of script, one with clear instructions about who's saying what and where they are when they're saying it. In other words, what we are looking for as we break down a script are scene numbers, information about locations, number of actors, props used, scene length, and more. At this stage we are *not* concerned with matters relating to theme, character, plot points, style, and so on. At least not directly. So, with that in mind, here is what a quarter page scene—properly formatted and ready to be broken down—will need to look like.

```
13      INT. MAX'S BEDROOM - DAY                                    13

            MAX rises from his bed and walks to the dresser. He looks at the
            bruise on his left eye in the mirror. Then he opens the bottom
            drawer and, from underneath his sweaters, removes a .22 caliber
            pistol. He checks to see if it's loaded. It is. Now he walks to the
            window taking out his cell phone and speed dialing a number.
            Outside, he notes a police car cruising by.

                                    MAX
                        It's me. I'm ready. Where are you?
```

Figure 7.5
[Credit: Illustration provided by the author]

And here is what Sc. 13 looks like once it's been *marked up*.

```
13      INT. MAX'S BEDROOM - DAY                                    13

            MAX rises from his bed and walks to the dresser. He looks at the
            bruise* on his left eye in the mirror. Then he opens the bottom
            drawer and, from underneath his sweaters, removes a .22 caliber
            pistol. He checks to see if it's loaded. It is. Now he walks to the
            window taking out his cell phone and speed dialing a number.
            Outside, he notes a police car cruising by.

                                    MAX
                        It's me. I'm ready. Where are you?
```

Figure 7.6 Marking up a scene means identifying the elements the production needs to have in hand in order to shoot the scene. The character of Max is highlighted in red, props like the pistol, cell phone and more are highlighted in purple, special makeup needs like the bruise have an asterisk next to them, and any picture cars are marked in blue. These colors, as assigned to various elements, align with the breakdown sheet which is created once a script has been marked up.

[Credit: Provided by the author]

Every element of the scene is assigned a color. Characters are highlighted in red. Props in purple. Makeup effects have an asterisk next to them, picture cars are assigned different font *color*. That information is transferred to a *breakdown sheet*, which is what we are going to look at next. So, at a glance, we can see what role/actor we'll need, where we'll need it, what time of day the scene takes place, what props need to be ready, and if there are any special vehicles (yes, a police car) required. The only thing not listed, which an astute and creative props person will remember to provide, are the bullets for the gun.

A quick reminder: the shooting script which cast and crew are looking for needs to contain information the camera can film and the microphone can record. Production people have little time or patience for script lines like:

```
Max, is really angry that he's being forced to kill his best
friend or the mob will kill his whole family.
```

The above line is very hard to visualize (much less to act out) in one or even a series of shots. It's less of a script line and more of a synopsis. But Scene 13, above, has all the information we are going to need to *mark up* our script before moving data to a breakdown sheet. For starters, Sc. 13 is numbered and identified as such. In passing, let's note that if an additional scene is written and inserted between Sc. 13 and 14, the new scene is labeled as 13A. Conversely, if we decide to eliminate Sc. 13 altogether, we continue to include it in future drafts, but instead of the actual text of the scene, we enter the word: OMITTED. Remember: once a scene has been numbered that number is forever assigned to that scene, whether it ends up being deleted or whether additional scenes are created.

Below is Sc. 13's data moved to the *breakdown sheet* (Figure 7.7). The assistant director or someone from the production team has simply migrated information from script form to the *breakdown sheet*, providing a *snapshot* of *who, what, when, and where* for the production.

It's all there. Everything from the script has been codified and turned into an *element* which the various production departments (*talent, hair/makeup, wardrobe, props, lighting, and sound*) can understand and act upon. But we're not ready to start filming—not even close. The *breakdown sheet* still needs to undergo a transformation into a *production strip* and become part of the larger *production board*, or *shooting schedule*.

Regardless of a scene's length every scene in a script is assigned a production strip. A scene may be nothing more than an exterior establishing shot of a building or it may be a 12-page action-heavy wedding scene with full cast and hundreds of extras all talking at once. It doesn't matter. It may be a single establishing shot or a three-page scene; it's assigned a number and gets *marked up*, entered into a *breakdown sheet*, and migrated to a *production strip* (Figure 7.8).

Once the entire script has been marked up and broken down, the resulting production strips provide complete control and flexibility scheduling-wise. Now, with the click of a mouse, *all of Max's bedroom scenes can be grouped together*—regardless of where and when they take place in the story. Grouping scenes together by location provides obvious advantages from a logistical and financial perspective. It is the number one criterion used when creating a shooting schedule, and good producers understand this. Furthermore, grouping scenes by locations immediately provides valuable information about how many days the production will have

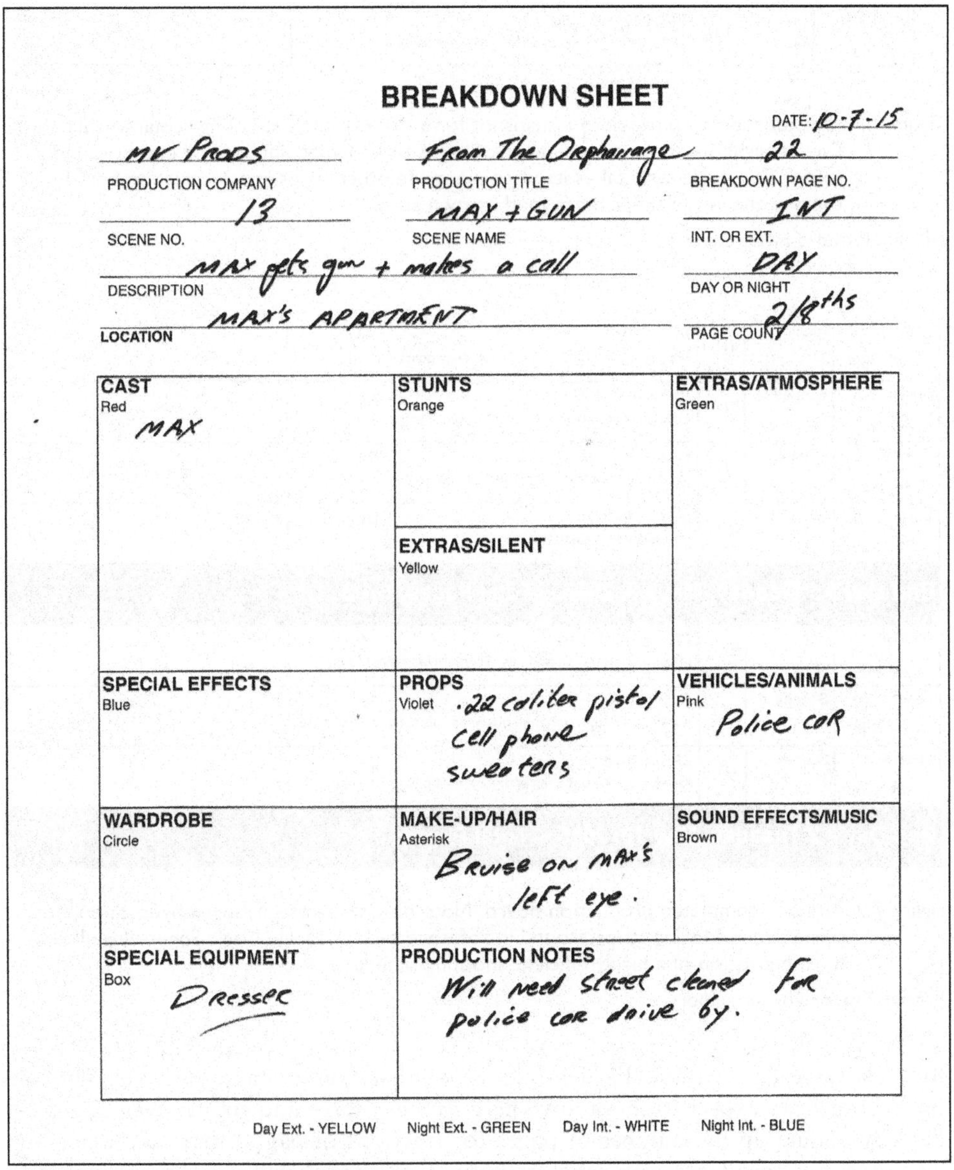

BREAKDOWN SHEET

DATE: 10-7-15

PRODUCTION COMPANY: MV PRODS
PRODUCTION TITLE: From The Orphanage
BREAKDOWN PAGE NO.: 22

SCENE NO.: 13
SCENE NAME: MAX + GUN
INT. OR EXT.: INT

DESCRIPTION: MAX gets gun + makes a call
DAY OR NIGHT: DAY

LOCATION: MAX'S APARTMENT
PAGE COUNT: 2/8ths

CAST Red	STUNTS Orange	EXTRAS/ATMOSPHERE Green
MAX		
	EXTRAS/SILENT Yellow	
SPECIAL EFFECTS Blue	PROPS Violet — .22 caliber pistol, cell phone, sweaters	VEHICLES/ANIMALS Pink — Police car
WARDROBE Circle	MAKE-UP/HAIR Asterisk — Bruise on Max's left eye.	SOUND EFFECTS/MUSIC Brown
SPECIAL EQUIPMENT Box — Dresser	PRODUCTION NOTES — Will need street closed for police car drive by.	

Day Ext. - YELLOW   Night Ext. - GREEN   Day Int. - WHITE   Night Int. - BLUE

Figure 7.7 The completed breakdown sheet for scene 13. All of the elements necessary to shooting the scene are available at a glance. Data is moved from the breakdown sheet to the production strip which becomes part of the production board, allowing for quick and accurate assessing of a scene's cost in terms of time and money.

[Credit: Provided by the author]

80 Getting to Work

| Sheet #: 24 2/8 pgs | Scenes: 13 | INT | MAX'S APARTMENT Max gets gun, makes phone call, sees police car. | Day | 1 |

Figure 7.8 A production strip provides a snapshot for a single scene's shooting requirements. Day or night, location, cast, number of pages to be filmed, interior or exterior, and so on. This single strip takes its place alongside other strips in a production board. Every scene in the script is assigned its own strip.

[Credit: Provided by the author]

Sheet #: 24 2/8 pgs	Scenes: 13	INT	MAX'S APARTMENT Max gets gun, makes phone call, sees police car.	Day	1
Sheet #: 76 2/8 pgs	Scenes: 7	INT	MAX'S APARTMENT Max and Karen plan trip to orphanage	Day	1, 6
Sheet #: 77 1 4/8 pgs	Scenes: 45	INT	MAX'S APARTMENT Max brings Lee back from the orphanage	Day	1, 8
Sheet #: 78 3 1/8 pgs	Scenes: 57	INT	MAX'S APARTMENT Karen comes to take Lee away.	Day	1, 6, 8
End Day # 1 Monday, May 18, 2015 -- Total Pages: 5 1/8					
Sheet #: 79 2 pgs	Scenes: 31	EXT	CITY STREET Max and Karen walk and talk. Then arrive to meet Biggs	Day	1, 6, 7
Sheet #: 80 1 pgs	Scenes: 45	EXT	CITY STREET Karen and Biggs exchange business cards, he tells her to ca	Day	6, 7
Sheet #: 81 4/8 pgs	Scenes: 27	INT	DRUGSTORE Karen buys AA batteries and gum, gets phone call, rushes ot	Day	6
End Day # 2 Tuesday, May 19, 2015 -- Total Pages: 3 4/8					

Figure 7.9 Part of a completed production board. Note how strips are arranged by location, not by scene order. Moving strips around in software such as Movie Magic Scheduling allows for the creation of a highly efficient shooting schedule.

[Credit: Provided by the author]

to spend at each location. Earlier I told you that—on average—independent film productions can expect to shoot anywhere between three and six or seven pages per day. By adding up the number of pages (or fractions of pages) that take place at a given location, producers can estimate how much time they'll need at—say—Max's apartment and they can, in turn, affix a cost to producing those scenes.

By examining all of the data entered into the production board/shooting schedule, producers can immediately assess what the production is going to be like. The shooting schedule *is* the production—*on paper*. It is a living document, changing and evolving with each new and sometimes unforeseen circumstance. Producers re-arrange strips to accommodate new realities. Delays cause slippage, forcing strips downstream, causing scenes to be shot at a later date. Conversely, time saved allows for more strips to be marked as *done* sooner.

But what exactly should a producer be *looking* for in the shooting schedule? After all, schedule creation is often the province of the assistant director or production manager working *in tandem with* the producer(s) and director. The *essential* questions good producers need to ask when reviewing the shooting schedule are:

How many script pages are being filmed per day? While it's true that some days may have scenes so complex that only one page or less can be successfully produced, by and large the production should aim for three to six pages per day. With that in mind, and since we're dealing with the creative arts, there are no hard rules. Some productions shoot up to ten or more pages per day, with features being made in bursts of ten days in a row. Producers need to be fair but firm. They need to push the cast and crew to complete as many pages per day without stressing the production or compromising the quality of the material filmed. During preproduction good producers listen to their team, take in everyone's perspective on how much can be realistically accomplished each day, then make an executive decision on the total number of days based on how much money is available.

Are the total number of days scheduled realistic and is there room for contingency days? Good producers develop a gut feeling about the overall production plan. They factor in the experience level of their cast and crew, the degree of difficulty presented by the project, the time and place where the filming will occur, and the amount of money they have to spend. They determine if the schedule is feasible and if there's room for additional shooting days. This ability, central to the producer's skill set, can only be learned from having been through this process at least once. In the absence of that experience, budding producers look to seasoned production people for help.

Once all scenes have been grouped by location, how does the schedule impact upon the actors? If the number one criterion when creating a schedule is to group scenes together by location, the second criterion is to group them together by actors. When scheduling, try to reduce the number of days an actor is on the project and try to group those days close together. Even though many actors are paid day rates, some actors request a *buy out*. Essentially this means the production is paying not just for the days the actor spends on set, but for the days spent *in between* their assigned shooting days. Unlike the production crew that comes on at the start of production and works until the wrap, actors are only needed for selected days. They have other projects, other commitments, and can be hard to pin down (*they're actors!*). Try to get them in, get their scenes filmed, and get them out in as few *consecutive* days as possible.

Is the schedule skewed towards getting all exteriors done first? Group as many exteriors as possible towards the first half of the shooting schedule. That way if it rains early on, the production can still adjust its plans and shoot inside. Using *cover sets*—as they are called—is a smart way to avoid problems later when all interiors have been filmed and it starts raining just when the production has to film outside.

Are there enough days off and how frequently do they occur? It is both unwise and illegal per the labor unions to require people to work seven days a week. The reasons are obvious. Exhaustion. Resentment. No down time. No personal time. These and other factors will all but destroy crew morale, compromise the quality of the material produced, and lead to errors or worse—accidents. Better to work five days with two days off, then six days, with one day off, then back to five. This is not an uncommon schedule for independent filmmakers, and some even hew to the five-day work week—often considered a luxury—for the duration of production. Good producers look at the shooting schedule to see if there are enough breaks, allowing cast and crew to go home, spend time with family and friends, re-charge their physical and psychological batteries, and come back to work refreshed and ready to perform.

FROM THE ORPHANAGE

Call Sheet

Production: MV Films
Producer: F. Muchnik
Director: Nick Arditti
Asst. Director: A. Phillips

Shooting Day: 1
Date: Monday, May 18, 2015
Crew Call: 7:00 a.m.

SET	SCENES	PAGES	CAST NOS.	LOCATION
MAX'S APARTMENT	13,7,45,57	5 1/8	1,6,8	82 Ridgedale Way

NO.	CAST MEMBER	PART OF	MAKE-UP	SET CALL	REMARKS
1	Alex Cook	Max	8:00 a.m.	9:00 a.m.	
6	Melinda Chapman	Karen	8:00 a.m.	9:00 a.m.	
8	John Groppe	Lee	10:00 a.m.	11:00 a.m.	

ATMOSPHERE & STANDINS	PROPS	SPECIAL INSTRUCTIONS
	Pistol	
	Cell phone	

OTHER CALL TIMES:		VEHICLES & OTHER:
Director	Camera	Need police car
First A.D.	Sound	
Second A.D.	Grips	
Prod. Asst.	Electric	
Craft Services	Art Dept.	
Script Supr.	Make-up	
Dir. of Photo	Wardrobe	

CHANGES AND OTHER INFO:

Figure 7.10 This simplified version of a call sheet provides cast and crew with an at-a-glance understanding of what's planned for a given production day. It's a product of all the planning work performed by the production team and, on a feature length film, it's all but impossible to complete without the aforementioned production strips and board. NOTE: This call sheet provides a very basic example of what call sheets are. It is presented for illustrative purposes only. Complete call sheets are the purview of assistant directors and unit production managers.

[Credit: Provided by the author]

The last step in this time tested method for creating a lean, mean, production machine is the creation of the *call sheet*. One call sheet is simply a snapshot—limited to one page—(front and back) of the *who*, *what*, *when*, and *where* for one production day. Generate 30 call sheets and you've got a 30-day shoot. Easy, right? Hang on, there's more. Before being distributed to the cast and crew the call sheet *must* be reviewed and authorized by the producer. There are literally hundreds of data points on a typical feature film call sheet. Many data points change at the last minute. Cast and crew take call sheets to be the definitive set of instructions about where they're supposed to be on any given day. Get the call sheet wrong and you risk not getting the people or places you've lined up. A call sheet has two types of data: reoccurring and new. The reoccurring data includes everything from the production's title, to the crew members' names and contact information, to the production office phone number and more. That data is—more or less—easy to enter. Do it once and—barring major snafus—you'll be able to carry that information to the next call sheet. The *new* data ranges from actor names and contact info, to listings of scenes and locations required, to weather reports, to number of pages scheduled to be filmed, and more. This data is critical to cast and crew. They live and die by it. A typical crew member on a film set is so busy working that when a call sheet arrives the only data they're concerned with is a) what's tomorrow's call time? and b) where is the location?

Hard copies of call sheets are distributed by the production managers on a daily basis. As a backup, they are also e-mailed to everyone. While it's essential that everyone knows *more or less* what scenes are going to be shot on what days (and where), the first round of call sheets can only aim to document the first four or five days of the shoot. There are simply too many variables, too many changes, too many unforeseen events that will impact the production. Subsequent days are cobbled together, the challenge being to stay ahead of the curve and to not let a day arrive that doesn't have a call sheet pegged to it. This is one reason why all feature films have two bases of operation: the location (or soundstage) where the cast and crew are working, and the production office, where all the planning ahead and administrative work takes place.

Chapter 8

Production

Commencement of principal photography is the phrase filmmakers enjoy using to denote the start of production. It sounds a little portentous, but who wouldn't want to make a big deal of it? Anyway, it does accurately convey what's happening: the start of filming. With that, the project has moved from preparation to execution. Why not celebrate the milestone with a highfalutin phrase? Well, there *are* reasons why we want to take the phrase with a grain of salt. The first and foremost is that the feeling and mindset on that first day of production is generally one of anxiety, exhaustion, and uncertainty. While it's imperative that producers and the entire cast and crew come to work with a positive mental attitude, there are always little or not so little fires that will need putting out. To borrow a concept from the world of business, the team is still in the *forming* stages. People are often meeting one another for the first time or, if they're friends, maybe they haven't talked in a while. There'll be some catching up to do over morning coffee, and very quickly, the topic will turn to work and the myriad tasks at hand. To continue with the business world concept, the *forming* stage is always followed by a period of *storming*. As the term suggests, during the storming stage, people will butt heads, test each other's limits, discover who's going to be their ally, who's not, and so on. In sum, conflicts (big and small) between people are addressed and hopefully quickly resolved so that attention can turn once again to the job at hand. Storming is an inevitable part of any team's evolution and growth and is followed by *norming*, that state where relationships and work routines are, well, normalized. During this stage people have worked out their differences as well as agreed upon how they're going to work together, how they're going to treat one another, and so on. But norming is not the end of a team's growth cycle. If it were, most projects would be—well—pretty normal. It's with the last stage, *performing*, that the team has a shot at achieving excellence. Performing is that stage where the cast and crew have transformed themselves into a lean, mean, production machine, where everyone takes a great deal of pride in performing their specific job, brings the best of themselves to the party, understands the project's *mission*, and instinctively knows how to contribute to it.

Forming, storming, norming, and performing. Good producers understand the inevitability of these four stages in the life cycle of production and allow for their natural development. The big question everyone wants the to answer is: *how fast can we reach the performing stage?* There is no predictable timetable for when a cast and crew reaches performance-level work. It can take as little a one morning or it can never arrive. However, on average, plan for two or three days of ramping up. This would be a good time to remind ourselves of the value of hiring department heads who come with their own personnel. Built-in familiarity among crew members increases the chances of a team reaching performance level work—but does not guarantee it.

One strategy good producers implement to increase their chances of reaching performance-level work is to schedule technically or artistically uncomplicated scenes during the first or second day of production. Keeping things simple at the outset allows cast and crew to gradually ramp up to the complex material all the while familiarizing themselves with their co-workers and ironing out differences. It's a marathon, not a sprint. Good producers let cast and crew work out their differences by themselves, stepping in to solve a problem only when necessary and only if their presence moves the team closer to performance-level work. Producers who micro-manage problems between crew or cast members lose sight of the bigger picture and incur resentment from the team for having interfered unnecessarily.

So what does a production feel like and what is the producer's role during the shoot? If the producer and his team have done their homework, if they've prepared the terrain well enough, if each member of the team is clear on what their roles and responsibilities are and is able to openly and freely execute them, the producer should, by and large, not be doing a whole lot of work. This is the producer's time to let the machinery take over. Production is when everything that the producer and his team have spent preparing is finally put to the test. Should there be any immediate needs for personnel changes, unforeseen financial considerations, or any other big picture items, the producer steps in and makes an executive decision. Otherwise, he is more of an observer, staying out of people's way but working to keep morale high and working conditions as good as possible.

Camera Setups and Block/Light/Shoot

A typical shooting day often begins at 6 a.m. when the first production assistants and perhaps the assistant director reach the location or studio. Craft services (the people who'll be serving coffee, juice, and pastries) also arrive and start setting up. Cast and crew members understand the term *call time* to mean the time they need to report to set. The *call sheet* (which I told you about earlier) details who needs to be where at what time. Most call times are set for 6 or 7 a.m., with 5 or 8 a.m. being too early or too late. Still, it happens. The majority of the crew usually has a 7 a.m. call time. Cast members are called later; they won't be needed until a set is dressed, lit, and ready. It's not uncommon to see actors called at 8 a.m., asked to get into wardrobe and makeup and be ready to rehearse and shoot by 9 a.m. Actresses are usually asked to arrive 90 minutes to two hours before they are needed on set. The thinking is that women need more time to go through makeup and wardrobe. This may or may not be true, but there it is.

Filmmakers use the term *camera setup* to define the moment a camera is moved to a new position on a film set. Depending on how different they are from one another camera setups can be very time consuming, or not. For example, when filming a conversation between two characters the camera may be pointed at both actors (a *two shot*), followed by a new setup with the camera positioned at ninety degrees from the two shot. The new setup may require only a little additional lighting time. Conversely, imagine going from a camera angle that's filming actors from a very low height (say, their feet), up to a very high angle shot (a *god* shot) of the actors as seen from the ceiling. Moving that camera and re-lighting the scene will be time consuming. For this reason there is no ideal or average number of camera setups per day that a production ought to *aim* for. Having said this, if a production is consistently averaging one or two camera setups per day, something is very wrong. Independent films can average between 10 and 20 camera setups per day with some productions working so fast they can hit 30 or more. Naturally, the risk inherent in a high number of daily camera setups is that the shots will be sloppy or even worse: useless.

As the director reaches the set, there are brief, initial meetings between him, the assistant director, the cinematographer, the sound recordist, and the art director. While actors are getting into makeup and wardrobe, the group looks at the script pages to be filmed today and starts to plan out how to go about it. Naturally, some planning has already taken place (during the location scout, for example, a general idea of how to shoot a given scene had been discussed among the group). As the director lays out his vision for a scene, he will ask the actors to come to set for a rough blocking out of the action. Actors, some of them in costume, some not, will briefly step away from the makeup room and join the group. At this point the director will instruct the actors where to move and when to deliver lines. He may also take a more hands-off approach and let actors do what they instinctively feel like doing. Both approaches can succeed or fail. Regardless, the goal of this *stumble through* of the scene is to give the assistant director, cinematographer, sound recordist, and art director a general idea of what's going to happen. However the director succeeds in conveying that vision is fair game. The important thing is to convey it.

With a general idea of how the scene will unfold, the actors are dismissed and the cinematographer can start to light the set, the sound recordist can plan what microphones to use and where to use them, and the art director can set props and furniture in places that align with what everyone has just seen the actors do. But this description of what happens only covers a fraction of what actually takes place. Alongside these steps, the rest of the crew is working in a support capacity, assisting the department heads, accelerating the process by quickly providing whatever resource it takes, be it human or material, to get the job done. And, concurrently, everyone is anticipating the next set up, the next scene, the next location, and planning and preparing for it. As you can see, there's a high degree of multi-tasking involved. No matter how slow things appear to be moving, the *work behind the work* continues.

Once the set has been lit and camera angles chosen, once the microphones have been set and the art department is done dressing the set, the actors are called. At this point shooting starts, usually preceded by a rehearsal, though sometimes the director will ask to film the rehearsal as well. No two directors work in exactly the same way. Some are happy with one or two takes, others can climb up to dozens of takes. Some like to call *action*, others like to have it called for them by the assistant director. Still others prefer not to hear the word as they believe it distracts the actors. Regardless of how a take is filmed, there is always the moment of the shot during which the *magic* will (or will not) take place.

During the actual shot cast and crew will be performing different functions. Producer and director may be stationed by the monitor, the cinematographer or her camera operator will be looking through the viewfinder, and so on. But the gaffers who have spent the past two hours at work lighting the set will probably be standing around with other electricians waiting for their next lighting setup in between shots. The crew members who were idle during the take will step in to adjust things. A gaffer may move a light, the makeup artist may touch up an actor's face, and so on. This cadence is part of every film shoot. There is the *moment of the shot*, and there is the *moment in between the shot*. With respect to this rhythm, the producer needs to ask this question: is the time *in between the shot being used effectively*? If so, great. If not, why and what must be done to fix things? One common explanation for when the *moment in between the shot* can be unnecessarily long is when every department is ready to move forward but no one knows that everyone's good to go. Here it becomes the assistant director's job to know *exactly* when everyone's ready to move forward and to call for a shot. Good producers delegate the cadence of a film shoot to the assistant director and trust them to know when the production needs to hold while adjustments are being made and when to know when everyone's set to go. If the assistant director is not aware of what every department is up to during every minute of the day, then *Houston, we have a problem*.

Production days can be divided into two segments; morning and afternoon. It makes little or no sense to attempt to slice the day into smaller segments. How an assistant director and unit production manager choose to spend time is a function of what needs to be filmed, where, with whom, and with what material resources. Myriad configurations are possible. For example, a morning may be spent filming an interior office location with full cast and crew performing a dialogue-heavy scene, followed by an afternoon shoot of exteriors with a *skeleton* crew and a handful of actors silently walking into and out of buildings. Or an entire day may be spent filming in a graveyard. Perhaps there's a morning spent on a street sidewalk and an afternoon inside a restaurant nearby. Some days may require considerable travel time and so only one location and one or two filmed script pages are possible.

Directing Actors

> Forgive me for staring at you. I'm just studying your attitude.—Robert Mitchum

> What's life-giving is doing something you don't know the answer to before you begin.—Sam Rockwell

Rehearsing. While stage plays require lengthy rehearsal periods leading up to opening night, filmmaking does not. But since we are operating in the creative arts there are always exceptions. Some directors insist on working with actors for weeks or months leading up to a shoot. Others meet the actors for the first time when they step on to the set. How productions choose to approach rehearsals (and whether to hold them or not) is a matter of personal preference. New York-based director Sidney Lumet—(*Serpico* (1973), *Dog Day Afternoon* (1975), *Network* (1976))—insisted on a rehearsal period leading up to the shoot. He would assemble his actors, mark the floor of the rehearsal space with masking tape to delineate the set, and block out key scenes. It made sense to Mr. Lumet to work this way; he started his career as a child actor in the theater before moving to directing, at first televised plays like *12 Angry Men* (1957), then theatrically released feature films. Earlier I told you about director Mike Leigh's long-term improvisational approach leading up to a shoot. That too is a form of rehearsing. But directors like Clint Eastwood or Woody Allen will eschew rehearsals altogether, preferring instead to focus on putting their actors in the right frame of mind once they are on the set, then letting them figure things out.

While the majority of film directors do not rehearse actors prior to filming, it is also true that they communicate with the actors about their roles before starting to shoot. It can be as simple as an informal conversation over dinner about character and story, or it may be as involved as sending an actor hired to play a soldier (for example) to boot camp, as film director Stanley Kubrick did for the film *Full Metal Jacket* (1987). The point here is that, regardless of whether or not rehearsals take place, directors and actors are conversing in a variety of ways about the work ahead.

Creating the conditions for great acting. Ask any working producer what they want to see on their film sets and they'll tell you: harmony. It's happiness, a desire to work, engagement, participation, and collaboration that leads to an atmosphere conducive to great acting. When they're working well actors have an extremely heightened degree of focus and concentration. Their senses are finely tuned in to everything happening around them, including other actors and the film crew. Actors will *know and feel* that something's not right. Out of the corner of their eye they may catch a production assistant nervously tapping their foot or a gaffer standing in their line of vision as they address another actor. Or a light may be poorly aimed right at their eyes, causing them to squint. These are simple problems that can be easily fixed. Much harder to accomplish is creating a high level of trust and support for the actor that'll allow them to reach an emotional space where great acting can occur. There is no silver bullet here. A producer has to simply know that actors must reach a level of comfort where they can open up and deliver a truly memorable performance. Creating that atmosphere isn't only the producer's or director's job. Many talented actors come onto a set and bring a disarming, fun, and comfortable vibe with them. Their energy is infectious and cast and crew loosen up and everyone gets to play together (as in kindergarten). One technique actors use to loosen up a set is to *play* to the room. They are not only acting to the other actor, but—in a sense—to everyone on the set. This is very hard to discern when we see finished films, but one need only look to blooper reels, outtakes, or other behind-the-scenes footage from a film to see how much cast and crew are communicating during and in between takes. When an actor knows that everyone is focused on the moment, when she knows everyone's in the *here and now* she will feel trust and support. It's not unlike what a pitcher might feel knowing he's got eight players watching his back, hoping he throws a strike. Good producers will recognize and encourage an actor's ability to loosen things up on a film set.

Any film set will be populated by actors of varying degrees of experience level and talent. While the job of directing actors falls mainly on the director, producers need to understand how to work with different actor types as well; it will make their off set interactions more successful and lead to better work.

Working with experienced actors. Experienced actors can be a blessing and a curse. The obvious benefits of working with a seasoned actor include having them show up on time with lines memorized and the ability to *hit their marks* without looking at the floor (to find the tape indicating where they're supposed to stop and deliver their lines). Additionally, experienced actors will have an understanding of the filmmaking process (block, light, shoot). Patience, discipline, cool headedness, these are some of the advantages to working with experienced actors. One of the major disadvantages to working with certain experienced actors is that they have their routine down to a, well . . . to a routine. They know their strengths and weaknesses, prefer to showcase their strengths, resist change, and eventually may be boxed in by their own tried and tested abilities. Experienced actors understand the need for a constant curiosity about every role they perform. Even if they've been typecast to play doctors dozens of times, they will still look at *this* doctor with a fresh pair of eyes.

Working with novice actors. It may seem obvious, but one way to spot a novice actor is to read their resume, if they have one at all. A novice actor's resume will have few credits listed, her picture may be poorly taken, or she may not remember to bring a headshot to the audition. It happens all the time. Yet many freshman thespians display a hunger and willingness to learn. Good producers capitalize on this eagerness. Novice actors are cast in films because they may display genuine talent, focus, and discipline at an audition, or because they physically and emotionally fit the part being cast, or because there is simply no money in the budget to hire an experienced actor. They may also be hired because they know the right people. A novice actor can bring an enormous amount of new energy to a film set. Many times this energy permeates the stiffness of a seasoned, perhaps somewhat wizened film crew, reminding them of their early days working on a film set when *this was just a whole lot of fun and now it's work*. Novice actors are more inclined to explore their role and try new and different ways to perform it. Sometimes the results are extraordinary, sometimes not. Sometimes new actors become easily frustrated at the *hurry up (we need you on the set right way) and wait (stand by while we light this scene)* routine intrinsic to all film shoots. They may not understand the relationship between themselves and the camera, or the director, or the other actors, or the rest of the crew. They may panic and freeze. Or they may simply not show up. Producers and directors choose certain novice actors over others because they sense they can trust them to show up and give the best of themselves.

Working with difficult actors. Experienced or novice, some actors will be difficult to work with. What is a difficult actor and what can be done to make them less so? If the actor comes to the audition on time, doesn't ask questions, does their best, and leaves promptly, allowing producers and directors to consider their options, there's a good chance that actor will be easier to work with. If an actor asks questions about the size of the role they're auditioning for, payment or the terms of their agreement before they are hired, then chances are they are going to be difficult. Once filming begins, a difficult actor may refuse to work unless certain needs are met. He may want to control the shooting order of scenes or the way and time scenes are shot (*"I want to shoot my close-ups first"*), or—in spite of his best efforts to be user friendly—he still can't manage to inhabit the role he's been cast to play, much less hit his marks. The first thing a producer or director does when an actor is being difficult on a film set is to take that actor aside—away from cast and crew—for a short, confidential meeting. This is done to ensure that the actor's attitude doesn't permeate the rest of the cast and crew, but it's also done to provide the actor with some way of *saving face* relative to everyone else on the production. No person, no matter how difficult they are to work with, wants their *issue* aired publicly and even if they do, be assured that good producers and directors do not. Skilled producers understand the need for confidentiality and have built in mechanisms for implementing it. Sometimes shaming a difficult actor in public will cause the actor to begrudgingly cooperate or, worse, walk off the set. Pulling a difficult actor aside and having a heart to heart talk about what's wrong is a much better idea. If diplomacy, listening, and negotiating with a difficult actor only leads to more difficulties, then the producer is empowered to fire her. Obviously there are major downsides to firing an actor during a production.

Will scenes need to be re-shot? Re-written? Is the role critical to the story? Who's going to replace the actor? The list goes on. More often than not producers weigh the pros and cons of firing an actor and opt to hunker down and wait it out, crossing the finish line with the stubborn thespian and vowing never to work with that actor again. Yet difficult actors often continue to find work, despite their reputation for being difficult. Why? Simply put: there are difficult actors who know what they're doing and deliver strong work. Good producers know how and when to keep—and when to fire—a difficult actor.

Working with non-actors. Non-actors are different from novice actors in that they do not see themselves as actors. These people are like you and I, individuals who go about their daily lives but which a producer or director decides are not only the best possible choice for a given role, large or small, but they are also user-friendly, meaning they can take direction.

There is a time-honored tradition of non-actors appearing in movies. From the Italian neo-realist films such as Vittorio De Sica's *Bicycle Thieves* (1948) and Roberto Rossellini's *Rome, Open City* (1945), to Satyajit Ray's *Apu Trilogy* (1955–59), to Robert Duvall's directorial debut, *Angelo My Love* (1983), which delves into the lives of gypsies, non-actors have brought a built-in authenticity to movies which many professional actors have been unable to match.

There is no single way to work with non-actors. Each individual must be handled on a case-by-case basis. The guiding principle, however, is that the non-actor was chosen for a part because they naturally exuded the characteristics of the role. It would be foolish to attempt to modify a non-actor's behavior to conform to a part they didn't naturally fit into. Good producers understand why directors may want to work with non-actors and work to create an environment conducive to a healthy collaboration.

Working with children. The old film industry adage that one should *at all costs avoid working with children* becomes problematical when a script calls for them. Much as producers would like to avoid it, sometimes working with kids is inevitable. Children, notably between ages five and 12, can be notoriously difficult to direct. They may have very short attention spans, may be easily distracted, may be unable to endure the rigors of a busy production day, may not be able to repeat their lines over and over again, may not be capable of memorizing their parts, and may suffer emotional distress and breakdowns on the set. They may shout, resist, get angry, laugh uncontrollably, or not understand what is happening around them. Some children may develop unchecked egos and come to believe the entire production has been organized around them and their character. While that might sometimes be the case, most of the time it's not. Producers and directors need to know what the implications are of casting children and they need to cast children who are, at best, talented, focused, and persistent, or at worst, occasionally capable of delivering their lines and hitting their marks. Fortunately there are some wonderfully talented and cooperative kids out there who'll come to work and deliver outstanding performances.

Casting directors are always on the lookout for these types of user-friendly kids, and are especially interested in identical twins. Identical twins provide producers with the ability to switch out actors, having one child work in the morning and the other in the afternoon. Doing so not only keeps kids fresh but also conforms to actors' union regulations about how many hours a child is permitted to work.

The key to working with children is to quickly get to know them and to make sure they understand they are being asked to listen to the director. The director, for his part, needs to develop a feeling of camaraderie between himself and the child, treating this production as something of a *game* they are playing together. Handling children with kid gloves on a film set is not always the best approach. Remember that children deal with all kinds of conflict and group dynamics on the school playground. A film shoot is often a tough undertaking and kids working with a good director will be able to handle it. Like most people, children don't like being patronized. They need to be treated as equals, co-conspirators in this *game of filmmaking*. Like everyone else on a *happy* film set, they want to have fun. Good producers and directors understand this and lead children *firmly but with empathy* through the shoot, getting authentic performances from them. Outstanding examples of films with excellent acting from children include films by Steven Spielberg (*E.T.*, 1982, *Empire of the Sun*, 1987, *A.I.; Artificial Intelligence*, 2001), Richard Linklater (*Boyhood*, 2014) and Francois Truffaut (*Small Change*, 1976, *The Wild Child*, 1970, *The 400 Blows* 1959).

Working with narrators/hosts. There are times when producers and directors need to work with an on-camera host, a "learned voice" who might introduce a story or help transition the movie from one scene to the next. This type of actor lives in between being themselves and inhabiting a character. Whether they appear on camera, or are merely heard through the (sometimes omniscient) *voice of god* narrator, their function is to communicate directly to the audience. Consequently, they must be good communicators. While there are narrator/hosts who can modify their performance, they often do not have the range actors have. What you see at the audition is going to be—give or take—what you're going to get on the set. Good producers understand that narrators/hosts tend to be one trick ponies with a demeanor and tone of voice that they've spent their careers cultivating and nurturing. To try to change a narrator/host's persona will almost certainly degrade the overall quality of the work, which brings us back to the importance of choosing the person most aligned with your vision of the host/narrator's type during the casting stage.

Working with stars. Audiences today seek out their favorite stars and flock to movies in which they appear. Stars are very much like brands. They have a great deal of built-in audience recognition and draw audiences in. Consequently, it is very difficult to make a movie without a star and expect audiences to come see it. Producers understand that movie stars are complex individuals who have entered into the public consciousness and who the public considers to be a personal friend. In reality, stars are similar to you and me; they don't approach a stranger and treat them like a personal friend; no one has a right to call a star a friend unless she really is one. Stars understand the power they exert over the rest of us; some of them don't use that power, some use it, and some abuse it. In most cases what you'll find is that the bigger the star, the better of a person they are to work with. The highest paid most popular stars don't need to be mean. It's the actors that live somewhere between stardom and non-stardom that often have difficulties on a film set. It's important here to add that most actors do not start out intending to become stars. Luck, hard work, talent, discipline all played a role—with luck at the top of the list. Stars have had to share their real, personal, and often complex lives with the rest of us. Our interest in stars and their lives away from the screen has a historical component worth mentioning here. Producers who understand this historical component will better understand how to work with them.

The Biograph Girl was the first movie star. Or, rather, let's call her a phrase. This Wikipedia entry says it best:

> The Biograph Girl was a phrase associated with two early-20th-century actresses, Florence Lawrence and Mary Pickford, who made black-and-white silent films with Biograph Studios (American Mutoscope and Biograph Company). At that time, all studios refused to give actors on-screen film credit; they did not want them to gain public celebrity status and command higher salaries. This had already happened with stage actors, and the studios did not want to repeat the trend on film.
>
> Because the actors were mainly anonymous, the public and news media began to call the popular actress Florence Lawrence the "Biograph girl". In 1910, Lawrence was lured away from Biograph by Carl Laemmle when he started his new Independent Motion Picture Company, known as IMP (he later founded Universal Studios in 1913). Laemmle wanted Lawrence to be his star attraction so he offered her more money ($250 a week) and marquee billing—something Biograph did not allow at the time. She signed on with him; Laemmle had rumors of her death circulated in the press and later took out advertisements criticizing the same rumors. This publicity, timed with the release of her first IMP film The Broken Oath (1910), made her a household name. She quickly became the first film star with celebrity status, and the first person to receive billing on the credits of her film. From then on, other actors slowly began to receive billing credit on film.
>
> After Lawrence left Biograph, Mary Pickford began gaining in popularity with the studio and was soon nicknamed the new "Biograph Girl" until she, too, received billing credits in her films.

This historical component is important because it shows the line of demarcation between the moment when an actress was a nameless face and property of the studio's (read: producer's) production company (The *Biograph* Girl) and the moment when that actress became a separate component; a movie star with a name, an identity, and her unique brand. Producers understand they're hiring stars for brand recognition and stars understand they are being hired because of their celebrity status as well as their talent.

Working with extras. Extras are people who want to be a part of a film production but have no specialized or marketable skill set other than their ability to populate a scene and hopefully give it a sense of authenticity. In the best of cases extras appear in a scene but the audience isn't *really* noticing them. In the worst of cases they are miscast, ill-dressed, obvious, and distracting. Generally speaking, a single extra won't have a great deal of impact upon a scene but a *group of extras* can have a formidable amount of influence.

Extras hear about film production work from local casting directors hired by producers to fill secondary or supporting roles. A producer will cast principal roles through an actor's agent, usually based in New York or Los Angeles, but smaller roles and extra work are a different story. Extras submit their headshots to regional casting directors and sign up to receive e-mails about casting opportunities. If an extra answers a call for work they'll be contacted by a casting associate or production assistant and told the time and place they're to report to. Pay is discussed as is what type of clothing to wear. Experienced extras know to bring reading material to the shoot because there will be a great deal of waiting before their few minutes on the film set arrives. They know not to bring their cell phones onto the set, know not to approach the stars, know to quickly perform the task that is asked of them, and know to avoid making suggestions about how to go about it. Seasoned extras accept their station in the hierarchy of a film production. They are at the bottom of the ladder, yet without them there can be no restaurant or shopping mall scenes.

Extras are told to mingle, dance, pretend to eat, shop, unite as an angry mob, disperse when a bomb explodes, collaborate in a complex series of moves designed to look natural, or sit still with the back of their head facing the camera. It's a thankless job and one wonders why people do it. There are plenty of excellent reasons and good producers understand this. Extras are sometimes called upon to stand in for stars while the lighting crew makes adjustments. An extra may be upgraded to speaking role because an actor was sick that day or because they just rub the director the right way. As the saying goes, "*90 percent of life is showing up.*" So extras choose to *show up* over *not show up*. Like Vegas gamblers at the slot machines, they hope to win something and will keep playing until they do. Unfortunately the odds are never in their favor. You can't beat the house. Still, many extras are reasonable, often highly educated, savvy, intelligent and very real human beings who take the work because they love it.

Film acting and stage acting. Watch any film from the silent era and you'll note a very different acting style from the one you're used to watching today. Before sound films arrived, facial expressions and body language were almost universally over the top, very histrionic, every move underlined, every emotion telegraphed, underscored, emphasized. While it's also true that many silent film stars were capable of delivering subtle, nuanced performances, the vast majority of film acting was, well, very theatrical and over the top. And justifiably so: many of the cinema's first thespians came from the theatre, film acting was still in its infancy, and artists were still finding their feet in the new medium. The invention of the close-up shot took a while to get used to (seen up close, a theatrical expression of—say—surprise—was truly overkill), and audiences were much less visually literate than they are today. These and other factors contributed to the mannered acting so prevalent in silent films. Today's filmmakers and their audiences understand the power of the close up and the need for restrained acting in order to sustain character believability. They understand audiences today are far more visually literate than they were 50, 75, or 100 years ago, and they know that a whole host of other tools in the filmmaker's kit (lighting, sound, color, framing, and more) are contributing to the overall emotional effect of a given beat or scene. Stage actors have been trained to *emote* and to *play to the back of the house* (meaning they have to reach audiences in the balconies—without the benefit of a close up). It goes without saying that theatrical, or histrionic acting may be required of a certain character in a movie. For example, Jack Nicholson's portrayal of The Joker in *Batman* (1989). And, of course, there are actors who've built entire careers on hamming it up. While Jim Carrey is capable of subtle, nuanced, modern acting in films like *Eternal Sunshine of the Spotless Mind* (2004) and *The Truman Show* (1998), his brand of outlandish acting, elastic facial expressions, and booming voices in films like *Dumb and Dumber* (1994) or *The Mask* (1994) are what we remember him for. Good producers know when acting is too histrionic for today's audiences and when over the top acting is called for by the story.

Another difference between stage and screen acting is best expressed by film star Al Pacino who likens acting for the stage to walking on a high wire without a net;

there's no room for error. No second chance. If you fail, it's over. Film acting, by contrast, is also like a high wire act but the wire's on the floor. If you fail, you can always shoot another take!

On-camera interview subjects and conducting interviews. More the province of documentary filmmaking, on-camera interviews nonetheless appear in fiction films. *Reds* (1981) or *Bernie* (2011) are good examples. Be it fiction or documentary, good producers understand how to coax the best material from a talking head interview. They know to make sure the director or person conducting the interview is capable of putting the interviewee at ease while at the same time—where necessary—disrupting or provoking them to reveal themselves and their story. Maintaining focus, appearing continuously interested in the subject, sustaining eye contact, guiding the conversation, and seizing unexpected opportunities to go deeper into a person's life or the story they're recounting in spite of their original intention to remain closed. These are the qualities of a good interviewer.

Working with the Crew

Shooting a film has nothing in common with working in an office. A producer who does not understand this will have an unhappy cast and crew. The crew is the lifeblood of the production. These are the people without whom nothing gets done. Crews travel in groups or teams. There is a high amount of inter-crew loyalty. A lead gaffer comes with his own gaffers, friends they are accustomed to working with, and who they like to bring on board. Ignore this fact at your own peril. If you pick good department heads they will in turn bring in good people that get along and you'll have a much more harmonious crew. A cinematographer has a preferred assistant camera who has a preferred second assistant who has a favorite focus puller. That said, if department heads are asking for too much, feel free to push back. The production designer may want an art director and two or more props people on board but you may feel that your production designer should be the art director and that the production only needs one props person. You're talking about salaries, meals, parking. You're talking about an additional human being on set. Sometimes the request for additional personnel is justified and you'd be wise to listen to the department head's reasoning. For example, you may need two props people in order for the second one to dress the advance location. Department heads do not want to impose their people on you. They're used to working under difficult conditions and they'll find a way to make what you give them work. But look for groups of people used to working together. Not individuals.

The Director

Film directors come in all shapes and sizes. Some like to be very involved in all of the minutiae intrinsic to filmmaking, others prefer focusing on a handful of details. Some like to work with their hands, handling props or adjusting sets or costumes, others don't. Some directors view the production stage as the crucible from which a great film will emerge. Others consider preproduction to be the most creative stage, with the filming being nothing more than a carrying out of instructions planned weeks ago. So the problem with writing about directors and directing is that there is no *best case* scenario. There are many types of successful and not so successful directors. For our purposes as producers let's unpack the *minimum system requirements* for the director we'd want to have on our set.

Regardless of how she accomplishes it, a director must *communicate* a vision for the film to the cast and crew. It's not essential that *everyone* gets what the director's communicating; just the department heads who can then direct their teams. It's not necessary that the director *get along* or even interact with everyone. What *everyone* wants, however, is an honest day's work and the knowledge that the person helming this film, the captain, isn't a psychopath.

At the very least, *all* film directors are—sooner or later—going to have to answer two central questions once they get onto a film set: where does the camera go and what do they tell the actors? Naturally, and inevitably, myriad questions are put to the director. From prop choices to wardrobe selection, from lighting considerations, to reviewing location stills for future shoots, the list is all but endless. Directors are asked literally *hundreds* of questions every day so the ability to decide quickly and effectively is an *absolute must* and part of the job description. Directors learn to nod or shake their head in assent or dissent and quickly move to the next question. Small wonder directors get moody or autocratic or worse. Experienced directors learn to pick their battles. They too, like the rest of the crew, have assistants they enjoy working with; people that will cover their backs and can anticipate or even decide for the director on matters both large and small. In the best of worlds good directors delegate the hundreds of questions to their trusted assistants and focus on the two questions I've itemized at the start of this paragraph. Let's unpack those two essential parts of the director's job description.

Where to put the camera

At first glance it would appear that this question ought to be addressed to the cinematographer, and to a great extent it is. But the opening salvo, the point of departure, during the blocking/rehearsal stage, comes from the director who subsequently *refines* the shot with the cinematographer. This is why it really helps to have a director that understands how to assemble a scene through various camera angles or shots, understands what different camera lenses are capable of, and understands when, where and how to *move* the camera and image, either physically or through a zoom in (or out). Good directors know when to stay *wide* and when to come in *close*. They know when to ask for a *two shot* and when to ask for an *over the shoulder* shot (also known as a *dirty single* because one actor's shoulder is visible in the foreground). When it comes to shot selection good directors have an unconscious competence which they've acquired from experience and from working with the script. Yes, that blueprint I unpacked earlier in the *Back Story* part of this book, the script, with its emotional and story-driven *beats*, its narrative *arc* and its character development will *direct the director*. What differentiates directors from one another is how they *interpret* the script. As an example, one director may choose to film the protagonist's big moment of realization through a close up of their face to convey the intensity of her big *aha!* moment, while another director may choose to film that same moment as a wide shot, isolating the heroine in an abandoned parking lot (for example), which might underscore the futility of that realization. The point here is that a director *must choose*. She must decide where to put the camera. Some directors become so adept at camera placement and shot choice that the camera itself becomes a character in the film. The very *way* in which the story is filmed becomes as important as the story itself. Classic examples of this type of camera work include Akira Kurosawa's *Rashomon*, Orson Welles' *Citizen Kane*, and Steven Spielberg's *Duel*.

What to tell the actors

Earlier we looked at the many types of actors a director must at some point deal with. To that section, there is little or nothing to add—at least not from an actor's perspective. From a director's perspective, however, which is what we are looking at here, there are a few items worth mentioning.

The first is what we might call the *traffic cop* approach to directing. Imagine an officer at the intersection of a busy city crosswalk. Cars and people are coming from four different directions and there are no street lights or stop signs. The officer stands in the middle, whistle in mouth, gesturing, telling people and cars when it's okay to move and when they need to freeze. Gridlock sets in and now the officer has to sort out cars and people and return the intersection to a place where things will flow. *Traffic cop* directors—and there are legions of them—concern themselves with—and only with—blocking. Their instructions to the actors are often limited to telling them where to stand, sit, gesture, what to say and when to say it. There is little more they are concerned with. And oftentimes not much more is needed. Some actors need minimal instruction, others are very high maintenance.

Other directors will sit near the actor, just out of camera range, and literally feed them lines, instructing them on precisely how they want lines delivered, often *acting* out the line off camera. Aside from potentially offending an actor, this approach means there'll be considerable sound editing in post-production as the director's voice is eliminated from the shots. But the technique can be effective and more than a few directors use it including David O. Russell and Claude Lelouch.

One misunderstanding actors often have about directors is whether or not they're delivering what the director *wants*. They misinterpret the director's silence after a take as meaning *not good enough* when in fact the director may be happy with the shot. Because actors tend to be insecure, because they are truly on the front lines and, in the audience's eyes, the *face* of the film, they need some affirmation that their work is good. But effusively praising an actor after every take is a waste of the director's energy and leads the actor to falsely believe everything's fine. If the director's goal is to keep the actor's performance spontaneous from take to take, constant praise will surely kill that spontaneity. Good directors will say something like *"if I don't say anything, it means I'm fine with what you're doing. If something's not working I'll let you know."* Actors who understand this can focus on their performance and not on what the director *thinks* about their performance. And some directors, in an attempt to balance out the actor's insecurities with the need to continue shooting a scene will say, *"That was excellent, everybody! Let's do it again, please."*

The Cinematographer

The current thinking about the profession of cinematographer is that because cameras have become so easy to use cinematography is a job title en route to extinction. As Mark Twain said: *"Reports of my death have been greatly exaggerated."* The point here is this: *Everything is lit*. Just because you or I can create video with our smartphones does not exempt us from having to *light and frame* our shot. Indeed, today we all frame and light video and we do this constantly. In a sense, we're all becoming cinematographers. But bring actors and a sophisticated camera and sound crew together and you can see that the cinematographer becomes essential. No one behind the lens? No movie.

The cinematographer's job boils down to three basic ideas: how to interpret the script, how to work with the director, and how to bring his own creative vision to the film.

To people not accustomed to watching a cinematographer at work, it can seem like an excessively time consuming, mysterious, and overly technical, complex job. Cinematographers move between the camera and the set, now looking through a viewfinder, now instructing a gaffer to adjust a light, now pausing to wait while yet another lighting fixture is set up and focused. They can be seen discussing a shot with the director, then working with the camera and lighting departments, then sitting idly by waiting some more. Lighting a scene is one of the most time consuming tasks to take place on a film set and it is often compared to watching water boil. How, producers may ask, is anything ever going to get accomplished at this pace? Directors tend to better understand how time consuming lighting a scene can be and the good ones are patient. Regardless of how a producer or director feels about the time it takes to light, everyone agrees that collaboration and cooperation are essential, not just to getting a scene lit, but for crew morale as well. Good producers understand cinematographers' need for time to light a scene.

Meals and Breaks

Productions will schedule a meal break approximately four and a half or five hours after the morning's call time. Waiting any longer to break for a meal begins to test the cast and crew's patience. Everyone is always willing to consider working for six hours before a meal break, but they must be asked to do so, not forced. And they must be unanimous or nearly so in their agreement to continue working. Five hours into a shooting day is when stomachs start to growl. Sugar levels will drop and so will productivity. People become more error-prone, things can go south pretty quickly, and tempers may flare up. Yet all of these problems are solved with food and drink. Even with a *crafts services* table nearby (a table laid out with candy, granola bars, fruit, bagels, water, juices, etc. for crew to nosh on while working), people will need a meal break. The break provides psychological, physical, and strategic benefits. It allows the producer and director to assess the morning and—if necessary—make adjustments to the afternoon's schedule. It gives the cast and crew a respite from the physically demanding work of making movies, and it allows for some non-work personal time for everyone.

But how exactly does the meal break work? This isn't an informal lunch that can go on indefinitely. Producers understand that money is being spent, even during a break, and that eventually everyone's going to have to get back to *performing* their jobs. So how does one feed cast and crew, which can be as small as a dozen people or as high as a hundred or more?

There are a set of time tested methods producers implement to get a cast and crew efficiently and effectively nourished. Let's unpack them.

- Provide coffee and bagels in the morning.
- Stage lunch early so it's ready when lunch is called.
- Try to make it a hot meal, and choose food that's easy to serve and eat.
- It's a buffet, not a restaurant with table service. People line up to a food table and help themselves.
- If possible, book an hour. Legally, the unions require it.
- Start timing that hour only after the last person in line has served themselves.
- Call out that the hour's begun.
- Call out that the hour's completed.
- Get the food out of the way once people are done but keep a crafts services table fresh and nearby.
- Tailor the meal experience to where you are shooting; if you're shooting in town, consider booking a restaurant instead of setting up tables and chairs on a sidewalk and having it catered. Tell the restaurant people to have all the meals ready by the appointed time. If they balk, look elsewhere. Negotiate a comparable price—or less than what your on set caterer is billing.

Common Problems

Production involves marshalling a set of resources, human and material, and creating the conditions for a group of people sharing a common vision to efficiently, effectively, and creatively produce the film. Patience is the name of the game. It's not an easy task organizing and managing the myriad logistics that need to come into play. There are simply too many elements that need to align. Here are some of the most common problems producers will have to work to solve on a film shoot:

Losing the light. It's a generally accepted notion that filmmaking is a race against time. Filmmakers are rising early, getting themselves to the location, dealing with myriad obstacles preventing them from getting to the moment of the shot, and then moving on to the next set of challenges. When filming outdoors nothing is more challenging to a production than the eventual and inevitable setting of the sun. Assistant directors walk onto a set knowing exactly what time the sun will be rising and setting and try to pace the day's work to conclude before the production *loses the light*. To make matters more vexing, the actual moment the sun sets is already too late; as the sun begins to set, about 40 minutes before it disappears behind the horizon line, the light—as everyone knows—starts to change color, moving from a bright yellow to a deep red. Called *magic hour* by cinematographers (for the way this red light appears to glow and for the flattering effect on people's face), it is both a blessing and a curse. A blessing for the aesthetic aspects I just mentioned and a curse because the constantly changing light wreaks havoc on a scene's *continuity*. Consequently, unless magic hour light is an aesthetic requirement, most productions try to wrap before it arrives. This means that the production day is shorter than the hours between sunrise and sunset listed on the *call sheet*. Producers understand that filmmaking is a race against time and they work to avoid losing the light. One obvious way to accomplish this is to schedule a film's production during the summer when days are longer. There is little that can be done, however, when a scene is incomplete and the sun has set. Two fallback solutions include *fixing it in post* (meaning: kicking the can down the road into the world of post-production and color correction) or, if the camera angles permit it, artificially lighting a scene to replicate sunlight, a time consuming task. Both fallback solutions work with varying degrees of success and, more often than not, producers prefer staying ahead of the sun.

Insufficient coverage. Getting *coverage* simply means filming a scene from enough camera angles (or *camera setups*) to allow for a variety of shot choices in the editing room. A classic problem is *lack of coverage* or: not getting enough material to make a scene work once it's cut together. Some directors are capable of visualizing and executing a scene so brilliantly that they do not require coverage. This technique, known as *in camera editing (*because the editorial choices have been made *inside the camera, by the director)*, is actually more hype than reality. Yes, geniuses like John Ford and Alfred Hitchcock are known for their lack of coverage, but the rest of us will always benefit from having shot choices in the editing room. Between takes, while waiting for actors or lighting adjustments, director Mike Figgis (*Leaving Las Vegas*, 1995), will point his camera at someone or something in the scene which, lo and behold, ends up being part of the finished film. Known as a *cutaway* (because we literally cut away from the scene momentarily) or an *insert shot*, this type of coverage can sometimes make the difference between a scene that works and one that doesn't.

Breakdown in communication. Earlier I told you that when *no one on the set knows that everyone is ready for the next shot* it means there is a major communications problem going on. The assistant director's job is to make sure this never happens. But there are other ways communication can collapse, from merely technical (dead walkie-talkies), to personal (resentful crew members that just want to go home early). If a film set is about one thing it's about communication. There are simply too many moving parts, too many people, and too many inter-locking pieces that will be compromised if people aren't talking to one another. Signs of communication breakdowns include cast or crew members standing around unsure about where they're supposed to be and what they're supposed to be doing, silence from the departments that may have sent people off set for errands, and instances of people talking past one another about different aspects of the shoot or scene. On every film set there must be a person who can call for order, clarity, and efficiency. A person who'll insist on open channels of communication at all times between all parties. Good producers play a pivotal role in encouraging this by assuring the best communicators are placed in the key positions and by keeping an *open door* policy between themselves and the rest of the production. Are there times when less communication is desirable? Of course there are. With rare exceptions, no one wants to see an intern *communicate* to a director how a scene should be filmed, or an actor *communicate* to a gaffer how to set up a light. There are channels of communication that should be adhered to, and there are times when communication is welcome, even necessary—and times when it's not.

Unforeseen costs. In a perfect world, once a film has been budgeted there would be no more discussion about money. A producer would simply refer to each line item in the budget and disburse funds accordingly. Producers would know what costs they're facing, how much to spend, who the recipients are, and when said payments will occur. But film shoots are never perfect. There are always going to be unforeseen events, unexpected costs, and unintended consequences. One way producers confront the sudden need for more money during production is to build a contingency plan into the film's budget. A contingency is a small but significant percentage of the budget's bottom line earmarked to cover additional costs during the production and post-production stages. We looked at it briefly in the earlier section on budgets, but for our purposes here, the contingency is the first line of defense against the sudden and urgent need for additional money. The contingency amount may be as little as 3 percent or as high as 10 percent (or more) of the production's overall budget and it is up to the producer to decide whether or not to use it for any given production-related problem or crisis. If the contingency has already been spent, or if it was never budgeted in the first place, a second approach would be to turn to the film's backers with a clear and detailed description of the problem at hand, how much money is required to solve it, and when it will be spent. Compassionate backers may write the production a check but not without the expectation of something in return. They may want a larger percentage of ownership of the film, or they may insist on creative input. In a word: approaching backers is an iffy proposition and producers should not expect positive results from it. The bottom line (pun intended) is that on an independent film production there often *are* unforeseen costs and there is simply no money to be had to meet them. Moreover, no alternative exists. Nothing can be bartered, exchanged, deferred, or offered *in kind*. There's simply no money and the production is compromised. End of story? Not quite. Good producers excel at confronting unanticipated costs. Earlier I showed you an illustration linking the producer, the script, time, and money into a malleable dynamic that is constantly shifting and re-prioritizing itself.

We can glean valuable advice from film history folklore here. American film director John Ford (*Stagecoach*, 1939, *The Informer*, 1935, *The Searchers*, 1956) was several days behind schedule and getting all manner of heat from his backers. "Mr. Ford," they told him. "You're seven pages behind schedule." Mr. Ford tore seven pages out of the script and answered, "We're back on schedule." True or not, the story provides us with two important lessons: the first is that, by thinking creatively, a production can save money by asking the basic question: what scenes can the story live without and how can the essence of those seven pages still be transmitted without actually filming them? The second lesson is this: *the single, most effective, most powerful and efficient way to cut costs on a film production is by reducing the total amount of shooting days.*

Technical difficulties. They will occur. No production is free of them. Whether it's a blown light bulb or a defective monitor, a flat tire or a damaged prop, something somewhere will go wrong. Experienced cast and crew members anticipate what might

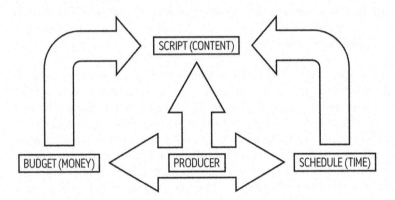

Figure 8.1 The three forces impacting on a producer's decision-making: time, money, and content.
[Credit: Illustration provided by the author]

break and plan ahead by bringing backup parts or the tools necessary to repair what's broken. Lighting and grip trucks are stocked with extra bulbs, accessories, and tools. Art directors work with carpenters to repair or adjust a broken flat or piece of furniture. The collaborative nature of filmmaking leads to the group banding together to solve whatever technical difficulties the production may be confronted with. When something breaks is when departments check in with each other to see if anyone can solve the problem. Collectively, the group is much smarter than they would be as individuals. If a technical problem can't be solved by the production (for example, an irreparable camera monitor), there are mechanisms in place for getting a replacement to the set as soon as possible. Good producers understand the inevitability of technical difficulties. They know that crews will collaborate creatively to solve the problem internally. And they know that if an outside solution is required there's a plan in place to effectuate it.

Inclement weather. While a film crew can withstand a wide variety of climates and working conditions, there are times when inclement weather makes working impossible. For starters, if it's raining and the script doesn't call for rain the producer must decide if she wants to add a line to the script like *"It's raining."* If a scene can be filmed under the rain without compromising a story's continuity or integrity, producers will signal to the director and assistant director to proceed, provided the director's on board with the rain. However, sometimes rain or inclement weather simply becomes too intense to allow cast and crew to work. Safety, especially for people, but also for gear, becomes a major consideration. Producers need to know if and when to cease production and wait until the weather clears up. No one can predict if inclement weather will pass quickly or not, yet the producer needs to make an informed decision—very hard to do when it comes to the weather. When cast and crew have been waiting for *hours* for the skies to clear, a state of diminishing returns sets in. It becomes economically and strategically unsound to keep everyone around. Producers huddle with the director and assistant director and a decision is made whether or not to keep filming. There are consequences with ceasing production early. Among them: script pages will have to be re-scheduled and filmed at a later date. Any pages filmed so far will have to match the re-scheduled pages in look and feel. There will be additional costs involved with getting cast and crew back to the location, and so on. But there are also a few advantages to an early release due to rain, among them: if needed, cast and crew can be called to set at an earlier hour on the following day. The *free* afternoon enables crew to better plan the next set of scheduled scenes. And leadership can spend that down time reviewing footage and adjusting their plan moving forward.

Long days. Shooting days that consistently extend beyond the times stipulated on the production call sheets will inevitably lead to a disgruntled cast and crew. Call it what you will. Mission creep. Slippage. Whatever. The point is that if producers insist on 14- or 15-hour days for too many days in a row, they will be rewarded with major headaches in the human resources department. Cast and crew members will quit what they will come to call *"this sh*t show."* News of the insane working hours will get around and replacing cast and crew becomes a chore no producer wishes upon his worst enemy. In a word: you can push a group of people only so far before they push back. No producer *ever* wants to lose cast and crew in the middle of a shoot. The damage to the production can be irreparable. Time spent filming is lost to time spent hiring replacements. Momentum, good will, and team spirit are lost. Everything has to be rebuilt from scratch. Better to stick to the playbook; if the call sheet stipulates a 12-hour day, producers stop working at the 12th hour—and that includes time spent wrapping the day, putting gear away, getting out of costume, etc. That way, once in a while, if a 14-hour day appears to be inevitable, the production will accommodate, knowing it is a rarity, not the norm.

End of Production

Just as there is a story that is unfolding from the pages of the script being filmed, there is a parallel story unfolding simultaneously. I am speaking of the narrative surrounding the film shoot itself. As with any activity involving groups of people over an extended period of time, a meta-narrative starts to develop which courses through the veins of the production. As with a work of fiction, there are protagonists, antagonists, objectives and obstacles, surprises, suspense, denouements, and closure. And, just as with a script, there are acts. In the first act of a production the team undergoes a series of challenges which I told you about earlier: forming, storming, norming, and performing. The second act becomes a kind of "point of no return," where everyone realizes—at about the half way mark—that there's no turning back, that good or bad, this is the project they've signed on to, these are the people they'll work with for a while, and we'd all better to get used to it now instead of later. The third and final act of a production is when the cast and crew start to sense the end of the shoot approaching and everyone begins to psychologically condition themselves to move on to the next project. This phenomenon bears mentioning here because good

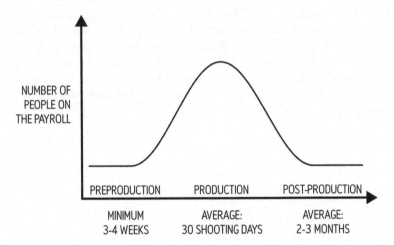

Figure 8.2 The bell curve above illustrates the dramatic increase in personnel a production incurs during the shooting stage of a film. The times indicated below each stage (preproduction, production, and post-production) are independent film industry averages. There is no average prep time for an independent film. It can take weeks or months to plan a low budget film shoot, but few—if any—feature length films ever see the light of day without a minimum prep of time of three to four (or more!) weeks. Post-production time refers solely to the editing stage, not the final mixing, mastering or marketing and distribution stages covered later in this book.

[Credit: Provided by the author]

producers need to understand that a film shoot is—in the end—not something they can ever *fully and completely* control. Much better to ride the group's natural behavior as production comes to a close and facilitate, encourage, and help to, however possible, get everyone across the finish line.

As production winds down fatigue sets in. Cast and crew may try to cut corners, which is one reason why good producers try to schedule key scenes early on when people are still motivated to work as effectively as possible. And, as production ends, there is a thinning out of personnel. Remember: when compared to the number of people on the shoot, the next stage, the editing stage (like preproduction) is staffed by a *very* small group of people.

As with every production, there's always the last shot of the last day. Called the *martini shot* (because, as folklore has it, the next shot is out of glass), it is preceded by the *Abby Singer*, named after an assistant director, which is the *second to last shot* of the day. For the record, the *Jonesey*, named after camera assistant Sarah Jones who in 2014 was killed by an oncoming train while on the job, is increasingly used to refer to the first shot of the day and a reminder that—above all—safety comes first and everyone needs to make sure all required safeguards are in place before filming starts.

And so there comes a time, on every production, when the *last day* of shooting arrives and with it the *last shot* of the production. The *martini* shot of the last day of production is a special one because after that there is nothing left to shoot. This milestone is worth celebrating, and there is no better way to do it than with a wrap party.

The wrap party is an important and necessary ritual because it's when cast and crew draw their working and personal relationship on a given production to a close. Producers budget for wrap parties because they know cast and crew need and want them. Some people will not go to the wrap party. That's fine. Those who do show up want to have a good time, they want to thank one another for completing the production, want to sort out or clarify anything that led to tension between them during the chaos of filming, and want to leave on good terms (or as close to good terms as possible) with everyone. There's rarely a wrap party that ends early. Suffice it to say there are always designated drivers . . .

Chapter 9

Post-production

> You start off with very great ambitions. You want to make 'Citizen Kane.' Then when you get in the editing room you realize that you screwed up so irredeemably that you'll edit the film in any configuration to avoid embarrassment. You put the beginning at the end, you take the middle out, you change things. The editing process becomes the floundering of a drowning man. That's been it for me from the start of my career.—Woody Allen

At the start of the *Getting To Work* section I told you that the five stages of production, (*Development, Preproduction, Production, Post-Production, and Marketing and Distribution*) are not as clearly delineated as their titles suggest. Rather they are more like overlapping processes with squishy borders sometimes unfolding simultaneously as opposed to sequentially. The post-production stage as it relates to the production stage provides us with a good illustration of this.

In order to make sense of the complexities of the editing and post-production stage, we are going to start with the image of a *football* and a phrase: *keep your eye on the ball*.

During the filming stage, while everyone was having fun on the set, an assistant editor was quietly setting up an editing facility. As scenes were being filmed (whether onto a hard drive or onto negative film stock) they eventually made their way into the editing room and the reliable hands of the assistant editor(s) and, now, the editor herself. Those scenes, that media, constitute the *football*, and are—simply put—the only material that counts now that the filming has ended. The moving of that football from the set to the editing room is so important, so critical, that the job is assigned to only the most reliable people on a production. Producers must never lose sight of where the media is, what state it's in, what needs to happen to that media in order to move it to the next stage of post-production, and what administrative, legal, and contractual tasks and agreements need to take place in order for that media to make it onto a multiplex screen, film festival program, online distribution network, cable television schedule, foreign market, and so on.

So, as you can see, post-production began with the first day of production when the first scenes were delivered to the editing room. The *football*—on a film shoot it is more often than not a hard drive containing media files—has been in play from the start of production.

If media has been reaching the editing room since day 1, it must mean that by the time the filming ends some degree of editing must have taken place. Some directors are also editors. They work with assistants who prepare rough cuts of scenes for them to view and refine at the end of their shooting day. Other directors don't want to see or edit anything until they're done filming. Others trust an editor to make important creative decisions, then react to that editor's work. Still other directors aim to have a rough cut of the film ready just days after the end of filming. This last strategy is clearly the most time saving of them all, though it can be fraught with the potential for error or poor artistic judgment. There is no *best* method. No two projects are alike. Producers understand the varieties of director/editor relationships and working methods and seek out the best creative team and workflow possible.

As cast and crew move on to other productions, the producer, director, editor and others continue working on the film. Compared to the chaos experienced during production, things get awfully quiet. Many filmmakers prefer the editing stage over the production stage. They feel that *this is where the film comes together (or not)*. To them, the film is made three times: when it's written, when it's shot, and when it's edited. Editing is something of a wondrous, even *magical* art. Anyone that's had the pleasure of watching a scene assembled, shot by shot, will agree. And just as a series of shots leads to a scene, a series of scenes leads to an act. And a set of acts, usually three, leads to a feature length film.

Earlier I told you about keeping your eyes on the ball. That was in reference to the importance of knowing where (and in what condition) the media from the filming stage is located and what needs to happen next—technically and managerially—in order to move that media closer to becoming a finished film. I'm referring to *workflow*. But there is an equally important ball producers *must* keep their eyes on during post-production: the story's structure.

Workflow and Story Structure

While the job of assembling the film falls within the province of the editor and her team working in tandem with the director, producers are often called into the editing room for their perspective on how a scene is coming along. Some producers insist on being in the editing room during the editing stage. Others only attend private screenings of the film once it's viewable from start to finish.

There are four stages to film editing, (not counting sound design, the mix, and color correction all done once picture editing is completed). They are:

- The assembly stage
- The rough cut stage
- The fine cut stage
- The picture lock stage

During the assembly stage editors string very loose versions of the scenes together from start to finish. An assembly respects the script's original structure. It's a visual representation in chronological order of what's on the printed page. Shots are intentionally left *long*, with *handles* (additional frames or even several seconds) left on both sides of a line of dialogue or an action. This is a good time to point out the importance of *reaction shots*; shots of actors listening to the other actors. Seasoned film actors understand how vital reaction shots are. Watching people listening and reacting often conveys more than when someone's talking. It's during the assembly stage that listening/reaction shots are discovered and kept (or not). An assembly's run time is often up to twice or even three times as long as the finished film. It may include several takes of one line, providing the director and editor with choices for alternate takes, but it rarely, if ever, includes music, sound effects, or transitions like dissolves or fades. Producers understand the need for an assembly. It's the only way to get to the next stage: the rough cut.

The rough cut stage is the most time consuming stage of them all. A film can remain in rough cut for months or even years. It's during the rough cut stage that major surgery is performed on the film. Scenes are deleted, re-ordered, and sometimes, money permitting, even re-shot. Woody Allen's quote at the start of this section describes the matter very well. The rough cut stage is when filmmakers make important, game changing editorial decisions. Should there be a voice over? Should the story be told non-linearly or, if the script contained flashbacks (or flash forwards), should they be kept where they occur? What about acting and character? Are weak actors going to get less screen time? Are characters thought to have been unimportant suddenly vital to the story's coherence? Is the story clear? What's preventing it from being so? It's called a *rough cut* for a reason; it's the stage where the material is tested and challenged. When there's no more room for improving the overall structure, tone, and style of the film, the rough cut stage is considered complete and the fine cut stage begins.

Rhythm, cadence, pacing, call it what you will. The fine cut stage is the stage that will determine if an audience will want to pay attention to the film or not. The fine cut stage is when the film gets up out of its chair and starts to walk, jog, or run. Temporary music tracks are tested, a few sound effects are thrown in for emphasis or mood, but not much more. Screen time is different from real time. An audience is *collectively* much smarter than they would be as *individuals*. By monitoring each other's reactions to a movie, a group has a way of capturing the purpose and meaning of a scene very quickly; sooner than if each audience member were to watch the film alone. Once an audience *gets* a scene they're ready for the next one. In order to come across as *normal* a film editor needs to subtly compress time. This is just the way the mind perceives screen time. Even *slow* scenes are edited using techniques that move things along faster than reality. Trimming one frame from a shot will impact an audience's experience of that shot. The fine cut stage brings the movie to a point where 99 percent of all editorial choices concerning rhythm and pacing have been made. It's followed by the picture lock stage, when—with only a few minor exceptions—all bets are off and the film is, visually, as good as time, money, talent, hard work, focus, and endurance allows.

With the picture lock stage (the stage where no additional picture editing is considered necessary), the attention in the editing room turns to audio. There are two essential reasons why picture comes first and audio second. For starters, they're not called *motion pictures* by chance; from the beginning, as far back as the silent era, movies were a visual medium. The primary way stories are told—unlike say, a radio drama—is through moving images. Second, consider the technical aspects of editing: look at picture and sound as if they were *tracks* and it becomes clear: there is only one picture track. It's the sequence of shots the audience is watching on the screen and they can be conveyed only one at a time. Shot, shot, shot. But sound can have an infinite number of tracks. Dialogue tracks, music tracks, sound effects tracks, or ambient sound tracks. Now take a step back and imagine having the editor create a complex, sophisticated multi-track sound design during the assembly or rough cut stages only to have the director or producer (or the editor herself), decide to eliminate the scene or drastically modify it. Audio comes second in the editing room not because it is aesthetically inferior to picture, but because it allows for a much more efficient workflow. Indeed, aesthetically, audio has become picture's near equal, and today's audiences demand much of it. Good producers understand this important workflow and make certain the best audio work possible is brought to the film, but only once picture has been locked.

A Note about Music

Today's big budget extravaganzas use music as *wallpaper*, putting it in from the first shot to the last. When asked about the role of music in his films Alfred Hitchcock said that sometimes it's not the music that matters but its *absence*. While he was absolutely spot on with regard to the power of silence, in one notable instance he was almost fatally wrong. His original intent was to have the shower scene from *Psycho* (1960) take place without composer Bernard Hermann's piercing violins, but after Hermann gently asked him to compare the scene with and without music, Hitchcock conceded he was wrong. One other important point to keep in mind: *music can be used to underscore what the image is showing, or it can be used to comment on it (contrapuntally)*. Here is film star Bette Davis on music: "... before I waste any more time on acting; who is going up those stairs to die; me or [composer] Max Steiner?!". What she meant was: a character walking up a staircase need not be accompanied by a musical crescendo melodically ascending with her. That is wallpaper. Conversely, at the close of Stanley Kubrick's *Dr. Strangelove* (1964), as we watch a montage of nuclear bombs exploding we hear the song *We'll Meet Again*. Kubrick is saying that humanity, as a species, is done. And he's saying it in a bittersweet, almost nostalgic way. The song *comments* on the action by offering this comic, albeit rather dark, point of view on the subject.

> **SIDEBAR INTERVIEW | Ann McCabe A.C.E./Editor. Features and television series. New York City.**
>
> FM: What's been your experience working with producers and what is the producer/editor relationship like?
>
> AM: The producer's role varies depending on whether it's a television show or a movie. And it also depends on what kind of producer it is because movies and television may have many producers. For example, there are line producers. That's the person that organizes things, costs things out, and does a lot of practical stuff. And then there are more creative producers; someone who's actually found the project and worked with the writers and the director and kind of overseen the whole creative process. Then there are producers that are all about raising money. And then there are producers that work in all of those areas. Some producers can be more influential than others and may be very much a part of the production process, while others are more hands off.

In television there's a producer/creator role called a show runner. That person creates the whole look and feel of the show and is a kind of be all end all of what the show's about. They're extremely powerful and have a lot of say. On a movie, you can also have an extremely powerful producer but you might also have a very powerful director who acts as the project's driving force. On a television show the director doesn't have nearly as much influence as they do on a movie.

With regard to the nature of the producer/editor relationship, it all depends. For television work I've gone on job interviews and met the show runner as well as several producers. On a movie I usually just interview with the director, but sometimes a producer is also present. Moreover, sometimes you have to go through multiple interviews before getting hired.

FM: What happens when you begin editing the project?

AM: During the editing stage the editor does a first pass of the film which is called an assembly. Then the director comes in. On a TV show it's for quite a short time; just a few days. But on a movie directors get more or less ten weeks of work with the editor. And in both of those scenarios they produce what's called a director's cut. Subsequent to that the producers will stop by and weigh in on the cut. Producers can be very involved and want to change things, and sometimes they'll collaborate with the director. It all depends on how everybody's getting along.

FM: Talk a little bit about the kinds of conversations you're having with the producer in the editing room. What is your best case scenario? How do you want to work with a producer in the editing room?

AM: On an independent movie the best scenario is a producer who is helpful. A solutions oriented person is great. A producer like that is somebody like Scott Rudin, who is very much about ideas and solutions. He's all about "Let's make this good." And sometimes producers are watching the money and they're saying things like "Okay, you've got this choice or that choice so you need to finish up."

Once you've gone through the assembly process you present the film to the producers and they will come up with ideas or reflect back and think about ways to make the movie better. And the best case scenario there would be to have a producer with really good ideas which you hadn't thought of. As the editor you're living with the footage and trying things and looking at the material over and over again, and you've become very close to it, so it helps to get a fresh pair of eyes on things. To me the best kind of producer doesn't overwhelm with a zillion ideas, saying we should change everything. It's someone that's very clever who has a couple of great ideas that can be extremely useful.

FM: So the producer comes in at various stages during the editing process?

AM: Yes. The best producer isn't in the cutting room every day because—honestly—having a lot of people in there is not such a great idea. It's better to present the cut. You send it to them, they watch it and they reply with a conversation or clever and insightful notes. Hopefully, notes that have to do with what was actually shot as opposed to notes that no one can do anything about. So the best producer is in touch with the project but not in there all the time.

FM: Looking back on your work so far, what frustrated you the most when working with producers, and what brought you the most satisfaction or joy?

AM: When somebody you respect likes your work, that's a great feeling. And if they feel like you've gotten the cut to a really good place quickly, that feels really good as well. The first movie I cut was Greg Mottola's *The Daytrippers* (1997). Steven Soderbergh was the producer but he's also an editor. And I was working, cutting the assembly, and Steven was going to come in and check on the cut, and it was certainly a great moment when we showed him the cut and he said he liked it.

More recently I cut the pilot of *The Newsroom* (2014). We had to put it together very quickly and we showed it to Aaron Sorkin, Scott Rudin, and Alan Poul—all heavyweight guys—and they were laughing and cheering. That was a fantastic experience.

In terms of negative experiences, sometimes you cut something and you get twenty pages of notes with a million requests for changes that are simply unachievable. Maybe they shot a movie on a very low budget in a really short period of time and there aren't very many angles, or the producers are critical of the way the movie looks and there's not enough coverage. And sometimes producers want to make it look like they spent a lot of money on what's actually a low budget film; doing that can be detrimental to the film. The charm of the movie gets sort of ruined. The whole thing about doing a small film is that you should be able to do interesting and experimental things.

The other thing that can happen sometimes is that on a film set everybody really liked a particular actor or actress and when they look at the cut they'll say, "Wait a minute there was that really funny moment when . . .". But sometimes when you cut it together what was really funny on the set doesn't translate well at all. Not that you should never try things on a set—but it won't always play well in front of an audience.

FM: What you're saying echoes what I've been hearing from people in other sectors of the industry about knowing what type of movie you're making.

AM: Right. Embrace the charm of the movie. It's what you shot and it's what you should most likely stick with. Don't try to slick it up later by spending a whole lot of money creating a bunch of effects that won't improve things.

FM: I'm curious about the conversations you might have with producers about a film's promotional materials. Do they come to you and say, "*Hey this is great, thank you for cutting the film. Now we need a trailer.*"?

AM: What happens is that they'll hire a trailer company to cut the trailer. It's a very different skill. Moreover, when I'm cutting a movie I'm very close to the material and I resist putting anything in the trailer because I don't want to give anything away! But cutting a movie trailer necessitates a skill which I do not have. So I'm not involved in that process. But I will look at trailers—and sometimes there are several versions—that producers send out, and sometimes a director or producer will ask me for my opinion on which one I like.

I've been involved in creating DVD extras but that's not happening quite so much anymore. Additionally, because the name of the movie often changes during the editing process, I might weigh in on the movie's title. But I don't have final say on that. It's more the producer's role.

FM: What is a producer looking for in an editor?

AM: Usually they're looking for somebody that has cut something they liked and was successful. They also want somebody who is able to work quickly, and has an opinion; they don't usually want somebody who's going to be completely passive. But on the other hand they don't want somebody who's going to be a huge pain in the ass. It's a very collaborative position. Producers will talk to other producers and directors who have worked with this person before. They'll look for recommendations. I think you have to have a lot of patience to be an editor, so I think producers look for an editor who is willing to try things but also someone who is not going to stretch it out for months and months and months and create delays.

FM: What gets you into the editing room? Why do you do this?

AM: I enjoy it. It's sort of like writing. It's very creative working to shape a story. And then there's the challenge of looking at footage and trying to come up with a way to tell the scene. It's actually a lot of fun! And the biggest satisfaction? Well, I just previewed something. It's a pretty challenging movie. A comedy with Robert De Niro, Zach Efron and Aubrey Plaza [*Dirty Grandpa*, 2016]. And we worked really, really hard on the movie. We presented it in front of three hundred people and they were cracking up like crazy, laughing. That was hugely enjoyable. Laughter is the real easy one. But other times, when you put a movie up in front of people and they are gasping, or crying, or you see their emotion or they cheer . . . I've been at screenings where people cheer and clap and it's hugely satisfying giving people that pleasure. And sometimes I like being by myself and just trying things. Try this, try that. Moreover, there's a lot of music involved with film editing and I really enjoy working with music. And sometimes it's like a puzzle and you're using your brain in a way that can be immensely satisfying. And—unlike working on a set—it's usually not eighteen hour days!

FM: How different is a finished cut from an assembly?

AM: It depends on the movie and the script. I've been working on comedies lately. And in comedies people tend to do an enormous amount of improvisation. So that creates a whole other layer of what gets changed and what gets kept. But I would say the biggest difference between an assembly and a final cut is that the film gets shorter. I've had assemblies that are three hours long. You put everything in and it's this huge, long, boring mess and then it's a matter of asking "Okay, what do we keep?"

And sometimes it's about reordering scenes. Or you'll have a scene and you break it up by cutting to somewhere else and cutting back. Additionally, we try to make people speak in a way that makes them seem smart. People in movies don't really speak the way they do in real life. I spend a lot of time taking out "ums" and "ahs" and any ramblings. I try to make the dialogue sound clever and I like to show people coming up with ideas very quickly. But I would say the biggest thing is making things tighter.

FM: "Cinema is life with all the boring parts cut out." Hitchcock.

AM: Right, right, exactly!

FM: Do producers ask you to visit the set during a shoot, or do you stay away?

AM: Occasionally they ask you to come by because they want you to weigh in on something, or they want you to stay connected to the director. And I've brought edited scenes to set and showed them. That can work well when you're cutting near the location or the studio. But editors have a ton of work. We have to watch hours and hours of footage and then try to put it all together. A trip to set can take a bunch of hours out of a working day.

FM: Do you have any insights on where filmmaking will be in five or ten years?

AM: I work on many different kinds of projects. Studio movies, independent movies, television. It's good to be versatile, and I'd say it's the same for a producer: it's a good idea to know how to do a lot of different things. I think the content of movies seems to be narrowing. I think there's always going to be a place for editors because there's somebody that's going to need to put it all together. Even if the technology changes you still need somebody to shape the story, choose the takes, and so forth. It's a lot of work and most directors would agree: they don't want to be the one doing that. They want to have someone else do it and they want to hire that person. So I'm not really sure where the industry is headed, though it does seem like there is more and more television. But, then again, I just read something the other day that says there seems to be too much television. Moreover, there don't seem to be as many independent movies as there were, say, ten years ago.

There are going to be a lot of people who'll learn how to edit. My kids know how to do use the basic versions of editing software like Media Composer, Final Cut, or Premiere Pro. They just start putting things together much more quickly, there's no mystery in learning how to make a cut anymore. That will change the industry as well. So I think we'll see a lot more movies done on smartphones, and they'll probably be some really good ones. But I'm hoping there's going to be a place for somebody to keep trying to shape a story.

Test Screenings and Finishing the Film

Once the film is in the fine cut or picture lock stage, test screenings can begin. Test screenings are for the general public, not for filmmakers and their families. This is an important distinction. Too much praise at a test screening may be the result of family, friends, co-workers, or colleagues showing up. The most effective test screening is one populated by strangers with little or no knowledge of the film. A test screening is a litmus test for the film's ability to reach an audience. There is no substitute for a room filled with 50 or 100 strangers watching your film. It's a very thrilling moment for the filmmakers. Even before the post-screening discussion and survey, producers gauge the film's impact on the audience by listening to their reactions and even watching them watching the film as it unfolds. A test screening yields valuable information like:

- Is the story clear? Are there any plot points that are unclear or—conversely—too obvious?
- Where does the story meander or where is it moving too fast?
- Is the audience empathizing with the characters?
- What beats are working and what beats need more work?
- Are there any dialogue lines that didn't make sense or were unclear?
- What about overall length? Are there redundant scenes? Are there missing scenes?
- What is the overall *takeaway* feeling for the audience?
- Would they recommend the film to a friend?

Producers who conduct test screenings come away knowing—often down to a specific shot—what needs to be done in the editing room to improve the film. Moreover, because test audiences can be fickle, good producers conduct two or more test screenings and look for recurring audience reactions. Test screenings are often maligned by filmmakers unwilling to keep an open mind about how to improve the film. They do this at their own peril. Moreover, filmmakers often listen only to praise for the film, not the criticism, which is often constructive. Good producers know how to sort and sift through the praise and the criticism. They know what notes to keep and what notes to leave out. They walk away from a test screening with a clear idea of what needs to be done next to move the film towards completion, and they implement a strategy to get there.

Finishing

By the time the film reaches the sound mix, a considerable amount of sound design has already taken place. But depending on the agreement between the producer and the mixing studio, additional and more sophisticated sound design may take place.

The lead sound mixer will be the person responsible for taking the many disparate sound elements (dialogue, sound effects, music, ambience tracks) and creating a seamless, perfectly equalized, clear, and engaging soundscape for the film. Filmmakers agree this is an indispensable part of post-production. After all, why commit so much time, money, and energy to a film's visuals only to compromise its sounds? Moreover, while distributors may understand the aesthetic reasons behind using a grainy, hand held, documentary shooting style, they are far less understanding of indecipherable dialogue, excessively loud music or technical flaws like static and audio saturation in the sound department. There's an intrinsic *push back* to poor sound from distributors—and audiences. The higher standard which audio is held to is one of the anomalies of filmmaking. Producers understand that if their film is going to have a shot at being seen at a festival, in theaters, or on television and the internet, a capable sound mixer is indispensable. The best sound mixers are not only technicians who can equalize, mix, and deliver a finished soundtrack. They are artists and skilled communicators and will engage the director in conversations about the film's theme, style, and more. They will point out unintended idiosyncrasies in the storyline and provide ways of downplaying them all the while accentuating the story points that require it. A great sound mixer will provide a film with an overall sound palette, an over-arching *feel* to the movie that would otherwise not be there.

Color Correction/Grading

While the film is being mixed, another critical step is taking place. Color correction, or *grading*, is the stage during which the film acquires its final and definitive *look*. Grading can fix problem shots, shots that may have been under or over exposed during the shooting stage. It can add or subtract color, contrast, hue, tint, saturation, gamma, and much more to one or more shots or scenes. Grading can change an entire movie's color palette. Some filmmakers use the grading stage to reinforce a film's *realism* or to make everything visually consistent from scene to scene. Producers and directors may instruct a colorist (as the position is called) to equalize or normalize everything so that audiences will focus more on the story and less on inconsistent color palettes. But some filmmakers will tell colorists to move away from realism and create a color palette that calls attention to itself. In other words, grading a film is not merely a technical stage during the final mastering of a movie. It's the visual equivalent of the sound mix and has the potential for as much creativity and innovation as every other stage of the filmmaking process.

Colorists work with a variety of tools and producers may deliver content to them in a variety of ways. The DaVinci Resolve software is currently a very popular color correction tool, but by the time you read this there may be a newer, better tool. Likewise, producers today may deliver high resolution Apple Pro Res 4444HQ files to colorists, but it's anyone's guess what they'll be delivering a year or two from now. So, in keeping with my opening statement about technology, I will refrain from unpacking today's tools. They'll be obsolete tomorrow. And besides: the internet will continue to bring filmmakers the latest/greatest updates on new tools and methods when they need them. For our purposes, let us agree that whether it's *invisible* (as when it's done in the service of *realism*) or *visible* (as when it serves a particular aesthetic style)—grading is a necessary and final step in terms of the film's image.

Master Files and DCPs

When the film's final—*graded and color corrected*—picture is combined with its final sound mix is when all bets are off and the film, come what may, is done. Obviously this is a major accomplishment and should be acknowledged as such. Yet, in our digital age, nothing is forever. There may be revisions, re-edits, and so on, but *this* master at *this* time is what will be duplicated and distributed around the world.

It can feel a little strange to see so much time, money, and effort reduced to a single digital master file, but that's exactly what the production process boils down to. Small films may never get beyond a high resolution Quicktime file while other films may have sophisticated Digital Cinema Packages, or DCPs. DCPs are hard discs which motion pictures are stored on using a universally agreed upon set of technical specifications. They are what allows a digital cinema in Paris, for example, to play the same film—using the same technology—as a digital cinema in Los Angeles. They are, for all intents and purposes, the digital equivalent of 35-mm film. DCPs look like they're here to stay, at least until distributors can beam movies via satellite across the planet and into cinemas or send them through super fast fiber optic cables (or whatever new technologies appear). Producers need to outsource DCP creation. It's not something that can be done in the editing room. Fortunately it's not an expensive process and many times distributors either pick up the total cost of DCP creation (an expense they'll apply against revenues to the producer, so be apprised!) or they'll split the cost with the film's production company. Things get a little trickier—and more expensive—if a film is being simultaneously released digitally on—say—a thousand screens. Now the cost of manufacturing 1,000 DCPs is not so affordable, though the potential for revenue has suddenly increased considerably.

With a finished film in hand one might think that putting it under one's arm and taking it to the marketplace should be akin to a walk in the park. After all, the film is finished and the market likes and maybe even *wants* it. The hard part is over. It's time for audiences to vote with their wallets. But you'll recall that earlier I told you that the five stages of filmmaking (development, preproduction, production, post-production, and distribution) are not as clearly delineated as they sound and that, in fact, they are fuzzy, squishy, amorphous stages that overlap, intersect, and often develop in tandem with one another. Now with this in mind think back to the early stages of scriptwriting and fundraising. Back then, the savvy producers weren't just developing a script and talking to investors. They were *already* in conversations with distributors, alerting them to the film's existence, sending synopses, cast lists, director bios, teaser reels and more to potential buyers. And as production moved forward with commencement of principal photography, producers alerted distributors of the start of filming. In many cases producers had already set up agreements with distributors who paid them a percentage of the film's budget in advance in exchange for distribution rights. Those distributors in turn had *pre-sold* the film to any number of territories (another word for countries) for a variety of platforms (theatrical, cable, on-demand, internet, etc.). Bottom line: if a producer finds themselves with a DCP or high resolution Quicktime file and no distribution prospects, there is no *walk in the park*. There's a lot of work left to be done. So much so that many filmmakers come to the conclusion that finishing a film doesn't represent the end of a journey. It's actually the half-way mark.

Deliverables

Every film that crosses the finish line must come with a set of deliverables. Ask 10 separate acquisitions people for their deliverables list and you'll get 10 different versions. Terminology, definition, order of importance, type of documentation, schedule of delivery dates, formats; it's all up for grabs. There are, however, about a dozen deliverables that are *not* negotiable. Additional deliverables are managed on a case by case basis. The list that follows is a good place to start. I've itemized it in order of importance. The latter part of the list provides optional deliverables. They are optional because, in the case of a film's poster art, a distributor will almost certainly conjure up their own version. Experience has taught distributors how to best position a film for the marketplace. Their poster will almost certainly be more audience-friendly than yours, which may be more artistic. Unless you are Stanley Kubrick, working with Saul Bass on the poster for *The Shining* (1980), a distributor that acquires your film will have final say on your film's poster, which is why delivering your poster art is an option and not a requirement. The same can be said about any trailer you and your editor concoct in the editing room. Good producers recognize their distributor's expertise when it comes to marketing and delegate poster and trailer creation to them.

Deliverables list:

- Master file of the completed film, color corrected and mixed.
- Mastered files of the music and effects tracks only
- Mastered files of the dialogue tracks only
- Chain of Title or Producer's Certificate
- Music cue sheets
- Word document containing full credit list and technical specifications
- Screenplay and certificate of authorship
- English dialogue list
- Location releases
- Actor releases
- High resolution images from the film

Optional deliverables list:

- Landscape and portrait style graphic of the film's poster
- Images of the director and cast
- Quicktime of a short interview with the film's lead actors
- Quicktime of a short interview with the film's director
- Quicktime of the film's trailer

Chapter 10

The Marketplaces
History, Deal Structures, Distribution, Exhibition, and Film Festivals

> For most of my lifetime a theatrical release has been simply, even in its most successful iterations, a loss-leader, a form of advertising that gave legitimacy to the product's "identity" as "cinema" in its actual economic life downstream on smaller screens.—James Schamus

Drive through any small town in the U.S. that still has a one-screen movie theater on Main Street and imagine a time when it was the *only way* audiences could see a movie. Across America, in cities large and small, cinemas drew weekly audiences numbering in the millions. Week after week, for decades, audiences for theatrically released motion pictures were larger than today's multiplex moviegoers by orders of magnitude. Moreover, on any given Friday or Saturday night the number of movies audiences could choose from were, by today's standards, microscopically small. It's strange for us today to imagine that for decades this was how movies were consumed by millions of people. There were no ancillary markets, no television, home video cassettes or DVDs, no cable, video on demand, or internet. And foreign markets weren't nearly as developed as they are now. Studios simply churned out hundreds of movies per year and shipped them to their cinemas. When a film completed its run it was shipped back to the studio, stored in a warehouse, and a new film was shipped out. No surprise that film historians equate the studio era with the image of a factory. It really was a time when, like widgets on an assembly line, a prodigious amount of movies were made. At its peak, during the 1930s and 1940s the studio system was churning out an average of 1,500 films *per year*. Sometimes a gem would emerge. *Casablanca* (1942), *It's A Wonderful Life* (1946), *The Wizard of Oz* (1939), or *Citizen Kane* (1941), but most studio films were pretty much boiler plate affairs, formulaic in story and style, and emblematic of the studios that produced them. It's hard to believe, but the vast majority of films made during the studio era are long gone, forgotten, or simply destroyed due to the fragile and perishable nature of nitrate-based motion picture film stock.

Eventually the federal government's anti-trust laws dismantled the studios' monopoly of the production, distribution, and exhibition of films, forcing them to divest themselves of one of their three principal entities. Wisely, they chose to give up their exhibition operations but held on to their production and distribution wings. And eventually even the distribution wings were dismantled.

The origins of today's *marketplace* for the exhibition of movies can be traced back to the studios' divestiture of their movie palaces. Moreover, the studios had developed their own specific *brands*. Warner Brothers, for example, was known for its dark social realism gangster films while Metro Goldwyn Meyer specialized in escapist musicals. As odd as it may seem to us today, during the studio era audiences often picked their evening's entertainment based on the studio that produced it. Today do we really care what studio is behind this weekend's blockbuster? With the possible exception of Disney/Pixar/Marvel, can we say that the studios have distinct and discernible brands?

I mention all of this because it helps producers see that today's marketplace for independent films is radically different from yesterday's marketplace, and that tomorrow's marketplace is going to be very different. By the time you read this, new distribution models using new technologies will have emerged. We can describe the present market for films but only if we accept that it will evolve into something else. That said, we can *also* describe perennial market forces that have remained unchanged since the marketplace first came into existence. Understanding this will help our movie make its way into the world.

What Distributors Want

Distributors demand films whose run time is somewhere between a minimum of more or less 70 minutes and a maximum of two hours. Movies that do not fall into this time frame provide distributors with a solid reason to *pass* on acquiring a film. Think about it. When was the last time you watched a 45-minute film, either at the multiplex or on television? The same can be said for the two-and-a-half-hour-plus film. It's a rarity. An outlier. The internet, however, is allowing films of *all* lengths, and—subsequently—*all* budgets. This game changing and highly disruptive environment is redefining film distribution. It is bringing back interest in the short subject film, be it fiction or documentary. It is changing viewing habits. It is inventing new economic models for financing, producing, and exhibiting audio visual content. It is commoditizing films to the point where audiences expect their content to be provided to them when they want it, on a wide variety of platforms (desktop, laptop, tablet, or smartphone) and for *free*. Moreover, today's (and most likely tomorrow's) independent film marketplace favors the distributor, not the producer. There are simply too many films available—many of them outstanding—and not enough theatrical, television, and computer screens to accommodate them all. Call it a *glut* of product. More supply than demand. Even wonderfully unique, deserving, brilliant, and innovative films fall by the wayside, disappearing into oblivion. Mysteriously (or, as we are about to see, not so mysteriously), awful movies, even ones made independently of the studios (and not privileged with large marketing and advertising budgets) end up in theaters, on television, and on your laptop or smartphone. There appears to be no rhyme or reason as to why a film does or does not *make it* in the marketplace. Is it really a free for all? Is it really the wild, wild west?

For producers, one way to tackle the question of *what the marketplace is looking for* is to ask the buyers. After all, distributors, exhibitors, film festival programmers, and audiences are the ones who'll spend money on your film. What do they have to say? Let's go back to scriptwriter William Goldman's maxim: *nobody knows anything.* He's right. Try to retrofit your film to the so-called *demands* of the marketplace and you will most likely fail. Make an outstanding, different, innovative, compelling movie and—while there are no guarantees—you at least increase your likelihood of success, so perhaps the better question to ask is not so much *what is the market looking for* but rather *what does it need to see to even consider your film in the running*? If we stick to practical matters, technical specifications, a universally agreed upon set of guidelines applicable to all markets, we at least give ourselves a fighting chance. With that in mind, the first question producers need to pose becomes: Is the film releasable?

Taking aesthetics and artistic achievement temporarily off the table, a releasable film is one whose permissions and technical specifications are in order. By permissions we mean that anything that is seen or heard during the movie has been *cleared* by the production; actors have signed release forms, location releases have been signed, and all music rights are either completed or en route to completion. Distributors often pick up the cost of clearing music or pay to have the film re-scored. That's a cost the distributor deducts from any future revenue earmarked for the producer.

A releasable film is one where all rights surrounding the story and script have been negotiated, cleared, and documented with a *chain of title*. The chain of title is what tracks the movie's ownership from idea to synopsis to script and finally to movie. Once a scriptwriter has penned a script, unless a chain of title stipulates otherwise, that script and its incarnation as a film belongs to that scriptwriter. Good producers make sure they have a clear, documented, legally binding chain of title that passes copyright ownership of a script into the hands of the production company which then passes it along to the film's distributor. No one in the business of acquiring a film wants to see a film without a clear chain of title. It's too risky—even with errors and omissions insurance (a type of insurance producers buy to stave off lawsuits when, for example, a trade marked brand appears in the film). In extremely rare instances, if a film has been written, produced, and directed by one entity, a chain of title may be considered more than adequate—and even a little comical—with sentences like: *"On June 12th, John Smith, scriptwriter, hereby transfers ownership of the script to John Smith Productions."* Followed by *"On September 3rd, Smith Productions hereby transfers the direction of the script to John Smith, director."* In these instances, distributors may forego the chain of title in exchange for a *producer's statement*, essentially a notarized letter assuring that the producer is indeed the owner of the film being released and has cleared all rights, protecting the distributor from any lawsuits, frivolous or not.

So why *do* "awful" films end up getting distribution deals? Well, for starters, we are dealing with the creative arts, and tastes vary. Your masterpiece is my trash. My masterpiece looks and sounds like complete junk to you. I'm sure you could have arrived at this conclusion without reading this book. Moreover, audiences often don't know what they like until they see it or are told it's good. Film critics make or break films, not as much as word of mouth does, but a rave in the *New York Times* will do wonders for a movie's box office take. Whether you will actually like it or not is another matter. So, all things being equal, why do *awful* studio or independent movies get distribution deals? If a less than average movie is in the theaters it must be because the distributor had no choice but to release it. And when a distributor has no choice but to release a film is when they have *advanced* money to the producer, oftentimes at the script stage, in exchange for the right to distribute the film. To quote Michael Corleone: *"It's not personal, Sonny. It's strictly business."* It does not get much more complicated than that. Here, the maxim, *follow the money* is especially useful. Studio or independent, big budget or small, if a distributor helps finance a film's production, it's going to get distributed regardless of how that film turns out. Once it's released the film may be in theaters for a week or six months—that is something for the paying public to determine. If no one shows up exhibitors will pull a movie from their screens. There are simply too many movies waiting in line for their turn to rise or fall.

So a *releasable* film is a film whose papers are in order. Distributors will not consider a film whose papers are not. Add the *artistic* and *entertainment* quotient back into the mix and it becomes clear that not every completed film is suitable for release. An incoherent storyline, unspeakably bad acting, lousy production values, and poor lighting, sound, and editing will make a film un-releasable just as much as one whose papers are not in order.

Let us now assume the best: a film whose papers *are* in order and whose artistic and entertainment quotient is more than acceptable, maybe even first rate. And let's say a distributor sees the film at one of the handful of film festivals where distributors actually acquire films. Negotiating a deal with a distributor is a highly complex undertaking. Good producers may work with entertainment lawyers to optimize a deal in their favor, but market forces will always play the decisive role in setting the terms for any distribution deal. It is beyond the scope of this book to unpack the varieties of distribution deals out there. What we *can* unpack are some of the basic industry percentages distributors offer producers, keeping in mind that they too will fluctuate depending on a host of conditions.

Deal Structures

Generally speaking, a standard distribution agreement has distributors advancing the cost of releasing a film and recouping that cost before a producer sees any money. Moreover, from the get go, the distributor must leave 50 percent of box office revenue with the exhibitor. One way to look at how money flows here is to work forward from the moment a paying customer walks up to the box office window and plunks down her $10 for a ticket to your movie. As noted above, 50 percent (or 5 of those $10) are kept by the exhibitor. There are, of course, variations. For example, over the course of a long run, say several weeks, the 50/50 split turns into 70/30 or 80/20 with the exhibitor keeping less and less in exchange for hosting a *hit* that guarantees a revenue stream (at least more than the next film, whose revenue potential is untested). Let's continue with the 50/50 split and see what happens to those five dollars the distributor has just collected. Recall that the distributor has advanced the cost of marketing and distributing the film. Standard distribution agreements stipulate that, give or take 5 percentage points, as much as 30 percent of the distributor's take goes towards recouping those costs. So for every $5 the distributor makes, $1.50 stays with them. That leaves $3.50. But the distributor's going to hold on to still more money. Marketing (buying advertising, social media, press junkets) and negotiating release dates and terms with exhibitors constitutes only part of the distributor's expenses. The distributor has also advanced the cost of manufacturing the digital cinema packages (DCPs) and promotional materials (including trailers, stills, poster art, and more). And then there's the distributor's operating costs. So, of that remaining $3.50, at the end of the day the filmmakers typically see about $1.00, and sometimes even less. Recall that we began with 10. With such poor returns a producer inevitably asks how—and when—will their film see a profit? The answer is—by and large—*never*. As the saying goes: *you can't make a living, you can only get rich*. Another way of putting it is to say that the only films that are going to generate profits for producers are the *hits*. The others, that is to say, the vast majority, are not. Distributors understand these odds and plan accordingly, releasing several films over the course of a calendar year, hoping their instincts are good and that one hit will cover the costs incurred by the flops. Small wonder that producers of hits often ask for—but rarely obtain—separate, film-by-film accounting for a distributor's slate of films. After all, if you've produced a hit would you want your film to *carry* a distributor's flops?

If the picture I am painting of the world of distribution is a bleak one, producers need not be discouraged. For starters, I am describing only *part* of the distribution landscape: the theatrical one. Moreover, as I stated at the outset, every year brings new distribution models and strategies.

SIDEBAR INTERVIEW | Francois Yon, Distributor. Feature films. Paris.

FY: I run an international film sales company, Films Distribution, which I started with my partner in 1995. We've got about forty people on board and we buy films that can come from anywhere in the world. About 90 percent of our acquisitions are made at the script level. We base our decisions on a number of parameters: script, director, the quality of the producer, the budget, and casting. If we decide to invest we usually finance anywhere from ten to thirty percent of the budget against worldwide sales rights and a commission.

FM: Describe your relationship with producers and production companies. What kinds of conversations do you have? Is it purely business? Are you involved with matters at the creative level?

FY: If you look at our company's track record the only stable parameter across all film projects is the quality of the producer. It almost means more to us than the casting. We are a very director-driven group so we tend to keep authors and filmmakers for a long time. But while directors have many great qualities, they don't have a whole lot of loyalty. They'll tend to change partnerships and work according to what the available budgets are. So, for us, the relationship with the producer is the important one. They are suppliers of quality films and there are only so many of them available. And for them we represent a place where they can find money to finance their movie. With regard to participation at the creative level, when you put money into a movie, you're putting money into your convictions. Consequently, you have a right to a say in matters. So if we put a million euros into a movie we get to have a serious discussion with the director about things like casting. If we think that the casting is—for example—too weak for the international market, we can bring that up. We can also discuss the length of the picture. Oftentimes that's something we discuss in advance. Moreover, in our contracts we include clauses about the maximum length of the movie. To be clear: if a script is 400 pages and we like it, we'll go for the movie. It's not like we're looking for short films. But if the movie is set to be about 100 minutes and the script is timed out to be 100 minutes and the movie comes in at two and a half hours, we have a problem.

FM: When do you begin showcasing the film to the world?

FY: It depends. If it's a highly anticipated film from a known director there's a good chance that marketing will start at the script stage. For example, on some scripts from known directors we make the script available to buyers worldwide. That script is our first marketing element and it can trigger presales. Another approach would be to provide any poster ideas. Anything we think will help us pitch the movie. Or we'll work on a promo-reel; that's a two or three minute excerpt of the film that showcases the project's production values and helps create audience awareness. That usually happens during the editing stage. Sometimes, when the film's nearing completion, we'll edit a second promo reel. So the marketing is something we usually start very early on. We're always thinking about the best way to make our project known to the world.

FM: Do you have a strict deliverables list or are you flexible?

FY: We have two types of deliverables lists. For movies with budgets above $10 million we require absolutely everything. For movies with smaller budgets we have a simpler deliverables list. We do this because smaller films can't always afford to deliver everything the bigger films can. In some cases we require films to be shot on 35-mm film, which still provides a better picture quality than digital.

FM: So, even if not many theaters in the U.S. project 35-mm film, you can shoot it in 35 and then project it on a digital cinema package (DCP)?

FY: Yes, that happens. But sometimes we insist the film be screened on 35-mm at a prestigious theater for discriminating audiences. When we do that people are reminded of the beauty of 35-mm film. Shooting in 35-mm also means we cannot afford more than two or three takes, so preparation is crucial.

FM: Talk about today's distribution landscape for producers, distributors, and exhibitors. How is it different than it was ten years ago and where do you think it's headed?

FY: The main shift has been in the diminished worldwide DVD market; their value has not been replaced by VOD (video on demand) revenues. On average, one DVD would bring a distributor somewhere between for or five euros, net—today it brings about one euro sixty per DVD. So this has been an enormous hit to distributors; one major source of revenue has disappeared. The other revenue stream that has disappeared is television. Television stations used to buy films, especially quality films, and they're—generally speaking—poor now. Moreover, *cinema* is not performing well on television. It's been replaced by television *series* and other types of programs. Distributors looking to make money from a film have to have a theatrical strategy, and films are made for that. They aren't made to be watched on computers alone in a room. They're meant to be a collective experience. That's what cinema is about. Films from Spain or Italy, Germany, Scandinavia, and other non-Hollywood production companies make money from the theatrical release of their films. But this shift in distribution has caused a traffic jam with the exhibitors. There are too many films and only so many films get to be distributed per year. Increasingly, the market is focusing more on the large art house films. For the smaller, emerging directors, in order to be relevant in the world, your film has to be a work of art. Ten years ago you could have had a small movie, made decent sales, gotten into festivals, and expected some revenue—it was a viable business model. As a distributor you might have twenty or thirty of those films per year and you could survive. Today, if you don't have two or three highly talked about, very anticipated non-Hollywood films, you cannot exist.

FM: What is your company's relationship to online watching and the internet? Do you deal with sites like Netflix or Hulu?

FY: When we sell a movie to the U.S., it's an *all-rights* deal. From there the buyer does whatever they want with the film. In France we deal with Netflix because we have a large library of about 800 movies and we made a deal with them for 200 of them, so we have a strong and good relationship. And—increasingly—we see Netflix coming into the international market; they're buying worldwide rights. They can stream throughout North America and now France. They already have Scandinavia and Holland and they're opening up in Italy, Spain, and Portugal. They can cover a good chunk of the world—they're opening up in Australia as well. And they love working with companies like us because they can strike worldwide deals before we sell to local distributors. So the deals we usually make with Netflix are very lucrative. We then go to the distributors and say, "Here's the movie. We'll give up all rights *except* for VOD. Here's what it's going to cost but you have to release the film by *X date*, because on that date the film will be on Netflix."

FM: To a budding producer wanting to make his first film, what advice does a film distribution person provide?

FY: You have to be provocative and outstanding in your talent. You have to stand out. Casting is not an issue for us. Budget is not an issue for us. We're just looking for talent. If you make yet another romantic comedy with an unknown cast shot in New York in black and white, we're not interested. On the other hand, if you come up with a story that's going to knock us out, or something new from a formal perspective, that's something. So I think you *have* to get noticed. I think a great first film is a film that doesn't care too much about the marketplace but cares more about how the filmmakers want to express their talent. If you obsess about the marketplace there's no way you're going to make a good first film. You'll always lose because there will always be a film that's *more* in the market than you are because it has the cast, the money, the reputation, and the name.

FM: As you know, there's a lot going in television now. Things like *Breaking Bad* or *True Detective*. Are you looking at television-based production and distribution models?

FY: We have looked at this question, but I think in the end we won't be able to go there because, given our size, it's not a business we can get into. Television is populated by large and complex media groups. If you want to be involved with a series, to play with the big guys you have to be prepared to put a hundred million dollars down. You're dealing with broadcasters. What we're seeing are television producers looking for talent but they're not getting the talent they want. So they look to *cinema*-based talent. We also see people coming from cinema, going to television to shoot a series, then coming back to cinema. The reason for this is that they consider themselves to be *auteurs* and see no opportunity for creative input in writing for television because the series' main storyline is set by the broadcaster and not by them. In the U.S. it's a little different; the market is so big and there's so much money in a television series

> that you can get the best talent you want. Actors, producers, writers, directors. You name it. That's not possible in Europe, so we're not so worried about the talent moving from cinema to television. What we *are* worried about is that audience tastes are changing and the cinema is perceived to be something for older people. Cinema, unlike series television, is no longer widely consumed by young audiences. That's a bit worrisome.
>
> FM: Any closing thoughts?
>
> FY: A lot of things will change in cinema. The shift in talent and shift in consumers has always been a worrisome topic. But we're always trying to find better talent and better films, and we're open to new ideas. It's a great game of survival. I'm not complaining.

Film Festivals

If you've never been to a film festival, go. The energy is infectious, and if the festival is well managed and offers a lineup of excellent films, even better. Film festivals dot the landscape like a fast food chain's franchisees. There are large ones, small ones, specialized ones, internationally recognized ones, obscure ones, in sum: there's a film festival for just about every type of film and filmgoer. There is even—and I am not making this up—The Internet Cat Video Festival which takes place in my hometown. Admission: $8. There is—no doubt about it—a film festival within an hour's drive of where you currently sit.

There's something enormously exciting and attractive about film festivals. For starters, they're one of the only places where discerning moviegoers can find and converse with like-minded people interested in films beyond the ones available at the multiplex. Additionally, film festivals provide the perfect venue for a producer, star, or director to meet and greet his or her audience in the flesh, and both parties benefit from the exchange. Some festivals carefully curate their lineup while others are less discriminating and book as many films as possible. Most festivals work with sponsors such as airlines or hotels and restaurants that provide transportation, lodging, and meals to visiting filmmakers in exchange for advertising in the festival's program, at the screening venues, and on the festival's trailer and website. Some festivals are brand new and on the rise. Others are older, have peaked, and are in decline. Just about everyone agrees that film festivals have become the de facto marketplace for independently produced feature films. If your film does not have a distribution deal in place, festivals are where you're going to get one, provided your film is accepted and that it generates a ton of buzz or, as one producer's rep likes to put it: *festival love.*

There is general agreement that when it comes to getting noticed by a distributor there are a half dozen world class film festivals that actually *matter*. Cannes, Sundance, Berlin, Venice, New York, and Toronto. These first-tier festivals essentially drive the acquisitions and distribution processes from year to year with many of the films playing already scheduled to come to a theatre, television, or laptop near you. Additionally, these first tier festivals set the agenda for programmers of second- and third-tier festivals like the festivals at Telluride, Chicago, Seattle, San Francisco, and Los Angeles. And so on, down the ladder it goes, until we get to the funky and fun regional festivals like the ones in Peoria, Dayton, or Albuquerque.

As it turns out, getting *into* any festival (and the one best suited to your film) is no easy task. For starters, there's the often cited problem of supply and demand; more supply (films) than demand (festivals). Submission ratios to desirable festivals are ridiculous (Number of slots at Sundance in 2015: about 175. Number of submissions: over 10,000). Film festival programmers bypass wading through the *glut* of submissions by focusing on a few simple strategies which include:

- Talking to other film programmers at other festivals and learning about what's hot and what's not, then booking the hot film.
- Cultivating relationships with directors that have premiered films at their festival in the past, banking on some degree of local audience recognition of that director from last year's fest.
- Booking star-driven films which bring name actors to their city, creating buzz for their festival.
- Dealing with producers' representatives whose job it is to cultivate long-term relationships with festival programmers and to navigate films through the highly political and murky waters of the so called festival *selection* process. Like most people, programmers enjoy doing business with people they know. A first time producer submitting a film will be treated differently than a producer's rep calling her programming pal at an international film festival to tell him about the film she's repping.
- Booking films that already have distribution deals, brought to their attention by studios and distributors seeking festival buzz prior to a theatrical release.

Programmers will reserve a number of slots for high profile films. Where possible they will work hard to increase the number of *brand* name films with known directors and stars. Subtract those slots from the total number of films to be shown and what remains are fewer slots for unknown or star-less films. So does it help to know people who know people? In a word: as much as one would like to believe that the festival selection process is a meritocracy, it isn't. There are, just as with most things in life, political aspects to film festivals. Programmers have their own agendas—and they don't always align with presenting new, unknown, outstanding, or different kinds of movies.

Yet, as imperfect as the festival circuit may be, it's the only circuit we've got. Every year a short list of *cool* films make the rounds, from Atlanta to Miami, and from Seattle to Los Angeles to San Francisco, with directors, actors, and producers in attendance. A fraction of these festival darlings may make it into theatres, but most will not, moving to video on demand, cable, DVD, Netflix and iTunes and more. The remaining festival films enjoy a *one off* screening followed by a Q&A with the director and a party with festival attendees before disappearing.

So, despite their shortcomings, festivals remain *the* place to see *new* product from around the world. Despite the studios' and the big indie films' influence (not to say ownership) of the festival lineups, festivals continuously provide a rare and much needed window into the diversity, eclecticism, beauty, and sheer entertainment quotient of movies from around the world.

SIDEBAR INTERVIEW | Larry Jackson, Producer's Representative. CEO of Persistence of Vision.

FM: What is a producer's representative?

LJ: The producer's rep is like a navigator. The filmmaker is the pilot, but the rep is the person that knows how to read the maps. In other words: the rep is the person that understands the politics of the film festivals, has connections with distributors, programmers, film critics, and journalists and can use those connections to help the filmmaker find their way through the labyrinth.

FM: Talk about what a producer is faced with today when they want to take a film from concept to market.

LJ: With the advent of digital, films can now be made for next to nothing. It means anybody can make a film. That's the good news. The bad news is that anybody can make a film, and anybody does, whether or not they have great ideas. The problem today for the producer is to find a way to navigate the marketplace and to be noticed. There is a glut of films competing for attention. There's never been so much chaos and confusion as there is now. In the first couple of years of the Sundance Film Festival there were about 350 submissions competing for about 125 screening slots. Now there are over ten thousand submissions competing for about 150 screening slots. Sure, a number of films can be made now that don't have high production values or a name cast, but they're more the exception, and their ability to get made and seen has more to do with the kind of story they're telling. More often than not they're genre pieces—like the *Paranormal Activity* (2007) films. Or *The Blair Witch Project* (1999)—which is by now a classic. So it's got to be something unique about the story. Something really attention getting—that will get it over the hump. Otherwise—and I'm not happy about this, but it's a fact—you need name actors to hang the film on. Casting becomes very critical here. So an internationally recognized name actor is very important, often more than the story, the director, or how well the film is made. It's much more about who's in it. Which brings us to the classic Catch-22 of the movie business: you've got to find a way to get to a name actor. The traditional path of going through an actor's agent is a very daunting one, because indie films don't pay very well—certainly not up front. Agents work on commission. An agent's job is to get their actor into the best paying work possible. They don't want to tie up their client for a small fee (even with the promise of a big paycheck on the back end) if there's any chance of getting their client into a movie that's going to pay more now. They want to know what their client is going to be paid—contractually—up front. So for an indie producer it becomes a matter of getting a cast—without necessarily going through their agent, but often having to go around the agent.

FM: Talk about the differences between the stand-alone theatrically released indie produced film and episodic or series television.

LJ: When I started working in the business in the late 60s, it was a time when cinema was being discovered as an art form. A whole generation was celebrating an art form in a way that hadn't been done before. There were a lot of exciting and new things happening. And, since there were only three television channels, movie-going was the dominant form of entertainment. People like me went out to the movies several nights a week. Working in the exhibition business back in the 70s—as I did—I started doing market surveys and I began to notice that year after year audiences for sophisticated films were getting just a little bit older. And, sure enough, what we've seen looking back is that the core audience for indie films has been the baby boom generation. But those boomers were never replaced with a new generation of college-aged movie goers. The new generation that came up wasn't trained to go out to the movies as often because they had hundreds of television channels, video games, other devices and distractions to choose from, and so attendance began to fall off. And today, independently made and theatrically released movies are no longer viewed as the single, mainstream form of entertainment.

With regard to television, there's some amazing stuff being done today; a kind of depth to character and plot development that takes place over a long period of time. Stuff that's difficult to do with an independently financed one-off film. That new type of television can be very rewarding.

FM: What advice can you offer to a budding producer?

LJ: If you move to one of the major production centers and start interning, you make the kinds of connections that will get you work. But that won't necessarily get you the chance to make films. If you have something you want to make, you have to have a good idea of how that film can be flexibly presented to audiences. You can't count on theatrical distribution. Even mainstream filmmakers no longer count on a theatrical release—unless their film is being financed by theatrical distributors. So, in conceiving your film, you have to have a good sense of what niche audience you'll be able to attract. Ask yourself: how can I use the flexibility of the new digital media and the new means of delivery to reach those niche audiences? How can I develop word of mouth through those niche audiences so that I can later expand or enlarge that audience? It's going to require planning, strategy, and solid casting. As fragmented as the distribution business is now, there's also a great opportunity because we're able to market films using social media and the Internet, targeting specific interest groups based on subject, story, style, cast, director, and even the setting. We can actually parlay those niche interests into an audience, and we can do that inexpensively and in a way that couldn't be done before when films were marketed to the lowest common denominator using traditional broadcast, shotgun style media. That's the new incentive. That's the new opportunity.

Submitting to Festivals

Submitting your film to a festival is without a doubt one of the most daunting processes in the entire marketing and distribution stage—and only more so if you are not working with a producer's representative or don't already have an *in* with the programmers at the festivals you choose to send your film to. Think of it as tantamount to a *cold call* in the sales world. By definition, cold calls have a very high failure rate, and a blind submission to a festival is more than likely going to result in an e-mail along the lines of "*This year's selection process was unbelievably difficult. There were so many wonderful films to choose from! Unfortunately, we regret to inform you that. . . .*" So, with that in mind, how does one get that e-mail that begins with "*Congratulations!*"? The simple answer is: make a great movie. But—as we've seen—that's only part of the answer. Is gaining acceptance at a film festival a numbers game? Should one simply submit to hundreds of festivals and let the laws of probability kick in? Wouldn't it be smarter to target the right festivals and hope for the best? Each producer develops their own strategy. Websites like filmfreeway.com or withoutabox.com provide one-stop shopping for festival entrants. Create one profile for you and your film, then happy submitting. Remember that—as I state above—blind submissions are tantamount to a cold call and that your chances are better when you work with a producer's rep.

There are signs that today's film festival landscape is changing. For starters, just as there are thousands of films being produced year after year, there are now more festivals than audiences are able to attend. It is no longer a rarity to go to a Thursday morning screening of an independent or foreign film with an audience of a dozen or less film fans, half of whom may be friends of the filmmakers. Things can get pretty awkward during the question and answer period; a cinema with 250 seats, 10 of which are occupied, does not make for a spirited conversation. Festivals and their programmers are well aware that they are playing in an increasingly crowded space. Moreover, filmmakers have begun asking for (and getting) screening fees ranging anywhere from $250 to $1,500 or more per film per screening. Programmers reluctantly pay the fees because the film in question has so much buzz surrounding it that not booking it makes their festival appear to be less important. Additionally, a new idea put forth by the filmmakers is starting to emerge: collecting a percentage of their film's take at the festival door. This model effectively turns the filmmakers into festival-oriented-distributors and may be the only opportunity producers get to experience any revenues for their film. But this scenario, were it to become standard practice, is still a few years away. Festivals push back on any kind of revenue sharing, and with good reason: most festivals are staffed by unpaid volunteers, are non-profit organizations, have substantial expenses to consider, and almost always operate at a financial loss. Running a film festival is no way to get rich. Besides, why pay filmmakers a percentage of the door when there are so many films to choose from with producers falling over themselves trying to get into the festival circuit?

Another change taking place in today's festival landscape is the move from *brick and mortar* to *online*. The [insert name here!] Online Film Festival type of event appears to be adding to the numerous options already available to filmgoers. Online film festivals come with the promise of quality films selected by discriminating programmers with taste and an understanding of what audiences want. But the reality is that, like conventional festivals, they vary greatly in quality. One method for discerning if an online festival is worth submitting to is to find out if a reputable and popular festival has an online *sidebar* of films shown during the festival days. Getting an online screening may or may not lead to a distribution deal but it does allow filmmakers to say they got in.

A third significant change is that film festival programmers have started booking television and internet series. It is a generally accepted fact that we are in the midst of a new *golden age* of global television production. Television series producers and festival programmers agree to show the first couple of episodes of their new shows at high profile festivals, generating word of mouth which translates into increased viewership. At the 2015 Toronto Film Festival audiences watched series from Argentina, Iceland, France, and the United States. Given their length (a 13-episode season of television is more or less equal to making four or five stand-alone independent features), series are very expensive to produce, are financed by large, centralized media groups (as opposed to private investors or independent producers), and are increasingly attracting feature film level actors and directors. Producing a television or internet series necessitates living and working near or in New York or Los Angeles where the media groups operate and where executives green light projects. Independent feature filmmaking is a more decentralized and regional (*as well as* New York and L.A. based) endeavor.

The Larger Distribution Landscape

The conventional wisdom in the film industry is that a theatrically released movie *drives* that movie's subsequent life on other platforms and territories. The thinking goes something like this: audiences and critics alike assign a sort of *seal of authenticity* that a *theatrically* released film is a legitimate movie bearing the characteristics we've grown accustomed to: a story, name actors, a certain level of production values, and so on. With this seal of approval, this blessing from the gods of the multiplex, distributors can market the film to network television, premium and basic cable, video on demand, DVD, the internet, and foreign territories with the expectation that the film will sell. Each of these platforms is referred to in the film industry as a *window*. Distributors speak of the window of time between a film's theatrical release and its appearance on cable, or the window between cable and DVD. That, as I say, is the conventional wisdom. But in the last 10 years an altogether different approach to film distribution has emerged. One that is radically different and in constant flux. To begin with, release windows are now finely tailored to each movie and in many cases are all but non-existent. Today a film opens at the multiplex and is simultaneously available on demand. This is called a *day and date* release. At first glance it appears as though the on-demand release of a film will bite into its theatrical revenue, but upon closer inspection it becomes clear that this is not the case. In fact, the noise surrounding a film's theatrical release causes home viewing audiences to note the film's on demand availability and they may become more inclined to renting it. Given the glut of product on the market, distributors have accepted that audiences now have literally thousands of movie choices. The game is no longer about windows. It's about being seen and heard in as many ways as possible—all at once.

Even more radical is a distribution strategy that makes a film available on demand *before* a theatrical release. Once unthinkable, today it is a common occurrence. And even more radical—and ever more frequently—are films released on the internet first and in cinemas later. The larger point here is that there is no longer *one way* to distribute a film, no conventional wisdom. Social media is now considered the new word of mouth. Films large and small have dedicated websites which often include the option to rent or buy the film. Films no longer need to depend exclusively on a distributor in order to be seen. A grassroots, fan-driven, online endorsement of a film can lead to a deal with a legitimate distributor and vice versa. Moreover, a savvy distribution strategy can now reach the remotest of audience members, including someone that may never set foot inside a movie theater.

Self-distribution and Four-walling It

If you're old enough to remember what the music industry was like before the introduction of the MP3 file format you'll recall that record companies manufactured compact discs and sold them in buildings called record stores. With the advent of the online distribution of music the record industry imploded, collapsing onto itself, leaving musicians and record companies scrambling to monetize whatever Napster didn't give away. Napster is gone now, replaced by Spotify, iTunes, and other pay-based music services. The online music distribution industry has gone legit. It's been able to monetize music via streaming and sales of MP3 files. It has done so at the expense to the makers of that music, including music producers. In other words: the money stays with the distributors. Unless you are Taylor Swift, Beyonce, or The Beatles. And the vast majority of us are not. Ms. Swift, an established, internationally recognized act, makes a lot of money from the online distribution of her music. She is a *hit*. Her success pays for the millions of *flops* that Spotify releases. I am using the words *hit* and *flop* in purely commercial, not artistic, terms. There is no doubt that great singer/songwriters who are *not* internationally recognized acts are putting beautiful music on Spotify—and making a dollar or two per year, if that. This new online distribution model has a name. It's called *the long tail* and it's probably here to stay. A few megastars reap the financial benefits of a new distribution model while everyone else gets a few pennies or nothing at all. Sound familiar? You can't make a living, you can only get rich.

To bring it back to movies, it's always been about hits and flops. During the studio era, production companies released a slate of films hoping that one (or more) commercial hit would absorb the losses incurred with the flops. Granted, it's somewhat disingenuous to speak only of hits or flops. After all, there are middling performers that eventually amortize their cost through, for example, foreign sales. But the numbers don't lie: a handful of movies make most of the money. With the prospect of turning over one's film to a distributor for a return of pennies on every spent, it can be mighty tempting to look into self-distribution.

Self-distribution is no longer a small sidebar alternative track. It's a full-blown industry replete with books, websites, expert consultants, and rags-to-riches stories of indie films that reached the masses through strategic campaigns. The story goes something like this: a group of young, unknown, entrepreneurial filmmakers make a great film. No one pays attention. Festivals pass on it, distributors don't return calls. The filmmakers pick a venue, say an art house cinema, in a hip, urban city. They take out local ads, generate buzz, and release the film for a week or two on a single screen. This practice, known as *four walling*, may or may not yield positive results. The film ends its run and nothing happens. Or it gains momentum and other art houses in other cities decide to show it. Undeterred or encouraged, the filmmakers create an online presence for the film. They amp up the social media, grow their mailing list, and offer the film as an online rental or purchase. Now a small distributor notices the film, sees it's gaining popularity, and steps in to help the filmmakers cross the finish line through international sales, making it available through iTunes, or helping with cable. If only it were that simple.

The scenario I've just described comes with unintended consequences all but guaranteed to stall or put and end to a film's release. To begin with no distributor is going to be interested in a film that has not had some kind of festival life. Festivals, as we saw, have become the proving ground for virtually *all* of the independent films produced around the world. Moreover, festival programmers covet the *seen here first* status. If a film's already been four-walled around the country, programmers aren't going to be as wild about it; there are simply too many other potentially great movies waiting for their turn to be discovered. So programmers and distributors alike view self-distribution as a strategy that detracts from their mission of discovering and generating revenue for independent films. Yet self-distribution can—and does—lead to the *occasional* rags to riches success story. The reason: the film is so good that the market and venue for it remains lucrative and interesting *despite* the fact that it's been self-distributed. We've come full circle: what gets a film distributed and into the world's best film festivals are quality, topicality, originality, authenticity, and innovation.

A final word about self-distribution. As of this writing there are literally *dozens* of online distribution services, from *Distrify* to *VimeoPro* that will host your film. These portals provide pay-wall players that may be embedded on your film's website or on a page created by the host. You get to set the cost of rental or purchase and the host takes a percentage, somewhere between 10 and 20 percent. At first glance it may seem like a great idea to set up your own online screening service and, as I've noted above, it may lead to a deal with a legitimate distributor. But regardless of whether you self-distribute or someone distributes for you, in both instances the film needs to be marketed and advertised. Setting up your film on, for example, *Distrify*, without an accompanying ad campaign is not going to do much for you.

Aggregators

Imagine you are in charge of acquisitions at Netflix. Given the glut of product on the market your e-mail's inbox is going to be swamped with hundreds of inquiries from filmmakers around the world. Your first reaction is going to be to delete those e-mails. Now imagine that you, as the acquisitions gal at Netflix, have an ongoing relationship with an outside company that sifts and sorts through the world's indie films, makes sure they conform to technical specifications, handles the deliverables, confirms the films are cleared of all rights, and can deliver exactly what you want at little or no cost to you. Moreover this company, known as an *aggregator*, can deliver not one or two, but dozens upon dozens of films at a time. Who are you going to want to work with? The aggregator or each and every one of the individual filmmakers that have been writing to you? Aggregators are the means by which independent filmmakers without a distribution deal get their films onto Netflix, iTunes, Amazon Prime, Hulu and the other large streaming services. Producers who fail at getting a distribution deal will hire an aggregator because having their film on Netflix legitimizes them in the eyes of the film industry which helps them when they start their next project. Moreover, when someone asks you where they can view your film it's much easier to say "*You can get it on Netflix*" than "*Go to my website. It's_____.com/movie and look for the embedded player.*" As of this writing, Distribber (www.distribber.com/faqs) is one among several aggregators who, for a fee, will work to get your film on one or more of the big streaming sites. Be assured that tomorrow there will be cheaper, better, and faster ways to get a film on Netflix. Want to see for yourself where things stand as you read this? Google *"stream my film on Netflix."*

In Closing

> I have been up against tough competition all of my life. I wouldn't know how to get along without it.—Walt Disney

> The only safe thing is to take a chance—Mike Nichols

In writing this book I have tried to provide you with guidance, insight, advice, and strategies for producing and releasing a feature film. If you've made it this far chances are you are serious about making a film and *The Strategic Producer* is going to be an invaluable resource moving forward. But, as they say, now you need to walk the walk. You are going to need talents and skills this book cannot provide. You're going to have to be *tenacious*. Stay *focused*, keeping your eyes on the end state all the while acknowledging where you are in the process. The only certainty in life is change, and you will be blindsided and sandbagged by events beyond your control. There will be a hundred reasons to give up and only one or two reasons to keep going. When that happens you're going to have to exhibit *endurance* and *leadership*. Leadership is part inspirational and part operational. Producers inspire cast and crew to *"come on this journey and, by the way, here's how we're going to travel."* So you're going to have to be good with people—as well being somewhat removed from them. You will have to develop close friendships that don't interfere with your job as producer and employer, and you are going to have to summon as much *business acumen* as possible, making savvy decisions that nudge your movie closer and closer towards completion. You will need *strong analytical and organizational skills*; the ability to think logically and to synthesize complex conditions into simple executable tasks, and you'll need to come up with creative solutions to hundreds of stubborn, real world problems.

Throughout this book I have refrained from talking about competition, about winning, and losing. My reticence is not unfounded. Art should not be a competitive enterprise. Commercial success or failure has little to do with whether a film opens up someone's mind or makes someone feel or is a work of art. But when it comes to the logistics of producing I believe that competition *is* absolutely essential. Competition against oneself, or even against other producers making similar films, but mostly against the ever present possibility of failure. I believe there *is* such a thing as a failed film. A failed film is a film that never fully sees the light of day. It's a film that—despite months or years of work—languishes, remains *unfinished* and eventually disappears, never to be screened or heard from again. What a terrible waste of time, money, and human effort! Naturally, everyone learns from failure. In fact, failure is the *only* way to actually learn, hence the term *failing forward*. But our society doesn't see failure as a learning experience, preferring to drive a final nail into the coffin of defeat and moving on to the *success du jour*, oblivious to the reality that today's hit movies are made by yesterday's failed filmmakers. So while it's okay and even necessary to lose, we prefer winning, and why not? After all, shouldn't all of our efforts and years of work be acknowledged and celebrated?

When I speak of success I can only speak about getting to work and getting the job done. *Completing* the best film possible. Once the film goes out into the world producers have little or no say as to whether it succeeds or fails, whether it *wins* or *loses*. That is something beyond anyone's control. My hope for readers of this book is that they succeed in bringing their feature length film across the finish line, and then some. If you do, more power to you. Be assured that I know how gratifying it is to produce a feature length film and lock in a distribution deal. Onward!

Appendix
The Business Plan

> This is show business, not show friend.—Linda Obst (among others)

The old joke goes that if you want to make a million dollars making movies start with 10 million. Kidding aside, making a profit with independently financed movies is all but impossible today. A cursory look at the landscape tells the tale: there are simply too many movies being made. Unless your film has a star on board, getting noticed is extremely difficult and even if you do, chances for success are slim.

The film marketing, distribution, and exhibition world is undergoing seismic changes. To attempt to describe them here is a fool's errand because by the time you read this the landscape will have changed yet again. As a moviegoer you need only look at your rapidly evolving movie going habits to understand the speed of change and where things are headed. If at one time you paid a few dollars to watch a film at the multiplex, today you expect your movies to be nearly free, available where and when you want them, and viewable on your smartphone. This is not to say that the multiplex is dying. Far from it. There will always be people looking to get out of the house on a Friday night. And as of this writing, lucrative 3D, Imax, and other large format platforms can only be seen at the multiplex (the verdict on home 3D television is still out). But the fact remains: there are more movies available on more platforms than there are audiences and the majority of these movies—regardless of their quality—are going to have a hard time making their money back. Everyone knows this and everyone agrees the system is in constant flux. So why do small films without stars break out and get noticed? Why does the system occasionally work? Why are there so many examples of successful and great movies? Because if you've made a film that people like, nothing you can do will keep them away. And if you've made a film people don't like, there's little you can do to get them to show up. What you are trying to do when you make a movie is to win *a popularity contest*. This belief in a Darwinian *cinematic survival of the fittest* is what prompts investors to back a movie. They believe that their project will survive—even thrive—through word of mouth, and bring them notoriety or profit. In other words, they believe they are the *exception*.

An investor's first documented point of contact with a movie is the business plan. The business plan gives the project context, paints a picture of the current filmmaking industry landscape, and educates the investor about how the film industry moves product and money. A business plan *makes the case for why the film should exist.* Informing an investor that you have a business plan is code for *I speak your language.*

An investor is initially going to look at two sections of the business plan: the opening *Executive Summary* and the closing *Financials* section. If those two sections work for them they'll look at the rest of the plan. Sandwiched between those two sections are sections on the current filmmaking landscape, marketing and distribution, risk factors, and information on the film along with more information about the company proposing to make it. Business plans describe the project at hand, talk about the production process, itemize what the deliverables consist of, list the team of key stakeholders, and offer an approximate timeline and a simplified budget.

A business plan is not a legally binding document. It is not a contract. A business plan is the project's first handshake to the world. It's a calling card, a mission statement, a marketing tool. It needs to be persuasive, engaging, revealing, promising, and make investors want to learn more. When it's well prepared a business plan conveys the all important *vision* that the producer wants investors to share. This shared vision, conveyed before any contracts are signed or money changes hands, is absolutely essential to the success of the project.

It's vital that the information in the business plan be reliable, authenticated, well researched, and truly representative of the project—artistic and commercial. As such, the plan cannot be pulled out of thin air. It can't be a product of your imagination. It has to be compelling, reasonable, data driven, and rooted in the realities associated with the project. In other words: the business plan is derived from previously existing documents: *the script and the budget*, along with verifiable data about the film industry. Put yourself in the investor's shoes. Would you fund a project without a draft of a script, a budget, and reliable numbers?

If luck favors the prepared, if an investor is genuine, if your pitch is compelling and your numbers are reliable, then talk of legally binding documents, investor offerings, and private placement memorandums can begin. Understand how a business plan works and how to make one specific to your film and you've increased your chances of getting funded.

One business plan I wrote contained the following sections with these titles:

- Executive Summary
- Company
- Film
- Industry
- Markets
- Distribution
- Risk Factors
- Financial Plan

Let's unpack each of these sections.

Executive Summary. Imagine you are the owner of a large chain of successful car washes. You've got a million dollars to spare and you'd like to get into the movie business but you don't know anything about the industry, the market, or the people that occupy it. All you know is what you see on the screen at the multiplex, on television, or on your laptop. So you're a shrewd businessman, having made a small fortune washing other people's cars, but before you invest in an independent film you're going to need to know more about the market, the amount of box office revenue it generates, nationally and internationally, and whether that market is growing or shrinking.

The executive summary's first job is to provide a *strategic opportunity* for the investor, offering reliable numbers on the size and scope of the worldwide film industry. You're showing that there's a legitimate market, it's global, and money flows through it.

Once you've provided data about the market and demonstrated to investors that there's a strategic opportunity, the next section of the executive summary introduces your *company*, its purpose, the project at hand, and the key players. In one or two short paragraphs the investor learns about your company's purpose (*to develop and produce films for theatrical release*), the project (*an original drama revolving around life in a small town and one family's struggle with addiction*), the project's approximate budget and timeframe (*. . . total budget is $5.5 million. The film will be produced over a one year period*), and who the lead producers of the project are (*The company's core team includes . . .*).

With a broad outline in place, the next step is to provide the investor with more details. In the subsequent segments of the executive summary, and more generally the entire business plan, the investor learns more about your company, the film, the industry, the markets, distribution, and the investment opportunity being presented. You've opened a wedge and now you're enlarging it through repetition, elaboration, and reinforcement

Company. You've introduced your company and its core team. In this section go into the company's role in the project, why it's producing this particular script, and what the company's standing is in the wider world of moviemaking. This is also where the business plan addresses the larger, perhaps *moral*, reason for making the film (*to raise awareness, to entertain, to _____*), not merely the financial reasons/benefits. It cannot be solely about making money. Investors, like producers and directors, are in it for a larger purpose. *Mission* is a good word here. Above and beyond making a profit, what are the company's *values*? After all, investors are more than human wallets. An investor who shares your vision, mission, or values will be *much* easier to work with than one who does not.

Film. Continuing the method of repetition, elaboration, and reinforcement, this section provides a more detailed synopsis of the script. But this section also places the project within the larger context of the world's media landscape and movie-going public, providing a rationale as to *why* this story needs to be told *at this point in time*. Additional information about the script, such as the title and (a brief) background of the scriptwriter, the current state of the script, and who controls script rights is also included here. Other *elements* mentioned here are the names of director, cinematographer, and the actors or stars who've *signed on* and committed to the project. A word about name actors: distributors will more often than not pass on a movie without a name actor—and so will investors. If you don't have a star on your business plan (and saying you do when you don't is the wrong way to gain an investor's trust), you can still say that once you have been funded you will actively seek out a name actor.

Industry. In order to make an informed decision on whether or not to back a film, investors must understand the film industry's nature, scope, and its current and future state. Moreover, they need to see that the filmmakers themselves are knowledgeable about the subject. Investors also need a clear explanation as to how films are made (the subject of this book). No need to go into myriad details; a brief explanation of preproduction, production and post-production will suffice. Lastly, a brief introduction to the principal distribution outlets (theatrical, television, on-demand, foreign distribution, etc.) will help investors see the larger picture. Again, no need to drill into all of the details here. You are providing summaries of topics which you will elaborate upon in the next sections. It's all in keeping with the strategy of repetition, elaboration, and reinforcement.

Markets. As an investor learns more about the film industry, they need to also understand how the film they're considering *fits* within it. Investors may be skittish about being the first ones to venture into new thematic territory. Others may not, preferring originality. Regardless, the business plan makes a compelling argument for either scenario. If the film is part of a traditional film genre or theme, the Markets section of the plan states this, citing specific films comparable to the one being discussed. Depending on the subject matter, the plan describes target audiences inclined to be interested in the film. For example, if the film is about alcoholism, mention the recovery movement as a viable audience. Or if the film is about boating, mention the burgeoning boating movement sweeping the nation. If the film is an outlier (meaning there's nothing else like it out there) say as much and position it as something unique and different that will stand out, eliciting attention from moviegoers interested in the new. While it will be harder to find comparable films that have performed well at the box office, there may be investors interested in the subject matter.

Distribution. Along with providing investors with a more detailed description of how films are distributed, this section also describes how the particular film being presented is going to be moved through the distribution pipeline. It helps to view distribution as more of a continuum. On one end is the wide release; the film that opens on thousands of screens around the world at once. On the other end is the narrow, or platform, release, with a film opening on a dozen screens or fewer in key markets. In between are the myriad varieties of distribution strategies, with DVD, television, cable, on demand, and the internet all playing a role at a key point in the film's distribution life. The days of one size fits all distribution strategies are long gone. They disappeared in the early 2000s when there was surge of independent film production. Today expert *boutique* distributors hand craft customized distribution strategies for each and every film they pick up, nurturing audiences through previews, word of mouth, social media, four-walling, branding, and more. Investors want to know the film they're considering comes with a distribution strategy and this section of the business plan is where that strategy is presented (even if it changes later, as it no doubt will).

Risk Factors. It would be foolish to assert that investing in a film is a risk-free proposition or—worse—that it will guarantee a return on investment. Doing so is not only unethical but a possible precursor to legal woes. That's why *all* film-related business plans address the risks associated with investing in the movie business. The risk factors section of the plan is—essentially—a disclaimer. It's where producers put their cards on the table and say *"hey; we're not soothsayers. We can't see the future any more than you can. Be apprised that, unless we produce a hit, you are not likely to break even or enjoy a profit from your investment."* The risk factor section is the plan's *reality check*. It's a clearly stated agreement between the production and the investor that there are no guarantees. And yet, as I noted earlier, the business plan *is* a marketing tool. It *is* designed to *persuade*. To *convince*. How, then, can the risk factors section not discourage? The answer is in the concept of *mitigation*. Embedded in this section is the idea that risk can be mitigated. It can be minimized. It can be attenuated. And, to some extent, it can through name actors, an experienced production team, great directors, a proven track record of success, and more. All of these elements help reduce—but never eliminate—risk. A producer sets these ideas to work in the investor's mind, then lets the cinematic chips fall where they may.

Financial Plan. In order to create a successful financial plan you'll need two documents. The first is a budget, the second is a shooting schedule. I do not recommend creating these documents on your own. In fact, I urge you to seek out a professional unit production manager or assistant director who can a) breakdown the script into its myriad components: number of actors, number of locations, any special effects work, any CGI needs, and so on, and b) assign costs to each of these components and compile said costs into a professional feature film budget complete with top sheet, above and below the line costs, and any and all related costs such as production overhead, fringes, union dues, social security, payroll taxes and fees, and so on. The final piece of the puzzle the unit production manager creates is the schedule—from which the budget is generated. A talented UPM will know how to *re-arrange the furniture*, so to speak. She will know how to schedule scenes out of narrative order (grouping all the car wash scenes together, for example) so as to best maximize the resources, (human, material, and financial), into what is often and on average—in the indie film world—a 25- to 35-day shoot.

What is the "right" amount of money for your film? This essential question is answered using hard data as well as intuition. As a producer your job is to determine—more or less—how much money your film is going to potentially earn. Would you spend more than what you estimate your film can *reasonably* make? Of course not. That would be foolish. So how do you know what your film can *reasonably expect to earn*? By looking at *comparable* films, their budgets, and their revenue. Just as no smart producer would ever give Woody Allen $100 million to make a film (because his films make far less than that), you seek funding that is commensurate with your film's earning potential. Producers know Tom Cruise is worth spending over $100 million on because, sooner or later (even if it takes 10 or more years), a Tom Cruise movie—even a Tom Cruise film that tanks—will make money (through overseas box office and long-term back catalogue licensing). So ask yourself: what is my film worth to the marketplace, then ask for less than that.

Things get more complicated when you are looking for films similar to *yours*. You cannot Google box office numbers for films similar to yours and slap those into your plan. Your *comps* need to be included in your business plan, in the financials section, and they need to be reliable and authenticated. One of the most commonly used resources for accurate numbers for a film's lifetime financial performance is the Baseline website (www.baselineintel.com). This is where producers preparing business plans can purchase reports on a film's national and international box office returns as well as data on how it did in every ancillary market and platform that can be documented. The financials section is going to be subject to close scrutiny by the investor. This is a language they understand—perhaps better than you—and if you want to close a deal, you need to speak in their terms, and you need to do it honestly. By *films similar to yours* I mean films that are thematically, stylistically, or psychologically/emotionally related. Think your film is too unique? Can't find a film that feels like the one you want to make? Keep looking. What you are looking for are films whose budgets, theme, scope, and feel resemble yours. Furthermore, you want to identify films that have been made recently, preferably during the last three to five years. So it's okay to mention films made over 10 years ago, just not in the financials section. The economics of today's film industry—along with its business structure—are very different from what they were 10 years ago. Remember that your numbers have to be reliable. If you're making a film about alcoholism it makes no sense to cite the *The Lost Weekend* (1945) in the financials segment. You can, however, point to it saying there is a long tradition of movies about alcoholism, which is why your film should be made. You might be able to get away with including *Leaving Las Vegas* (1995) in your comps. A film like *Flight* (2012), on the other hand, was made recently enough to merit inclusion in your comps list.

The following business plan owes much to the work done by Louise Levison in her book *Filmmakers and Financing: Business Plans for Independents* (Focal Press). For anyone wishing to go deeper into business plans, I recommend reading her excellent book.

Sample Business Plan

Mighty Visual Productions
Business Plan for
"Northeast Kingdom"
(Working Title)
Feature Length Theatrical Motion Picture

This document and the information contained herein is provided solely for the purpose of acquainting the reader with Mighty Visual Productions and is proprietary to that company. This business plan does not constitute an offer to sell, or a solicitation of an offer to purchase securities. This business plan has been submitted on a confidential basis solely for the benefit of selected, highly qualified investors and is not for use by any other persons. By accepting delivery of this business plan, the recipient acknowledges and agrees that i) in the event the recipient does not wish to pursue this matter, the recipient will return this copy to Mighty Visual Productions at the address listed below as soon as practical; ii) the recipient will not copy, fax, reproduce, or distribute this confidential business plan, in whole or in part, without permission; and iii) all of the information contained herein will be treated as confidential material.

Controlled Copy

Issue to:

Issue date:

Copy No.:

For information contact:

Table of Contents

1 Executive Summary
2 Company
3 Film
4 Industry
5 Markets
6 Distribution
7 Risk Factors
8 Financial Plan

1 Executive Summary

Strategic Opportunity

- North American box office revenues in 201_ were $__ billion.
- Revenues for independent films in 201_ were $__ billion, or X% of the total North American box office.
- Worldwide revenues from all sources for North American independent films were over $_ billion in 201_.
- Worldwide box office revenues for 20_ were $__ billion.
- The overall filmed entertainment market is projected to reach $__ billion in the United States in 201_ and $___ billion worldwide.

The Company

Mighty Visual Productions (MVP) is a startup enterprise engaged in the development and production of motion picture films for theatrical release. MVP will film an original drama revolving around life in a small town and one family's struggle with addiction and the drug trade. Currently titled *Northeast Kingdom*, the movie is designed to capture the attention of individuals, families, and communities interested in a socially relevant, entertaining story about the illicit drug trade and addiction. *Northeast Kingdom* will provide a compelling and dramatic story about a subject that will entertain and resonate with audiences.

    The Company's four-year plan for the film is to produce the film over a one year period and to collect revenues from distribution over the subsequent three years. The total budget for production and subsequent distribution of the film is $5.5 million. MVP's core team includes President and Executive Producer Ms. _____, and Producer Mr. _____, with additional producers and a director to be brought on board once financing is in place.

The Film

Set in a small New England town, *Northeast Kingdom* tells the story of Kevin Dunham's struggle to save Madeline, his 19-year-old daughter, from the scourge of heroin and prescription drugs all the while uncovering and dismantling a local drug lord's hold on the region.

The Industry

The future for low-budget independent films continues to look impressive, as their commercial viability has increased steadily over the past decade. Recent films that are thematically related to *Northeast Kingdom* such as *Dallas Buyers Club, Promised Land, Homefront, Side Effects, Requiem for a Dream, Thirteen,* and *A History of Violence* are evidence of the strength of this market segment. The independent market as a whole has expanded dramatically in the past 15 years. At the 2005 through 2014 Academy Awards, over 50 of the 70 films nominated for the Best Picture Oscar were either in part or wholly independently financed. Technology has dramatically changed the way films are made, allowing independently financed films to look and sound as good as those made by the Hollywood studios while remaining free of the creative restraints place upon an industry that is notorious for fearing risks. Widely recognized as a "recession-proof" business, the entertainment industry has historically prospered even during periods of decreased discretionary income.

The Markets

Entertaining action-oriented dramas with family-themed stories about addiction and the illicit drug trade appeal to a wide market. Films such as *Traffic, Drugstore Cowboy, Requiem for a Dream, The Basketball Diaries,* and *Dallas Buyers Club* have proved that a variety of people will go to a topical and newsworthy movie that informs, inspires, and speaks to their interests and concerns and which they can tell their friends and relatives about. For teens there are *morality plays* and cautionary tales about the risks and dangers associated with addiction, while adults can learn how best to talk to their kids. Whole communities can benefit from a film's *solutions-oriented* story. And for audiences looking for an entertaining story, a character-driven drama combined with surprising twists and turns in the story provides action, suspense, and thrills. The independent market continues to grow and prosper. As an independent company catering to this market, MVP can distinguish itself by following a strategy of making films for this well-established and growing genre.

Distribution

The motion picture industry is highly competitive, with much of a film's success depending on the skill of its distribution strategy. As an independent producer, MVP aims to negotiate with major distributors for release of *Northeast Kingdom*. The production team is committed to making the film an attractive product in theatrical and other markets.

Investment Opportunity and Financial Highlights

MVP is seeking an equity investment of approximately $5.5 million for development and production of *Northeast Kingdom*. Using a moderate revenue projection and an assumption of general industry distribution costs, we project (but do not guarantee) gross worldwide revenues of $34.5 million, with pretax producer/investor net profit of $13.1 million.

2 Company

MVP is a privately owned limited partnership corporation that was established in June of 20__. Our principal purpose and business are to create theatrical motion pictures. The Company plans to develop and produce *Northeast Kingdom*, an entertaining, action-oriented, and inspiring drama.

The public is ready for a film about family, addiction, the new and growing illicit drug trade in America's small towns and how to deal with the challenges these topics pose. In addition, we see news media reports on addiction and the drug trade on a daily basis. Today's drug epidemics stretch across all national boundaries, as does the illicit trafficking of drugs. In the United States, heroin and other drugs, many of them manufactured by pharmaceutical companies and distributed as legitimate painkillers, are appearing in once drug-free small communities and towns.

MVP's goals are as follows:

- To produce a quality film that is topical, newsworthy, provides entertainment, action, and a moral storyline designed for both enjoyment and education.
- To make a film which will leave audiences with the understanding that it takes a village to solve the current drug epidemic and illicit drug trade.
- To portray drug users not as criminals but as people suffering from the disease of addiction.
- To produce *Northeast Kingdom* as a feature film in its first year with a budget of $5.5 million.
- To develop a distribution strategy for *Northeast Kingdom* and track its release throughout a three year period.

We believe we can make an exciting film for $5.5 million without sacrificing quality. Newsworthy dramas that present socially relevant topics bring people together. They initiate a dialogue and can provide hope and solutions. We plan to change the conversation about addiction from fear to empathy. And we want to show how the drug trade can almost destroy a community but how that community can work together to remove drugs from its streets and homes. Historically, films about addiction and the drug trade have stopped short of offering solutions, limiting themselves to portraying a dark world whose characters never emerge. *Northeast Kingdom* will take additional steps, showing how after a period of conflict and violence a community can learn and begin to move towards peace, healing, and recovery.

Production Team

The primary strength of any company is in its management team. MVP's principals, _____ and _____ have extensive experience in business and in the entertainment industry. In addition, the Company has relationships with key consultants and advisors who will be available to fill important roles on an as-needed basis.

_____ Executive Producer

_____, Producer

[Add bios.]

3 Film

Currently MVP controls the rights to the screenplay for *Northeast Kingdom*. As MVP's Executive Producer and lead writer, _____ has researched, developed, and written the screenplay for *Northeast Kingdom* on his own time and at his own expense. Once financing for the film is in place Mr. _____ will receive payment for authoring the screenplay. As production begins he will receive additional payments for re-writes and polishes.

Set in a small New England town, *Northeast Kingdom* tells the story of Kevin Dunham's struggle to uncover and dismantle a local drug lord's hold on his town and to save his 19-year-old daughter Maddy from becoming addicted to heroin. At first Kevin is indifferent to his town's problem but things change when he learns his daughter is using. Kevin's first priority is his family and he selfishly focuses his attention solely on Maddy. When he learns that saving Maddy isn't as easy as he thought he becomes vindictive and uses force. In so doing he uncovers and, in a violent denouement, ends the illicit drug trade plaguing his town but at a high personal price. In the end Kevin learns that curing addiction and stemming the influx of drugs requires compassion and the collaborative efforts of not just law enforcement, but of everyone. The projected budget for *Northeast Kingdom* is $5.5 million with _____ executive producing, and _____ producing. We are currently in the development stage with this project. The initial script has been written, but we have no commitments from actors or a director. Casting and the search for a director will commence once financing is in place.

Media coverage of the current heroin and prescription drug epidemic has been very strong. The entire region—and the rest of the nation as well—is being challenged to come up with a solution to a horrible and seemingly insurmountable problem. This epidemic is real, it is expanding, and it will continue to grow for a long time. Regardless of when this epidemic abates, it has already inflicted significant damage to the region. Its effects will be felt for generations to come.

A fictional film about a small town's heroin epidemic needs first and foremost to be authentic. But it can also act as instrument for social change. By providing audiences with an accurate and compelling rendering of the problem and a thorough understanding of the myriad issues surrounding it, a film about this epidemic can provide audiences with a roadmap towards a solution.

MVP is aware of the risks, both artistic and social, inherent in making a fiction film about this very real story. It is vital that the film get the story right, if only out of consideration for the thousands of victims whose voices will never be heard. All people from all walks of life—from law enforcement to faith based organizations to caregivers to ordinary citizens, dealers small and large, users, addicts, and victims—will identify with this movie. Yet, unlike a documentary or a movie based directly on actual persons and events, a fiction-based narrative movie can tell an authentic story while remaining a product of the moviemaker's imagination as well as respecting the subjects' choice to remain anonymous.

4 Industry

The future for independent films continues to look impressive, as their commercial viability has increased steadily over the last decade. Recent films, such as *Winter's Bone*, *Out of the Furnace*, and *Homefront* are evidence of the strength of this market segment. In addition, every year since 2006, an independent film has won the Academy Award for Best Picture: *Crash* (2006), *The Departed* (2007), *No Country For Old Men* (2008), *Slumdog Millionaire* (2009), *The Hurt Locker* (2010), *The King's Speech* (2011), *The Artist* (2012), and *Argo* (2013). As studios cut back, equity investors have been moving into the independent film arena. Lately, falling salaries, rising subsidies, and a thinning of competition have weighted the financial equation even more in favor of the investor. In addition, revolutionary changes in the manner in which motion pictures are produced and distributed are now sweeping the industry, especially for independent films.

The total North American box office in 201_ was $___ billion. The share for independent films was $___ billion, or ___% of the 20__ total. Revenues for North American independent film from all worldwide revenue sources for 201_ are estimated at more than $__ billion. Worldwide box office revenues totaled $___ billion in 201_. Once dominated by the studio system, movie production has shifted to reflect the increasingly viable economic models for independent film. The success of independent film has been helped by the number of new production companies and smaller distributors emerging into the marketplace every day, as well as the growing interest of major U.S. studios in providing distribution in this market. Also, there has been a rise in the number of screens available for independent films.

Investment in film becomes an even more attractive prospect as financial uncertainty mounts in the wake of Wall Street bailout, the economic downturn in real estate and the international stock market slides. Widely recognized as a "recession-proof" business, the entertainment industry has historically prospered even during the periods of decreased discretionary income.

Motion Picture Production

The structure of the U.S. motion picture business has been changing over the past few years at a faster pace, as studios and independent companies have created varied methods of financing. Although studios historically funded production totally out of their own arrangements with banks, they now look to partner with other companies, both in the United States and abroad, which can assist in the overall financing of projects. The deals often take the form of the studio retaining the rights for distribution in all U.S. media, including theatrical, home video, television, cable, and other ancillary markets.

The studios, the largest companies in this business, are generally called the "Majors" and include NBC Universal (owned by Comcast Corp.), Warner Bros. (owned by Time Warner), Twentieth Century Fox Film Corporation (owned by Rupert Murdoch's News Corp.), Paramount Pictures (owned by Viacom), Sony Pictures Entertainment, and The Walt Disney Company. MGM, one of the original Majors, has been taken private by investors and is being run as an independent company. In most cases, the Majors own their own production facilities and have a worldwide distribution organization. With a large corporate hierarchy making production decisions and a large amount of corporate debt to service, the studios aim most of their films at mass audiences.

Producers who can finance independent films by any source other than a major U.S. studio have more flexibility in their creative decisions, with the ability to hire production personnel and secure other elements required for pre-production, principal photography, and post-production on a project-by-project basis. With substantially lower overhead than the studios, independents are able to be more cost-effective in the filmmaking process. Their films can be directed at both mass and niche audiences, with the target markets for each film dictating the size of its budget. Typically, an independent producer's goal is to acquire funds from equity partners, completing all financing of a film before commencement of principal photography.

How It Works

There are four principal steps in the production of a motion picture: development, pre-production, production, and post-production. During development and pre-production, a writer may be engaged to write a screenplay or a screenplay may be acquired and rewritten. Certain creative personnel, including a director and various technical personnel, are hired; shooting schedules and locations are planned; and other steps necessary to prepare the motion picture for principal photography are completed. Production commences when principal photography begins and generally continues for a period of not more than three months. In post-production, the film is edited, which involves transferring the original filmed material to digital media in order to work easily with images. In addition, a score is mixed with dialogue, and sound effects are synchronized into the final picture, and, in some cases, special effects are added. The expenses associated with this four-step process for creating and finishing a film are referred to as its *negative costs*. A master is then manufactured for duplication for release prints for a *fifth step:* theatrical distribution and exhibition, but expenses for further prints and advertising for the film are categorized as P&A (for *prints and advertising*) and are not part of the negative costs of the production.

Theatrical Exhibition

Per the most recent report of the MPAA there were more than 39,000 theater screens in the United States and 135,000 theater screens worldwide. Film revenues from all other sources are often driven by the U.S. domestic theatrical performance. The costs incurred with the distribution of a motion picture can vary significantly depending on the number of screens on which the film is exhibited. Although studios often release a film on up 3,000 to 4,000 screens on opening weekends (depending on the budget of both the film and the marketing campaign), independent distributors open their films on far fewer screens. Theatrical revenues are considered an engine to drive sales in all other categories. Not only has entertainment product been recession-resistant domestically but also the much stronger than expected domestic theatrical box office has continued to stimulate ancillary sales, such as home video and digital, as well as raising the value of films in the foreign market.

Television

Television exhibition includes over-the-air reception for viewers through either a fee system (cable) or "free television" (national and independent broadcast stations). The proliferation of new cable networks since the early 1990s has made cable (both basic and premium stations) one of the most important outlets for feature films. Although network and independent television stations were a substantial part of the revenue picture in the 1970s and early 1980s, cable has become a far more important ancillary outlet. The pay-per-view business has continued to grow thanks to continued direct broadcast satellite (DBS) growth. Pay-per-view and pay television allow cable television subscribers to purchase individual films or special events or subscribe to premium cable channels for a fee. Both acquire their film programming by purchasing the distribution rights from motion picture distributors.

Home Video

In 201_, overall consumer spending on home video totaled $____ billion, according to the Digital Entertainment Group, consisting of $__ billion from DVD/Blu-ray sales and rentals and over $_ billion from digital download (including electronic sell through, video on demand [VOD], and subscription streaming). VOD grew by % in 201_. At the same time, total penetration of Blu-ray disc playback devices—including set-top box and game consoles—reached __ million households in 201_, an increase of nearly ___% from 201_. Consumers also purchased more than __ million HDTV's during 201_, raising HDTV penetration to __ million households. The VOD market for paid rentals is currently ruled by pay TV services, but the Internet-on-demand (iVOD) market is growing in strength.

International Theatrical Exhibition

Much of the projected growth in the worldwide film business comes from foreign markets, as distributors and exhibitors keep finding new ways to increase the box office revenue pool. More screens in Asia, Latin America, and Africa have followed the increase in multiplexes in Europe, but this growth has slowed. The world screen count is predicted to remain stable over the next seven years. Other factors include the privatization of television stations overseas, the introduction of DBS services, and increased cable penetration. The synergy between international and local product in European and Asian markets is expected to lead to future growth in screens and box office.

Future Trends

Revolutionary changes in the manner in which motion pictures are produced and distributed are now sweeping the industry, especially for independent films. Web-based companies like Movie-link (owned by Blockbuster), Amazon's Video on Demand, CinemaNow, and Apple's iTunes Store are selling films and other entertainment programming for download on the Internet, and websites such as Netflix and Hulu (through Hulu Plus) stream filmed entertainment to home viewers as rentals. New devices for personal viewing of films (including Xbox, Wii, video iPod, iPhone, and iPad) are gaining ground in the marketplace, expanding the potential revenues from home video and other forms of selling programming for viewing. Although there may not be a notable impact of the new technologies at present, their influence is expected to grow significantly over the next five years.

5 Market

The independent market continues to prosper. The strategy of making films in well-established genres has been shown time and time again to be an effective one.

Although there is no boilerplate for making a successful film, the film's probability of success is increased with a strong story, and then the right elements—the right director and cast and other creative people involved. Being able to green-light our own product, with the support of investors, allows the filmmakers to attract the appropriate talent to make the film a success and distinguish it in the marketplace.

Although we expect *Northeast Kingdom* to have enough universal appeal to play in the mainstream houses, at its projected budget it may begin at specialty theaters as the blockbuster *Dallas Buyers Club* did. Because of the film's low budget, exhibitors may wait for *Northeast Kingdom* to prove itself before providing access to screens in the larger movie houses. In addition, smaller houses will give us a chance to expand the film on a slow basis and build awareness with the public.

Target Markets

FAMILY DRAMAS

Family dramas appeal to the nearly the widest possible market, with *Northeast Kingdom* having a multigenerational audience from teens to grandparents. *Variety* and industry websites have said that family films boost the box office. "Movies that have a good message for [young people] that adults enjoy are universally embraced," says Tom Rothman of Twentieth Century Fox.

TOPICAL, NEWSWORTHY, AND SOCIALLY RELEVANT

In addition to the family-centered market, *Northeast Kingdom* will appeal to audiences looking for topical, relevant, and community-oriented stories that inform and uplift; stories that speak to their lives, offering solutions to real-world problems while entertaining and educating them. Character-driven dramatic movies with some action like *Out of the Furnace, Homefront, Courageous,* and *Broken City* all play to this market with great success and distributors and exhibitors know this as well as knowing how to reach it.

ADDICTION, RECOVERY, LAW ENFORCEMENT, COMMUNITIES, CLERGY

Anyone in the recovery movement, be it recovery from drugs, alcohol, or any number of other addictions, will find *Northeast Kingdom* to be appealing helpful, and instructive. And the recovery movement—both nationally and internationally—is growing every year, with more and more people finding the key to curing their addictions. These individuals are part of a large, global network of healing and they are looking for stories they identify with. Word of mouth is very strong among this group and a recommendation from colleagues with shared experiences travels quickly. In the law enforcement community there is still a great deal of debate around how best to solve the drug trafficking problem; from strong arm tactics to decriminalization and everything in between, *Northeast Kingdom* provides a thoughtful, compelling, and inspired story on the matter. Communities and municipalities, both large and small, will look to *Northeast Kingdom* as a film that will illustrate the problem and then model policies conducive to reducing addiction and the influx of drugs. Faith-based organizations, from established churches to grass roots recovery groups, will respond to *Northeast Kingdom*'s message of compassion and hope for addicts. In the past, films such as *Clean and Sober, The Lost Weekend, Smashed,* and *Flight* have all resonated with audiences around the world.

Demographics

MOVIEGOERS AGED 14 TO 90

Northeast Kingdom is designed to appeal to everyone from young adults to their grandparents. It plays especially well to the two largest age ranges of frequent moviegoers: the 18 to 24year olds and the 25 to 39 year olds. *Northeast Kingdom* also plays well to the 40+ audiences. The MPAA counts all moviegoers from ages 12 to 90 in specific groups in their annual *Theatrical Market Statistics* analysis. The combined audience share of moviegoers aged 18 to 49 in 2013 was 44% with an additional 34% for audiences aged 50 and up. Older audiences have emerged as a powerful force at the box office. Aging baby boomers have time and money to spend on compelling family dramas with a strong story, name actors, and high quality production values while younger audiences look for action and suspense which *Northeast Kingdom* also provides.

Social Media and Self-Marketing

An important marketing component for any film, especially during its opening weekend, is word of mouth. Without incurring additional costs, it is possible for the filmmakers and their many colleagues to supplement the marketing strategy of a distribution company by working through niche channels to spread word of mouth about the film. Typically, film companies use the Internet to great effect with viral marketing. It is a strategy that encourages individuals to forward an email or video marketing message to others, creating the potential for exponential growth in the message's exposure and influence. The recipients of those emails then forward them to friends. As with any mainstream marketing, the strategy starts with the people at the top, the opinion makers or influencers and their channel partners, and it extends through the ranks to the people who see the films the first weekend. They then spread the word to everyone else.

Complementing this approach are the more purely social networks. It is a multi-billion-industry which continues to grow yearly. Facebook, Twitter, LinkedIn and other social networking sites have more than doubled since 2007, according to Forrester Research. Facebook (1.2 billion users in the first quarter of 2014 according to Statista) and Twitter (255 million users in 2014 according to Statista as well) in particular have clearly become one of the focus sectors in media and entertainment. With their large communities, finding friends with similar film tastes in a social network is fairly easy. Twitter has become a force in the success of many films. Fans blog reviews on their own web pages or even make a video recording of their reactions and post these on YouTube, their own sites, or a social networking page and then tweet the link to their followers, informing friends and Web surfers about a film and influencing their opinions. In addition, some celebrities gather huge followings on Twitter, using the website to address their fans directly and plug their projects not at time of release but also throughout filming to create anticipation.

There are also websites that are web-based marketplaces where filmmakers and fans connect via crowd sourcing to make independent films happen through small individual contributions to funding and other forms of support. Fans get the opportunity to discover and impact the films of tomorrow while getting insider access and VIP perks for the contributions.

6 Distribution

The motion picture industry is highly competitive, with much of a film's success often depending on the skill of its distribution strategy. The filmmaker's goal is to negotiate with experienced distribution companies in order to seek to maximize their bargaining strength for potentially significant releases. There is an active market for completed motion pictures, with virtually all the studios and independent distributors seeking to acquire films. The management team feels that *Northeast Kingdom* will be an attractive product in the marketplace.

One important venue in the film's distribution strategy will be film festivals. MVP will aim to show *Northeast Kingdom* at one or more of the world's key film festivals like Sundance, Cannes, Toronto, Berlin, New York, and others. The goal will be to attract distributor interest through a positive festival response. Distributors attend all the key festivals and often acquire films on site. MVP plans to make a film that festival programmers and distributors want.

Distribution terms between producers and distributors vary greatly. A distributor looks at several factors when evaluating a potential acquisition, such as the uniqueness of the story, theme, and the target market for the film. Since distribution terms are determined in part by the perceived potential of a motion picture and the relative bargaining strength of the parties, it is not possible to predict with certainty the nature of distribution arrangements. However, there are certain standard arrangements that form the basis for most distribution agreements. The distributor will generally license the film to theatrical exhibitors (i.e., theater owners) for domestic release and to specific, if not all, foreign territories for a percentage of the gross box office dollars. The initial release for most feature films is U.S. theatrical (i.e., in movie theaters). For a picture in initial release, the exhibitor, depending on the demand for the movies, will split the revenue derived from ticket purchases (gross box office) with the distributor; revenue derived from the various theater concessions remains with the exhibitor. The percentage of box office receipts remitted to the distributor is known as *film rentals* and customarily diminishes during the course of a picture's theatrical run. Although different formulas may be used to determine the splits from week to week, on average a distributor will be able to retain about 50% of total box office, again, depending on the performance and demand for a particular movie. In turn, the distributor will pay to the motion picture producer a negotiated percentage of the film rentals less its costs for film prints and advertising.

Film rentals become part of the *distributor's gross* from which all other deals are computed. As the distributor often re-licenses the picture to domestic ancillaries (i.e., cable, television, home video) and foreign theatrical ancillaries, these monies all become part of the distributor's gross and add to the total revenue for the film in the same way as the rentals. The distribution deal with the producer includes a negotiated percentage for each revenue source; for example, the producer's share of foreign rentals may vary from the percentage of domestic theatrical rentals. The basic elements of a film distribution deal includes the distributor's commitment to advance funds for distribution expenses (including multiple prints of the film and advertising) and the percentage of the film's income the distributor will receive for its services. Theoretically, the distributor recoups expenses for the costs of its print and advertising expenses from the first initial revenue of the film. Then the distributor will split the rest of the revenue monies with the producer/investor group. The first monies coming back to the producer/investor group generally repay the investor for the total production cost, after which the producers and investors split the money according to their agreement. However, the specifics of the distribution deal and timing of all money disbursements depend on the agreement that is finally negotiated. In addition, the timing of the revenue and the percentage amount of the distributor's fee differ depending on the revenue source.

Release Strategies

The typical method of releasing films is with domestic theatrical, which gives value to the various film "windows" (the period that has to pass after a domestic theatrical release before a film can be released in other markets). Historically, the sequencing pattern has been to license to pay-cable program distributors, foreign theatrical, home video, television, networks, foreign ancillary, and U.S. television syndication. As the rate of return varies from different windows, shifts in these sequencing strategies will occur.

The business is going though a changeover between screens that play 35-mm films and those that accept digital, which makes a difference in the cost of what we usually call *prints*. Traditional 35-mm prints typically cost $1,200 to $1,500 each. Using film prints a high profile studio opening on as many as 3,000 to 4,000 screens in multiple markets (a wide release) can have an initial marketing expense of $3.5 to $6 million, accompanied by a very high-priced advertising campaign. The number of screens diminishes after opening weekend as the film's popularity fades.

By contrast, independent films typically have a *platform* release. In this case, the film is given a build up by opening initially in a few regional or limited local theaters to build positive movie patron awareness throughout the country. The time between a limited opening and a wider release may be several weeks. This keeps the cost of striking 35-mm or digital prints to a minimum, in the range of over $1 million, and allows for commensurately lower advertising costs. Using this strategy, smaller budgeted films can be successful at the box office with as few as two or three prints initially and more being made as the demand increased. In the new digital system, the distributor pays an $800 to $900 fee per theatrical screen on which the film is exhibited. For independent films that are in theater for at least two months on an escalating number of screens, adhering to the platform release pattern, the overall distribution cost can still run between $1 and $2 million.

Distributors plan their release schedules not only with certain target audiences in mind but also with awareness of which theaters—specialty or multiplex—will draw the audience. How much is spent by the distributor in total will depend on the release pattern that best serves each film.

7 Risk Factors

Investment in the film industry is highly speculative and inherently risky. There can be no assurance of the economic success of any motion picture since the revenues derived from the production and distribution of a motion picture depend primarily upon its acceptance by the public, which cannot be predicted. The commercial success of a motion picture also depends upon the quality and acceptance of other competing films released into the marketplace at or near the same time, general economic factors and other tangible and intangible factors, all of which can change and cannot be predicted with certainty.

The entertainment industry in general, and the motion picture industry in particular, are continuing to undergo significant changes, primarily due to technological developments. Although these developments have resulted in the availability of alternative and competing forms of leisure time entertainment, such technological developments have also resulted in the creation of additional revenue sources through licensing of rights to such new media, and potentially could lead to future reductions in the costs of producing and distributing motion pictures. In addition, the theatrical success of a motion picture remains a crucial factor in generating revenues in other media such as DVDs, television, and online. Due to the rapid growth of technology, shifting consumer tastes, and the popularity and availability of other forms of entertainment, it is impossible to predict the overall effect these factors will have on the potential revenue from and profitability of feature-length motion pictures.

While formed and currently in operation, the Company itself is still subject to all the risks incident to the creation and development of a new business venture with its current minimal net worth. In order to prosper, the success of *Northeast Kingdom* will depend partly upon the ability of management to produce a film of exceptional quality at a lower cost, which can compete in appeal with higher-budgeted films of the same genre. In order to minimize this risk, management plans to participate as much as possible throughout the process and will aim to mitigate financial risks where possible. Fulfilling this goal depends on the timing of investor financing, the ability to obtain distribution contracts with satisfactory terms and the continued participation of the current management.

Strategy

MVP proposes to secure development and production film financing for *Northeast Kingdom* from equity investors, allowing it to maintain consistent control of the quality and production costs. As an independent, MVP can strike the best financial arrangement with various channels of distribution. This strategy allows for maximum flexibility in a rapidly changing marketplace, in which the availability of filmed entertainment is in constant flux.

Financial Assumptions

For the purposes of this business plan, several assumptions have been included in the financial scenarios and are noted accordingly. This discussion contains forward-looking statements that involve risks and uncertainties as detailed in the Risk Factors section.

Table 1: The *Projected Income Statement (low, moderate, high)*. Table 1 summarizes the estimated income for the film to be produced. The *Domestic Rentals* line reflects the distributors share of the box office split with the exhibitor in the United States and Canada, assuming the film has the same distributor in both countries. *Domestic Other* includes home video, pay TV, basic cable, network television, and television syndication. *Foreign Revenue* includes all monies returned to distributors from all venues outside the United States and Canada.

The film's *Budget*, often known as the production costs, covers both above-the-line (producers, actors, and directors) and below-the-line (the rest of the crew) costs of producing a film. Marketing costs are included under Print and Advertising (P&A), often referred to as releasing costs or distribution expenses. These expenses also include the costs of making copies of the release print from the master and advertising and vary depending on the distribution plan.

Gross Income represents the projected pretax profit after distributor's expenses have been deducted but before distributor's fees and overhead expenses are deducted.

Distributor's Fees (the distributor's share of the revenues as compared to his expenses, which represent out-of-pocket costs) are based on 35% of all distributor gross revenue, both domestic and foreign.

Net Producer/Investor Income represents the projected pretax profit prior to negotiated distributions to investors.

8 Financial Plan

Table 2: *Projected Cash Flow Based on Moderate Profit*. Table 2 summarizes projected cash flow based on the moderate case scenario from Table 1. The *Cash Flow* assumptions used for Table 2 are as follows:

a) Film production should take approximately one year from development through post-production, ending with the creation of a master print. The actual release date depends on finalization of distribution arrangements, which may occur either before or after the film has been completed and is an unknown variable at this time. For purposes of the cash flow, we have assumed that distribution will start within six months after completion of the film.
b) The largest portion of the print and advertising will be spent in the first quarter of the film's opening.
c) The majority of revenues generally will come back to the producers within two years after release of the film, although a smaller amount of ancillary revenues will take longer to occur and will be covered by the investor's agreement.

Table 3: *Comparative Films With Varied Genres*. Table 3 provides data for five films released between 2000 and 2010. The films chosen are the basis for the projections shown in Table 1 for *Northeast Kingdom*. They relate in theme, style, feeling, or budget to *Northeast Kingdom*. It should be noted that these groups do not include films of which the results are known but that have lost money. In addition, there are neither databases that collect all films ever made nor budgets available for all films released. There is, therefore, a built-in bias in the data. Also, the fact that these films have garnered revenue does not constitute a guarantee of the success of this film.

Table 4: *Summary of Comparative Films released between 1989 and 2009.* Table 4 provides data for comparable films with budgets ranging from $2.5 to $53 million. The table provides budgets and box office (worldwide, except where noted).

Table 5: *Summary of Comparative Films released between 2010 and 2013.* Table 5 provides data for comparable films with budgets ranging from $0.2 to $30 million. The table provides budgets and box office (worldwide, except where noted).

For **Tables 3, 4, and 5**, we have chosen films that relate in genre, theme, and/or budget to the film we propose to produce. The *low* scenario indicates a case in which some of the production costs are covered but there is no profit. The *moderate* scenario represents the most likely result for the film we propose to produce and is used for cash flows. The *high* scenarios are based on the results of extraordinarily successful films and presented for investor information only.

Due to the wide variance in the results of individual films, simple averages of actual data are not realistic. Therefore, to create the moderate forecast for Table 1, the North American box office for each film in the respective comparative tables was divided by its budget to create a ratio that was used as a guide.

The North American box office was used because it is a widely accepted film industry assumption that, in most cases, this result drives all the other revenue sources of a film. In order to avoid skewing the data, films with excessively high or low ratios in each year were not selected.

The remaining revenues were added and then divided by the sum of the remaining budgets. This gave an average (or, more specifically, the *mean variance*) of the box office with the budgets. The result was a number used to multiply times the budget of the business plan's proposed film in order to obtain a reasonable projection of the moderate box office result. In order to determine the expense value for the P&A, the P&A for each film in the comparative tables was divided by the budget.

The ratios were determined in a similar fashion, taking out the high and low and arriving at a mean number. For the high forecast, MVP determined a likely extraordinary result for each film and its budget. The remaining revenues and P&A for the high forecasts were calculated using ratios similar to those applied to the moderate columns. In all the scenarios, and throughout these financials, ancillary revenues from product placement, merchandising, soundtrack, and other revenue opportunities are not included in projections.

Distributor's Fees are based on all the revenue exclusive of the exhibitor's share of the box office (50%). These fees are calculated at 35% (general industry assumption) for the forecast, as MVP does not have a distribution contract at this time. Note that the fees are separate from distributor's expenses which are out-of-pocket and paid back in full.

TABLE 1 --- MIGHTY VISUAL PRODUCTIONS

NORTHEAST KINGDOM

PROJECTED INCOME
LOW, MODERATE, HIGH RESULTS
(Millions of Dollars)

		LOW	MODERATE	HIGH
U.S. BOX OFFICE		4.82	9.11	16.08
REVENUE				
Domestic Rentals	(a)	2.41	4.56	8.04
Domestic Other	(b)	10.02	11.26	16.08
Foreign	(c)	12.06	18.76	26.80
TOTAL DISTRIBUTOR GROSS REVENUE		24.50	34.57	50.92
LESS:				
Budget Cost		5.36	5.36	5.36
Prints and Advertising		2.60	4.02	5.36
TOTAL COSTS		7.96	9.38	10.72
DISTRIBUTOR'S GROSS INCOME		16.54	25.19	40.20
Distributor's Fees	(d)	8.57	12.10	17.82
NET INCOME BEFORE ALLOCATION TO PRODUCERS/INVESTORS		7.97	13.10	22.39
ROI		0%	40%	109%

Note: Box office revenues are for reference and not included in the totals.
(a) Box office revenues are for reference and not included in the totals. 50 percent of the box office goes to the exhibitor and 50 percent goes to the distributor as Domestic Rentals.
(b) Domestic Other Revenue includes television, cable, video and all other nontheatrical sources of revenue
(c) Foreign Revenue includes both theatrical and ancillary revenues.
(d) Distributor's Fee equals 35 percent of Distributor's Gross Revenue

Prepared by Mighty Visual Productions

[Credit: Provided by the author]

TABLE 2 - - - MIGHTY VISUAL PRODUCTIONS

NORTHEAST KINGDOM

PROJECTED CASH FLOW*
BASED ON MODERATE PROJECTION
(Millions of Dollars)

	YEAR 1				YEAR 2				YEAR 3				YEAR 4	
	Qtr. 1	Qtr. 2	Qtr. 3	Qtr. 4	Qtr. 1	Qtr. 2	Qtr. 3	Qtr. 4	Qtr. 1	Qtr. 2	Qtr. 3	Qtr. 4	Qtr. 1	
Budget	(1.3)	(1.6)	(1.6)	(0.8)										(5.4)
Prints and Advertising							(2.1)	(0.5)	(1.0)	(0.4)				(4.0)
Domestic Rentals							3.4	0.7	0.5					4.6
Domestic Other									5.6			5.6		11.3
Foreign Revenue									5.4	4.5	2.8	4.5	1.5	18.8
Distribution Fees								(1.4)	(8.2)				(2.5)	(12.1)
TOTAL	(1.3)	(1.6)	(1.6)	(0.8)	0.0	0.0	1.3	(1.3)	2.3	4.1	2.8	4.5	4.6	13.1
CUMULATIVE TOTAL	(1.3)	(2.9)	(4.6)	(5.4)	(5.4)	(5.4)	(4.1)	(5.3)	(3.0)	1.1	4.0	8.5	13.1	

* For reference only. How and when monies are actually distributed depends on contract with distributor.
Prints and advertising are usually paid back first, then the production budget.

Note: Totals may not add due to rounding.

Percentage projections
for budget of film   5%   10%   66%   19%
for printing and advertising
for foreign rev calc   0.29   0.24   0.15   0.24   0.08

[Credit: Provided by the author]

TABLE 3 - - - MIGHTY VISUAL PRODUCTIONS

SELECTED COMPARATIVE FILMS WITH VARIED GENRES*
NORTHEAST KINGDOM
WITH BUDGETS $2 TO $32 MILLION
U.S. BOX OFFICE AND BUDGETS ONLY
USED TO CALCULATE RATIOS AND MODERATE REVENUE SCENARIOS*

(Millions of Dollars)

FILMS	BUDGET	BOX OFFICE
REQUIEM FOR A DREAM (2000)	4.5	7.4
THIRTEEN (2003)	1.5	10.1
A HISTORY OF VIOLENCE (2005)	32.0	60.7
A SERIOUS MAN (2009)	7.0	40.2
WINTER'S BONE (2010)	2	6.5

* The amounts obtained by these comparable films do not constitute a guarantee that *Northeast Kingdom* will do as well.

[Credit: Provided by the author]

TABLE 4 - - - MIGHTY VISUAL PRODUCTIONS

SELECTED COMPARATIVE FILMS WITH VARIED GENRES*
NORTHEAST KINGDOM
WITH BUDGETS $2.5 TO $53 MILLION
U.S. BOX OFFICE AND BUDGETS ONLY**
YEARS 1989 to 2009
(Millions of Dollars)

FILMS	BUDGET	BOX OFFICE (worldwide except where noted)
DRUGSTORE COWBOY (1989)	2.5	4.7 (North American only)
REQUIEM FOR A DREAM (2000)	4.5	7.4
TRAFFIC (2000)	48.0	124.0
BLOW (2001)	53.0	83.1
THIRTEEN (2003)	1.5	10.1
A HISTORY OF VIOLENCE (2005)	32.0	60.7
LITTLE CHILDREN (2006)	14.0	20.5
A SERIOUS MAN (2009)	7.0	40.2
CRAZY HEART (2009)	7.0	84.0

* The amounts obtained by these comparable films do not constitute a guarantee that *Northeast Kingdom* will do as well.

[Credit: Provided by the author]

TABLE 5 - - - MIGHTY VISUAL PRODUCTIONS

SELECTED COMPARATIVE FILMS WITH VARIED GENRES*
NORTHEAST KINGDOM
WITH BUDGETS $0.2 TO $30 MILLION
U.S. BOX OFFICE AND BUDGETS ONLY**
YEARS 2010 to 2013
(Millions of Dollars)

FILMS	BUDGET	BOX OFFICE (North American only except where noted)
WINTER'S BONE (2010)	2.0	6.5
THE GRACE CARD (2010)	0.2	2.4
KILLING THEM SOFTLY (2012)	15.0	38.0 (worldwide est.)
HOMEFRONT (2013)	22.0	43.0 (worldwide est.)
SIDE EFFECTS (2013)	30.0	63.3 (worldwide est.)
DALLAS BUYERS CLUB (2013)	5.5	27.0
COURAGEOUS (2013)	2.0	35.0
HOME RUN (2013)	1.2	2.9

* The amounts obtained by these comparable films do not constitute a guarantee that *Northeast Kingdom* will do as well.

Note: Domestic ancillary and all foreign data generally are not available until two years after a film's initial U.S. release; therefore, this table includes *North American box office only* and, where available, worldwide estimates.

[Credit: Provided by the author]

Index

above the line 72
access 63–64
actors 70–71, 81; casting 60–62; children 91–92; conditions 89; difficult 90–91; director 97; experienced 89–90; extras 93–94; interviews 95; narrators/hosts 92; novice 90; rehearsing 88–89; stage and screen acting 94–95; stars 92–93
acts 35
adaptation 25
advance locations 63
aggregators 131–132
Allen, W. 88, 105
American Film Market (AFM) 52
Angelo My Love 91
The Apartment 32
Apu Trilogy 91
art 12–16, 21–22
art direction 65
assembly stage 106–107
assistant director 88
The Atomic Caf 30, 54
audience 22, 28, 31

Bass, S. 115
Batman 94
beat 33
believability 26
below the line 72
Bernie 95
Betrayal 29
Bicycle Thieves 91
The Biograph Girl 92–93
Birdman 30
Blair Witch Project 20
blocking 87–88, 97
Bowes, M. 68–70
box office potential 50
Boyhood 58
brain trust 71–72
brand recognition 41
breakdown sheet 78–79
breaks 98–99

Brick 30
Bruckheimer, J. 39
budget 55–56, 68, 71–76 *see also* money
business entities 51
business plan 135–136; company 137, 143; distribution 138, 150–151; executive summary 136–137, 141–142; film 137, 144; financial plan 139–140, 153–158; industry 137–138, 144–147; markets 138, 147–150; risk factors 138–139, 152–153; sample 140–158

Cain, J.M. 37
call sheet 81–83
call time 86
camera: cinematographer 97–98; department 74–76; director 96–97; setup 86–88
Carrey, J. 94
Cassavetes, J. 19
casting 60–62
categories 17–19
cave painting 7–8
chain of title 119
Chaplin, C. 7
character 26–28, 59
child actors 91–92
China 7–8
Chronicle 20
cinema: evolution 12–20; origins 7–12, 16 *see also* distribution
cinematographer 97–98
Citizen Kane 97
Close Encounters of the Third Kind 29
Cloverfield 20
color 12, 15; correction 114
communication 55–56, 100
competition 132–133
compilation film 53–54
complexity 17
computer generated imaging (CGI) 13
computer-based editing 2–3
concept art 44

content 56, 70, 101
contingency 72, 100–101; days 81
contracts 50–51
corporation 51
costs 57, 100–101
coverage 100
craft services 86, 98–99
creativity 21–22, 25
crew 66–68, 95–98
critics 119
cutaway 100

Davis, B. 108
day and date release 129
DBA 51
De Sica, V. 91
deals: cast and crew 67–68, 70–71; distributors 120–121
deliverables 115–116, 122
demos 44
departments 74–76
desire, character 27
development 41–44
dialogue 15
difficult actors 90–91
digital cameras 2–3
Digital Cinema Packages (DCPs) 114–115
director 87, 95–97; editor relationship 105–106; location scouting 62–63; producer relationship 42–43, 47, 68; script 35–37
Disney, W. 132
Distribber 131
distribution 47, 113–115, 121–124, 129–132; deal structures 120–121; distributor s wants 118–120; film festivals 124–125, 127–129, 131; history 117–118
documentaries 17, 20
doing business as 51
Dr. Strangelove 108
Duel 97
Dumb and Dumber 94
Dune 43
Duvall, R. 91

Eastwood, C. 88
economic models 19–20
Edison, T. 9, 16
editing 2–3, 105–112
empathy 28, 31
Eternal Sunshine of the Spotless Mind 94
Europe 47–48
exhibition 117–118, 120
experienced actors 89–90
exteriors 81
extras 93–94
failure 132

fairy tales 21
Falk, B. 58–60
Fantastic Mr. Fox 30
fantasy 18
favored nations 67
festivals *see* film festivals
fiction films 17–18
Figgis, M. 100
film acting 94–95
Film Com 52
film festivals 124–125, 127–129, 131
fine cut 107
finishing 113
five stages 39–40, 45
Ford, J. 100–101
The Fortune Cookie 32
four walling 130–131
free locations 64–65
Full Metal Jacket 89
furniture 75–76

genre 17–19
Godard, J-L. 21, 49
The Godfather 35
Goldman, W. 35, 118
Good/Cheap/Fast 75–76
grading 114
grand total cost 72
Greek civilization 7, 9

hand-held look 19–20
Hermann, B. 108
Herzog, W. 39
hiring 66–68, 70–71
Hitchcock, A. 21, 28, 100, 108
holding area 65
Hollywood 1, 16–17
hosts 92

images 7
in camera editing 100
inclement weather 102
incorporation 51
independent producers 1–2
insert shot 100
intellectual property 41–42
internet 118, 123, 128–130
interviews 67, 95 *see also* sidebar interviews
investors 50–51; producer relationship 49–50, 70; script 35–37; sources 52
Italian For Beginners 30

Jackson, L. 126–127
Jackson, P. 43
Jaws 28
Jodorowsky, A. 43
Jodorowsky s Dune 43

Kagemusha 49
Kinetoscope 9, 11
King, S. 21
Kubrick, S. 89, 108, 115
Kurosawa, A. 43, 49, 97

Latham Loop 12–13
Latham, W. 12
Leigh, M. 32, 88
Lelouch, C. 97
lighting 16, 86–88, 97–100
Limited Liability Corporation (LLC) 51
Limited Partnership (LP) 51
Linklater, R. 58, 92
location: costs 64; owners 65; production strip 78, 80; scouting 62–65
Locke 30
Lord of the Rings 43
Lumet, S. 88
Lumi re brothers 7, 9–10

McCabe, A. 108–112
marketing *see* distribution
marking up 77–78
martini shot 104
The Mask 94
master files 114–115
material *see* stories
meals 98–99
Melies, G. 18–19
Memento 29
money 42, 49–54, 101; budget 55–56, 68, 71–76
morality 26–27
movies *see* cinema
multiplex 10
Murder on the Orient Express 29
music 44, 108
mystery 29

narrative *see* stories
narrators 92
negotiating: cast and crew 67–68, 70–71; distributors 120–121
Netflix 131–132
Nichols, M. 1, 132
Nicholson, J. 94
night shoots 57–58
no budget filmmaking 53
noir 37
non-actors 91
novice actors 90

Obst, L. 32
on demand 129, 131–132
one page/one minute metric 57
option 42

oral storytelling 23
originality 29–30
overwriting 34

pacing 107
Pacino, A. 94–95
Paranormal Activity 20
Patterson, J. 22
payroll 68
performance 85–86
personal money 52
picture lock 107–108
Polanski, R. 25
post-production 105–106; cost 72; deliverables 115–116; editing 105–112; finishing 113–115; test screenings 112–113
poster art 44
preproduction 55–58; budget 71–76; casting 60–62; location scouting 62–65; scheduling 76–83
problems, production 99–103
process 39
producer s representative 126–128
production 85–86; actors 88–95; block/light/shoot 87–88; camera setup 86–87; crew 95–98; end of 103–104; meals and breaks 98–99; problems 99–103
production schedule 55–58, 80–81, 101
production strip 78, 80
projectors 12
projects 59, 70
proof of concept 43
properties 41–42
proscenium shot 12
protagonist 26–27
Psycho 108

radio-friendly script 44
Raiders of the Lost Ark 35
Rashomon 97
Ray, S. 91
reaction shots 106–107
realism 18
Reds 95
regional economy 67–68
regionalism 70–71
rehearsing 88–89
Reisch, P. 44–48
relationships 46
releasability 119–120
return on investment 50–51
rhythm 107
Rome; Open City 91
Rosselini, R. 91
rough cut 107

Russell, D.O. 97

scene 33–34, 78
Schamus, J. 53, 117
scheduling: preproduction 76–83; production schedule 55–58, 80–81, 101
Screen Actor s Guild 70–71
screenwriter 42
script 31–35, 55–57, 59–62; location scouting 62–63; preproduction 77–78; style 35–37
self-distribution 130–131
sequence 35
setbacks 13–16
Seven 29
Sex, Lies, and Videotape 29
Seydoux, J. 43
shadow plays 7–8
Shaye, R. 43
The Shining 115
shoot 87–88 *see also* production
shooting schedule *see* production schedule
sidebar interviews: Ann McCabe 108–112; Brian Falk 58–60; Francois Yon 121–124; Larry Jackson 126–127; Mike Bowes 68–70; Piotr Reisch 44–48
Singin in the Rain 15
skills 45, 58–59, 69, 132
smartphones 9, 11, 15
software 56
sole proprietorship 51
Sorkin, A. 31
sound 12–14, 107–108, 113
soundstage 66
sources, investor 52
speculative script 41–42
Spielberg, S. 32, 92, 97
stage acting 94–95
stage managers 66
star actors 92–93
stealing locations 64–65
stories 7, 21–23, 41–42, 59, 69; character 26–28; mystery 29; originality 29–30; script 31–37; suspense 28–29; suspension of disbelief 25–26
storyboards 44

studios 1, 117–118
style, script 35–37
submissions 127–128
surprise 28–29
suspense 28–29
suspension of disbelief 25–26

talent coordinator 71
Tarantino, Q. 7
Tarkovsky, A. 34
tax credit 67–68
technical problems 101–102
technology 2–3, 12–16, 19–20
television 58, 109, 122–124, 127–129
temp music tracks 44
test screenings 112–113
theatrical release 129
time, locations 63 *see also* scheduling
Timecode 29
top sheet 72–73
transformation 27, 31
travel 63–64
Truffaut, F. 92
The Truman Show 94

underwriting 34
unforeseen costs 100–101
USA 47–48

Vachon, C. 42–43
values 27–28
viewing context 9
Voyage dans la lune 18–19

wants, character 27
weather 102
Welles, O. 97
Wilder, B. 32
window 129
Workers Leaving the Lumi re Factory in Lyon 7, 9, 18
working days 58, 81, 102–103
wrap party 104
writing 25, 34 *see also* script; stories

Yon, F. 121–124